TOTAL HOCKEY TRAINING

Sean Skahan

Human Kinetics

Library of Congress Cataloging-in-Publication Data

Names: Skahan, Sean, 1975-
Title: Total hockey training / Sean Skahan.
Description: Champaign, IL : Human Kinetics, [2016] | Includes
 bibliographical references.
Identifiers: LCCN 2015031654 | ISBN 9781492507093 (print)
Subjects: LCSH: Hockey--Training.
Classification: LCC GV848.3 .S535 2016 | DDC 796.962--dc23 LC record available at http://lccn.loc.
gov/2015031654

ISBN: 978-1-4925-0709-3 (print)

This publication is written and published to provide accurate and authoritative information relevant to the subject matter presented. It is published and sold with the understanding that the author and publisher are not engaged in rendering legal, medical, or other professional services by reason of their authorship or publication of this work. If medical or other expert assistance is required, the services of a competent professional person should be sought.

The web addresses cited in this text were current as of August 2015, unless otherwise noted.

Acquisitions Editor: Justin Klug; **Developmental Editor:** Laura Pulliam; **Managing Editor:** Nicole O'Dell; **Copyeditor:** Patricia MacDonald; **Cover Designer:** Keith Blomberg; **Photograph (cover):** Xinhua/Zumapress/Icon Sportswire; **Photographs (interior) and Photo Production Manager:** Jason Allen; **Visual Production Assistant:** Joyce Brumfield; **Art Manager:** Kelly Hendren; **Associate Art Manager:** Alan L. Wilborn; **Illustrations:** © Human Kinetics; **Printer:** Versa Press

We thank Parkland College in Champaign, IL, for assistance in providing a photo shoot location for a portion of the photos in this book. We thank Ultraslide (www.ultraslide.com) for providing the slide for the photo shoot.

Human Kinetics books are available at special discounts for bulk purchase. Special editions or book excerpts can also be created to specification. For details, contact the Special Sales Manager at Human Kinetics.

Printed in the United States of America   10 9 8 7 6 5 4 3 2 1

The paper in this book is certified under a sustainable forestry program.

Human Kinetics
Website: www.HumanKinetics.com

United States: Human Kinetics
P.O. Box 5076
Champaign, IL 61825-5076
800-747-4457
e-mail: info@hkusa.com

Canada: Human Kinetics
475 Devonshire Road Unit 100
Windsor, ON N8Y 2L5
800-465-7301 (in Canada only)
e-mail: info@hkcanada.com

Europe: Human Kinetics
107 Bradford Road
Stanningley
Leeds LS28 6AT, United Kingdom
+44 (0) 113 255 5665
e-mail: hk@hkeurope.com

Australia: Human Kinetics
57A Price Avenue
Lower Mitcham, South Australia 5062
08 8372 0999
e-mail: info@hkaustralia.com

New Zealand: Human Kinetics
P.O. Box 80
Mitcham Shopping Center, South Australia 5062
0800 222 062
e-mail: info@hknewzealand.com

E6500

TOTAL HOCKEY TRAINING

Contents

Preface. vi

Acknowledgments vii

Chapter 1 **Seasonal Scheduling and Logistics . . . 1**

Chapter 2 **Testing and Tracking Progress 7**

Chapter 3 **Position-Specific Training 17**

Chapter 4 **Pretraining 25**

Chapter 5 **Core 47**

Chapter 6 **Strength and Power. 103**

Chapter 7 **Acceleration and Speed. 171**

Chapter 8   Flexibility 197

Chapter 9   Conditioning 207

Chapter 10 Off-Season Training Programs 219

Chapter 11 Preseason Training Programs 269

Chapter 12 In-Season Training Programs 279

Bibliography 293

About the Author 294

Preface

The game of hockey has certainly evolved over the last two decades. The sport is now played at a much higher level. Players are bigger, stronger, faster, leaner, and more mobile than they once were. Strength and conditioning programs have to reflect the changes of the game moving forward.

As a player, do you want a strength and conditioning program that will help you improve your game? If you are a coach, do you want to know how to design a strength and conditioning program for your team?

Total Hockey Training will take you step by step through a season-specific strength and conditioning program. The off-season, preseason, and in-season periods are all included. Strength training, speed training, plyometrics, conditioning, and recovery methods are addressed so that you will always know what to do at any time during the year.

This comprehensive training program is for any player at any level. This book is also a resource for team coaches and strength and conditioning coaches. Athletes today want to know why and how training methods can help them, so each exercise and drill contains an explanation of its application to hockey. *Total Hockey Training* reflects my years of coaching players in strength and conditioning at the professional and collegiate levels. I hope you enjoy it!

Acknowledgments

This book would not have been possible without the help and support of my wife, Hillary, and sons, Will and Wyatt. Their support throughout the entire process from start to finish has been tremendous.

I would also like to thank Justin Klug and the Human Kinetics staff for their guidance and assistance and their belief in me.

I would also like to thank those who have mentored me and had a positive effect on my career in more ways than they know. Strength and conditioning coaches and educators such as Mike Boyle, Glenn Harris, Al Vermeil, Brad Arnett, Paul Chapman, Mike Poidomani, and Avery Faigenbaum have all been instrumental. Much of what you will read in this book wouldn't be included without their guidance.

Also, thanks to all the hockey coaches and management personnel who have given me opportunities to work with their teams.

Chapter 1

Seasonal Scheduling and Logistics

A calendar year for any hockey player should include three main components: the off-season, the preseason, and the in-season. Each component represents times of the year where different parts of an all-encompassing program are emphasized more than others. However, strength training will always be consistent. For example, although training for speed off the ice will not be emphasized during the in-season, strength training will be consistent on a year-round basis. Hockey players should always try to get stronger.

In this chapter, all aspects of the yearly program are identified and described. The ultimate goal is for hockey players who embark on this program to apply the principles to help them become the best players they can be.

OFF-SEASON

The off-season is when players are away from the competitive demand and stress of the game of hockey. It is a time of year when they can make positive changes to their bodies with the intention of improving on-ice performance. A high-quality strength and conditioning program is very important at this time. With hockey being such a high-pace game, every hockey player should be training to increase his strength and power while also improving his conditioning levels. This will also help reduce the chances of injury. The off-season is the optimal period for these changes to happen.

In *Total Hockey Training*, the training is broken down into blocks of 3-week phases. During the off-season, there will be 4 of these 3-week phases to make up a 12-week off-season. Each phase consists of several exercises that will progress from the previous phase in terms of difficulty or set and repetition ranges or both. This allows for training variety to prevent boredom and to apply different stresses to the body, with the intention of building a stronger and faster hockey player who is resilient to injury.

Off-Season for a High School Player

At the high school level, the entire off-season could be from March through November. High school hockey players may also be multisport athletes, which is beneficial for athleticism and conditioning. During the fall, they could participate in football, soccer, volleyball, or other fall-season sports. During the spring, they may participate in sports such as baseball, softball, or lacrosse. Whether they play multiple sports or not, the nine-month period should involve two to four weeks of active rest when the hockey player needs to get away from the game of hockey

The summer months (June, July, and August) are for strength and conditioning. The 12-week off-season program (at least four days per week) consists of exercises for flexibility, core strength, acceleration, speed, plyometrics, lower and upper body strength, and conditioning.

Off-Season for a Junior Player

Junior hockey players, whether they are at the Tier-I, Tier- II A, or Tier III A, B, C, or D levels, will have a much shorter off-season program than high school players. Their season could end in March or in late May (depending on the level of play). A junior hockey player should also embark on a 12-week off-season strength and conditioning program during the summer months. Players at the junior level are probably not participating in other sports. These players have already made the decision to specialize in hockey.

Off-Season for a Collegiate Player

The collegiate hockey player will have an off-season that is longer than the junior player but shorter than at the high school level. This will usually be from May through August. This allows for a postseason phase of four to six weeks after the in-season phase and before the off-season phase. Although there might be some multisport athletes at the collegiate level, for the most part, these players are committed to playing just hockey. At the Division I level, athletic scholarships are awarded to players. It is a full-time commitment to be a scholarship athlete who focuses on academics and hockey.

At the higher levels of collegiate hockey, the athletic department will most likely employ a strength and conditioning coach who works with the hockey team. Most university hockey programs that award athletic scholarships have this luxury. The strength and conditioning coach's job is to look after all aspects of the team's strength and conditioning program on a year-round basis. During the off-season, some programs will ask their players to take summer school classes so they can train as a team. This pays huge dividends down the road for team-building purposes. Since most NCAA Division I programs have outstanding facilities, a really good off-season program and hardworking culture can be developed.

Off-Season for a Professional Player

The professional level's off-season is a little different. A player on a team that doesn't qualify for the playoffs will have a much longer off-season than someone who plays for the championship. For example, a Stanley Cup–winning player's off-season will be much shorter. There is a big difference between a 16-week off-season and a 9-week off-season. If you ask any professional player, he will always opt for winning the Stanley Cup and worrying about the off-season after.

Professional players can do whatever they like in the off-season. When the regular season concludes, they are on their own. Many professional players do not live year-round in the city in which they play. They return to their off-season homes and either train on their own or with a personal trainer or strength and conditioning coach. Although the team provides a strength and conditioning program, ultimately the player has the option of following the program or completely disregarding it. Players who stay in the team's location throughout the off-season have the benefit of working with the team's strength and conditioning coach.

Junior, collegiate, and professional players should participate in a comprehensive strength and conditioning program during the off-season. Although players should get away from the rink at the beginning of the off-season, they should get back on the ice as the off-season concludes. Power skating and pick-up hockey sessions are great options toward the end of the off-season.

PRESEASON

During the preseason, players get together with their teammates to practice and participate in the strength and conditioning program as a team. Any players who haven't done much team training over the last few months can get on the same page as their teammates. This is a crucial part of the year for the team's success. Teams can start to develop camaraderie through preseason practices and strength and conditioning sessions.

Preseason for a High School Player

The preseason phase for the high school player will only be a few weeks. This will usually be in late November through early December. For example, in the state of Massachusetts, high school hockey always begins on the Monday following Thanksgiving. The preseason phase runs from the first practice until the first scheduled game. Early-morning practices and afternoon strength and conditioning sessions (or vice versa) should be scheduled to accommodate the school schedule.

Preseason for a Junior Player

At the junior level, the last part of August and the beginning of September is when the preseason occurs. This is highlighted by on-ice practice sessions and strength and conditioning sessions. Preseason games also take place while rosters are being formed. Players will either make the team or not make the team. There is no junior varsity or minor leagues at the junior hockey level.

Preseason for a Collegiate Player

In collegiate hockey, the preseason phase will usually last four or five weeks. This would be from late August or early September through early October. This coincides with when students report back to campus for the fall semester. During this time, on-ice coaches are only allowed to work with players for two hours each week for three weeks. However, the strength and conditioning coach can lead the team through six hours of strength and conditioning per week. This includes strength and conditioning sessions in the weight room and conditioning sessions on the ice without the use of sticks and pucks. The players on the team will also execute their own drills and play scrimmages on their own.

Preseason for a Professional Player

In professional hockey, the preseason could be divided into two parts: the pre-preseason, and the preseason. The pre- preseason would be the time period from when all of the players on the team report back to the team's training facility on their own before the training camp officially starts until the official start of training camp. The pre- preseason consists of on-ice practices conducted by the players themselves and five to six days of strength and conditioning in the weight room. The official preseason period is the three- to four-week phase from when all the players on the team report to training camp until the first regular season game. This would be the official training camp period that consists of several on-ice practices, preseason games, and strength and conditioning in the weight room.

At this level, players are expected to come into training camp and pre-season phase in good condition. The emphasis on playing games starts right away, as preseason games begin approximately two days after the players report for camp.

What is consistent about the preseason at all levels of hockey is that it is an important period for team building. Usually, there are new players coming in as freshmen, or, in the case of the professional ranks, rookies. There could also be new players coming in via trades, free agency, or transfers from other schools. No matter what, the players need to learn how to work with one another collectively in order to become a team. The teams that can figure out that aspect the quickest will be more successful. Strength and conditioning sessions and on-ice practices should focus on getting the team to work together as a group in a competitive environment where teammates can push one another and start to build something for the long season ahead.

IN-SEASON

The in-season is all about playing hockey. Wins and losses are most important, no matter the level. The goals of the strength and conditioning program are to decrease the chance of injury and to increase performance by delaying the loss of strength, power, and conditioning gains that were attained during the off-season and preseason. This is very difficult at all levels because less time can be dedicated to the strength and conditioning program as the focus switches to winning games on the ice. The strength and conditioning coach needs to have a plan for the duration of the season.

In-Season for a High School Player

At the high school level, the in-season period is three or four months long. The schedule usually runs from late November or early December through the month of February and even into the beginning of March. There are usually 20 to 25 games, meaning a high school team plays two or three times per week. This is a really good schedule for in-season strength and conditioning. Again, like the off-season period, the in-season period is divided into three-week phases.

In-season strength and conditioning programs at the high school level can be either easy or difficult to administer. Depending on the school, a weight room could be a well-appointed facility with adequate space and equipment or it may be a closet in the hockey arena (if there is one). The best philosophy on administering a strength and conditioning program at any level is to make the best out of what you have to work with. The key is to get in two or three sessions per week and get better at basic exercises, whether you're working in a spacious weight room before the school day starts or outside the locker room at the rink with no equipment at all.

In-Season for a Junior Player

More games are played at the junior level than in high school. Depending on the level of hockey, junior hockey seasons can run any time from September through May, which can be very demanding for 16- to 21-year-olds.

At the higher levels of junior hockey, the schedule and culture are very similar to professional hockey. The increased number of games presents more barriers for the implementation of a good in-season strength and conditioning program. However, strength and conditioning at this level is very important. Since the young men are in the 16 to 21 age range, it is critical that they do strength and conditioning work.

During the 1990s and early 2000s, all that may have been available to a junior team was one exercise bike. Since then, strength and conditioning in junior hockey has improved. Some high-level junior teams now have full-time strength and conditioning coaches and large weight rooms.

In-Season for a Collegiate Player

At the collegiate level, most of the games are played on weekends, with occasional midweek games. It isn't uncommon for teams to play each other on a Friday and a Saturday night. The collegiate schedule is ideal for implementing an in-season strength and conditioning program. A college hockey strength and conditioning coach can get in a minimum of two training sessions per week.

In-Season for a Professional Player

At the professional level, each team has a full-time strength and conditioning coach, and some may also employ a full-time assistant strength and conditioning coach. Some teams at the American Hockey League (AHL) level (which is the next level down from the NHL) also have strength and conditioning coaches. Most of the lower levels of professional hockey do not, which makes it more difficult for a professional player to move to the next level of hockey.

An in-season strength and conditioning program is very difficult to administer at the professional level. The number of games that are played is ultimately the main barrier. A professional player will play up to 82 regular season games over the course of six months. With half of those games being an away game throughout the United States and Canada, scheduling training sessions is challenging.

Some teams will conduct training sessions immediately after a game. Some take a different approach and conduct most of their training sessions on practice days. It all depends on the strength and conditioning coach's philosophy. The minor leagues have schedules similar to NCAA hockey, where most of the games are played on the weekend. For example, a typical AHL schedule has games on Friday, Saturday, and Sunday with the possibility of playing on Wednesdays. More time can be devoted to working on skill development at practice as well as off-ice strength and conditioning. The NHL plays more games during the week and never plays games on three consecutive nights, so program design is different at this level.

FACILITY LOGISTICS

One of the main factors to consider when designing a strength and conditioning program for whatever level of hockey you coach or play is your facility. The size of your facility and the quality of your equipment will determine the program. The key is to make the most out of what you do have.

Unfortunately, strength and conditioning is still relatively new in the sport of hockey, and some hockey arenas were built a long time ago without the idea of including a weight room. At most levels, finding space and transitioning it into a weight room is going to be a challenge. The reality is that a weight room doesn't need much more than some barbells, free weights, squat racks, chin-up bars, and dumbbells. Kettlebells, sleds, stability balls, and foam rollers are nice to have but aren't vital. Machines that isolate muscle groups not only take up space (since only one person at a time can use them) but also may not be the best way to exercise the muscles you want to strengthen. Which is better: having one player performing leg extensions on a machine while the rest of the players are waiting or having multiple players performing an exercise like a split squat?

No matter what level of hockey you coach or play, devising a quality training program will depend on your ability to come up with the best program with what you have. Again, you don't need the newest weight training machines to make this happen. This book shows how to implement a training program with minimal equipment.

The hockey season is one of the longest in all major sports, and the training structure needs to be year-round. A properly designed training program will progress nicely from each part of the year to the next, from the in-season period to the off-season and then into the preseason period.

Chapter 2

Testing and Tracking Progress

The assessment process is an important aspect of a year-round hockey training program for older players (age 16 and above) to measure the results of all the work they put in as well as track their progress over time. Power, speed, strength, and conditioning are attributes that coaches and strength and conditioning coaches can continue to evaluate as a player matures.

Note that testing isn't recommended for younger players. Younger players shouldn't be subjected to testing among their peers and coaches. They shouldn't be evaluated from a physical perspective because they will not have the necessary physical or neuromuscular ability to perform well on some tests. Kids just want to play and have fun and not be embarrassed in front of teammates.

It is important to designate periods of time when testing will take place. The most common time is during the preseason when players can be evaluated to see if they have improved as a result of the off-season strength and conditioning program. It is also a chance to compare each individual player with teammates. The number of tests conducted at this time of year is usually higher than any other time. Another appropriate time for testing is the postseason, depending on the level of hockey. In collegiate hockey, where the team will most likely participate in a phase of training after the season, it would be appropriate. Players can establish a baseline and set individual goals to achieve throughout the off-season. In the professional ranks, postseason testing is less common, although some teams conduct strength and conditioning assessments before departing for the off-season. Important areas to assess and address include body composition, leg power, leg strength, upper body strength, conditioning, and speed.

BODY COMPOSITION

It is important to test body composition because it indicates the percentage of a player's weight that is adipose (fat) tissue. A high amount of body fat is unnecessary, and carrying extra weight can make hockey players slower.

When players are younger, the talented player who has more body fat than others is going to be even more talented when he loses the unnecessary fat. Unfortunately, most players won't have the amount of talent to allow them to be good with higher amounts of body fat. For young players who are heavier, nutrition intervention is a must. Parents need to help their kids succeed by providing them with proper nutrition at home. The player usually isn't the person who is buying the groceries and deciding when to eat out at fast food establishments.

For male hockey players, a body fat percentage of 10 percent or less is recommended. A player with a body fat percentage in the single digits is giving himself the best chance to succeed at any level of play. From practical experience that includes several years of working with professional and collegiate players, body fat percentage ratings are as follows:

- Below average: >12 percent
- Average: 8 to 12 percent
- Above average: <8 percent

The best advice is to get body fat assessed by a fitness professional if it could be an issue. There are several methods for measuring body fat percentage, including skinfold calipers, underwater measurements, the Bod Pod, and even some scales. As long as body composition is analyzed by the same person over and over again and the person administering the test is using the same device, the readings should be reliable. Some would say the best way to check body fat is to look in the mirror. If a player can't see the abdominal muscles or the serratus anterior muscles (the muscles attached to the ribs under the armpits), then losing some body fat should be a priority.

LEG POWER

Lower body power is another key attribute of a successful hockey player. More important, and what should always be a goal, is the continual improvement of leg power throughout a strength and conditioning program. Hockey players both young and old should always try to improve their leg power. In fact, as a player reaches 30, leg power should become the priority as this is one of the first things to diminish with age (Mascaro, Seaver, and Swanson 1992). Plyometrics, Olympic lifting, and leg-strength exercises will help improve leg power.

The vertical jump is a popular method for assessing lower body power in hockey players as vertical jump measurements have correlated highly with on-ice speed (Mascaro, Seaver, and Swanson 1992). The broad jump is another method of assessing lower body power. From practical experience, the vertical jump is an easier and safer test to administer. In the broad jump, less than adequate body mechanics while taking off and landing are more common.

For testing the vertical jump, the Just Jump mat or the Vertec are the better options for assessment tools. The Just Jump mat is a device that measures the time spent in the air between takeoff and landing. It is quick and effective, especially for measuring a large group of athletes. Like any other test, there are methods of cheating. However, an experienced tester should be able to recognize cheating with the Just Jump mat. With the Vertec, the athlete jumps up and hits the colored sticks with the hand. Some players prefer this method because it allows them to reach for something while they jump. A popular cheating method is not reaching up as high as possible when the reach measurement is conducted. Since the total score is the highest jump measurement minus the reach measurement, a lower reach will help the player get a better score. Another more logistical flaw is that you must take two measurements (reach and jump) and always readjust the device to allow for higher jumps. From practical experience that includes several years of working with professional and collegiate players, vertical jump ratings (both feet, no pause) are as follows:

- Below average: <25 inches
- Average: 25 to 27 inches
- Above average: >27 inches

Whatever method you use, keep a record of the scores. At the end of the off-season strength and conditioning program, repeat the test to see if the program helped improve leg power.

Vertical Jump Test

Just Jump Mat

To perform this test, set the device attached to the mat to "just jump." The athlete steps on the mat with both feet and simply jumps as high as he/she can and then lands with their feet flat. Ideally, they will not cheat by re-bending their knees while in the air and land on the heels. The mat has the ability to convert the amount of time spent in the air to inches, thus providing a score. The test administrator allows the athlete to complete as many trials as necessary until he is unable to improve on the last test completed.

Vertec

To perform this test, the person administering the test places the colored sticks in the ready position so they are within reach of the athlete overhead. The athlete stands up straight, with both arms straight overhead and hands over each other, and slowly walks through while remaining as tall as possible. The test administrator records the athlete's reach (where his hands contact the sticks). The administrator then adjusts the Vertec so that the sticks are now higher, and the athlete prepares to jump.

With both feet on the floor, the athlete jumps as high as possible while reaching as high as possible for the sticks. The test administrator allows the athlete to complete as many trials as necessary until he is unable to improve on the last test completed. The difference between the jump measurement and the reach measurement is the score. For example, if a player has a 95-inch reach and jumps 120 inches, then the score is 25 inches.

LEG STRENGTH

Developing leg strength should be the priority of any hockey player at any level. Leg strength combined with power development will result in a more explosive hockey player. The most popular way to measure leg strength is the back squat using a barbell. The back squat has been the king of all lower body exercises in strength and conditioning circles for some time. Most strength and conditioning programs in hockey use the squat or a variation of it to develop lower body strength. For beginners to strength training, however, the squat is not an appropriate exercise, especially for testing purposes. The athlete must be technically proficient at the squat before adding load.

In *Total Hockey Training*, the off-season program uses the front squat rather than the back squat for several reasons (discussed in chapter 6). If your athletes have learned how to do the front squat properly and you would like to get a benchmark, then obtain a three- to five-rep max on the front squat during the testing period.

At the professional level, not many teams test with the squat because it may not be worth the risk of injury. Unlike the NFL where teams have organized off-season programs at their training facilities, the professional hockey leagues don't require that players use their facilities or work with their team's strength and conditioning coach during the off-season. Regardless of the level of hockey, if a coach doesn't see most of the roster for the entire off-season, there is no way he can possibly test heavy squats in the preseason after players return from their off-season break. The squat (front or back) must be performed over and over throughout the training process, under the supervision of a strength and conditioning coach, before a three- to five-rep max can be tested. In hockey, there is no way to tell who has been doing squats in the off-season.

A safer alternative to the squat for assessing leg strength is the single-leg squat using a 12- to 14-inch (30 to 35 cm) box. This exercise should be a priority in an off-season hockey program, so it makes sense to add it to a testing protocol. Lower back stress is minimal, and few things can go wrong as far as safety goes, so the risk of injury is significantly lower. A strength and conditioning coach can feel comfortable prescribing this exercise when players are training on their own during the off-season. Also, asymmetries (the differences between the right and the left) can be identified and corrected as needed.

Front Squat Test

The athlete stands with feet shoulder-width or slightly wider than shoulder-width apart and grasps the bar appropriately, with the elbows high (see figure *a*). The athlete takes a deep breath and then descends until the tops of the thighs are parallel to the floor (see figure *b*). While keeping the elbows up and torso perpendicular to the floor, the athlete ascends back to the starting position while exhaling the breath.

Note that before beginning this test, the administrator must know the load to use for the test set. The load must be a weight the athlete can safely lift for three to five repetitions. I recommend that the athlete have some experience with this exercise before attempting a test set. This is not for a beginner who hasn't done the front squat with load on the bar. After using the front squat as an exercise during the off-season, the athlete will have a good idea of what load to use for the test set.

Also, a few warm-up sets are recommended in order to prepare the musculoskeletal system and nervous system for the test set. Increase the warm-up load with each set until the athlete reaches

the amount of weight he will use for the test set. For example, if an athlete is attempting a 225-pound (102 kg) test set, then the recommended sets would progress as follows:

Warm-Up Sets

- Empty bar × 5 reps
- 135 pounds (61 kg) × 3 reps
- 185 pounds (84 kg) × 2 reps
- 210 pounds (95 kg) × 1 rep
- 220 pounds (100 kg) × 1 rep

Test Set

- 225 pounds (102 kg) × 3-5 reps

If any of the repetitions are not up to standard, the set is stopped. The test is scored by how many repetitions within a minimum of three and maximum of five are performed with proper form. If the athlete can repeat this test with either more repetitions or more load at the next testing period, then he has increased strength.

Single-Leg Squat Test

The single-leg squat test requires a 12- to 14-inch (30 to 35 cm) box. For players who are 6-foot-2 and above, the box should be higher (a 14-inch box with an Airex pad on top). It is up to the coach or test administrator to decide how much weight the athlete should hold in each hand. For example, a young midget-aged player may hold 5-pound (2.5 kg) dumbbells, while a professional player may wear a 25-pound (12 kg) weight vest while holding a 25-pound dumbbell in each hand.

To perform this test, the athlete stands on one foot next to the box, with the free leg extended straight to the front and arms to the sides (see figure *a*). The athlete squats until the glutes touch the box and simultaneously raises the arms until they are both parallel to the floor (see figure *b*). The athlete returns to a standing position.

The athlete performs up to 10 repetitions on each leg. If any of the repetitions are not up to standard, then the set is stopped. The test is evaluated by the coach's observation of the athlete's ability to maintain proper form. If the athlete can repeat this test with either more repetitions or more load at the next testing period, then he has increased strength.

UPPER BODY STRENGTH

The maximum number of pull-ups an athlete can do is one of the best ways to assess upper body strength and endurance. Nothing beats the pull-up for assessing posterior shoulder strength. Being able to perform pull-ups properly is an indication of a healthy posterior shoulder girdle. Overhand pull-up ratings are as follows:

- Below average male: <10
- Average male: 11 to 18
- Above average male: >18
- Below average female: <6
- Average female: 6 to 8
- Above average female: >8

Athletes do a variation of the pull-up twice per week in the off-season aspect of *Total Hockey Training*. As a result, they are working their shoulders both in training and during assessment in training camp, helping to prevent injuries by regularly strengthening the joint. They should be well prepared for a pull-up test.

Pull-Up Test

The athlete grasps the bar (or handles) in an overhand grip, with arms straight (see figure *a*). The width of the hands is the athlete's choice. In most cases, the wider the hand grip, the more difficult the pull-up will be. The athlete pulls himself up until the chin is over the bar or higher than the hands (see figure *b*). He then lowers to the starting position, pauses for 1 second, and repeats as many times as he is able. Repetitions must be done under control without any swinging or kipping.

CONDITIONING

Adequate conditioning is important for hockey players at any level. They must be able to repeatedly skate at a high intensity for shifts lasting anywhere from 30 seconds up to 1 minute, with 2 to 4 minutes of rest in between. The conditioning program in *Total Hockey Training* will help any player improve the ability to work hard for each shift while also being able to recover before the next one.

In hockey, all three energy systems of the human body come into play: the ATP–PC (adenosine triphosphate–creatine phosphate) system, the glycolytic system, and the oxidative system.

- ATP–PC system: This system is active in the first seconds of an activity.
- Glycolytic system: This system is used after the ATP–PC system and is relied on for the next 30 to 45 seconds. Athletes feel the burn in their legs when this system is used up.
- Oxidative system: Any activity that happens after the ATP–PC and glycolytic systems have been exhausted is fueled by the oxidative system. This system helps restore energy in order to repeat the cycle again.

A good conditioning test for hockey that assesses all three energy systems is the 300-yard (300 m) shuttle test. This running-based conditioning test (or a variation of it) is done by some collegiate hockey teams and some professional teams during the preseason. However, coaches and trainers must ensure the players have adequately prepared for this test. Ideally, players should be supervised while they are training for at least a few weeks until this test is completed. A hockey player can't just show up unprepared and do a good job.

Since the off-season program in *Total Hockey Training* consists of a logical progression of running 150-yard shuttles and then 300-yard shuttles, a player who gives each conditioning session 100 percent effort would do fine on a 300-yard shuttle test.

300-Yard Shuttle Test

The 300-yard shuttle test is probably best done on a football field with grass or with the field turf. To perform this test, the athlete starts at the goal line and on the coach's whistle, he runs to the 25-yard line, touches the line, returns to and touches the goal line, and repeats five more times for a total of 300 yards. The athlete's score is measured and recorded when he crosses the goal line.

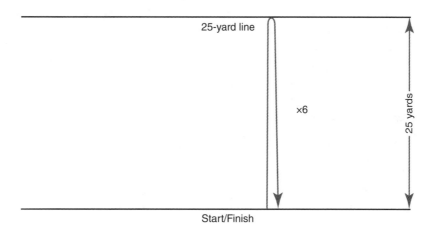

25-yard line

×6

25 yards

Start/Finish

THOUGHTS ON $\dot{V}O_2$MAX TESTING

The $\dot{V}O_2$max test may be the most scrutinized fitness test in hockey. It has probably been the most popular test administered at all levels since hockey started embracing physical testing many years ago. This test is used by several professional teams for their preseason fitness testing and is also one of the tests administered at the NHL's annual predraft scouting combine. Yet some teams do not use it, and not all strength and conditioning coaches support it.

As with any tests administered in training camp, players will prepare to do the best job they possibly can. In the past, in trying to improve $\dot{V}O_2$max scores, most players would likely include steady-state long-distance work on the stationary bicycle throughout the entire off-season. They might do two or three 60- to 90-minute steady rides per week at 65 to 75 percent of maximum heart rate range. At the time, this was the only known way to prepare for a test that measures aerobic capacity. It is also what hockey players would have done for any conditioning work before reporting for training camp back when there was no such thing as strength and conditioning for hockey. Today, a small number of players are still implementing steady-state aerobic work as their only conditioning method during the off-season. What can be more detrimental is the trickle-down effect to the lower levels of hockey because sometimes the thought process is "This is what the pros do."

Total Hockey Training prescribes an aerobic base phase for conditioning during the first three weeks of the off-season. This phase of conditioning includes some long-distance running and steady-state cardio two days per week. Most players are coming off a two- to four-week period of active rest after the conclusion of the season.

Recently, Joel Jamieson, a strength and conditioning coach who works with MMA athletes, has done a great job of elaborating on proper conditioning methods for athletes (Jamieson 2009). He talks about the roles of cardiac output, left ventricle hypertrophy, resting heart rate, and the importance of the aerobic energy system. Hockey players could probably benefit from work in the heart-rate range of 120 to 140 beats per minute (bpm) for longer periods, especially at the start of the off-season when they have been less active for up to 4 weeks. When hockey players are performing interval training both on and off the ice for 42 to 45 weeks out of the year, six or so steady-state aerobic sessions done on days when they are also doing the usual strength and power work will not have a negative effect on strength and power gains.

Toward the end of a $\dot{V}O_2$max test, players will get into the 170- to 200-bpm range. Those who have done interval training with their heart rates in the maximum range of 85 percent-plus are able to get to higher levels on the $\dot{V}O_2$max test. They are conditioned to working above their anaerobic threshold. As a result, they are more prepared to work at that higher stage on the $\dot{V}O_2$max test. Interval training will help develop leg strength and power while also getting an aerobic effect as the athlete's heart rate will not drop significantly in the 1 to 2 minutes of rest between the intervals. Players who report to camp without following an interval training program will not be able to get to the higher levels because of lack of conditioning.

An important job of a strength and conditioning coach is to make sure players follow the conditioning aspect of the off-season program. In reality, if players come into training camp with average scores on the $\dot{V}O_2$max test and improvements in strength and power, the strength and conditioning coach should be pleased. The players who don't perform interval training will also have a low $\dot{V}O_2$max score. Most important, they will not be conditioned for hockey.

A rest period follows, but there is some debate as to how much rest is ideal. The traditional 300-yard shuttle test has a 5-minute rest period. Some collegiate and professional teams may use a shorter time such as 1, 2, or 3 minutes. The traditional 5-minute rest period is recommended in *Total Hockey Training*.

The player repeats the shuttle after the 5-minute period, and that score is recorded. The average of the two shuttle scores is the final score.

SPEED

From an on-ice standpoint, in the assessment of speed and acceleration, a sprint from the goal line to the near blue line is a good test. Most hockey players at the higher levels can skate fast. However, the ability to accelerate faster than others is what separates the good from the really good. The test is simple: Take three trials and record the best score. Progress is measured from one testing period to the next. If the times are lower, the athlete is getting faster.

The strength and conditioning coach should assess the players several times throughout the year. The players should be evaluated in the preseason to assess their performance gains during the off-season program. In the case of a long season, assessments could be done at the midpoint to ensure that the in-season program is maintaining (if not improving) strength, power, and conditioning. Another time to assess the team is at the start of the off-season program. This gives the strength and conditioning coach and the athlete some direction and goals for the off-season program.

There are many other fitness assessments that can be done throughout the season. However, the strength and conditioning coach doesn't need to make this process complicated. The coach's job is to help the players get stronger, faster, more powerful, and in better condition. The tests described in this chapter will determine whether a prescribed program is working. Another advantage of these tests is that they can be done at different times of the year. Physical tests and other assessments are conducted on a year-round basis during a proper training program.

Chapter 3

Position-Specific Training

Hockey has three different positions that are simultaneously on the ice for each team: forwards, defensemen, and the goaltender. Although there are three forwards, two defensemen, and one goaltender on the ice during even-strength regulation play, each position is made up of different kinds of players. For example, a forward may be an offensive-minded player who has minimal defensive skills and is suited for the power-play unit rather than the penalty-kill unit. A stay-at-home defenseman whose defensive skills outweigh his offensive skills would make a good defender and penalty killer. Hockey is the ultimate team sport—getting these positions to work cohesively as one unit toward the goal of winning the game is key.

FORWARDS

The forwards are relied upon to score goals. In a typical game, 11 or 12 forwards suit up. It is usually 12, but sometimes a team may decide to play 7 defensemen instead of 6, which removes a forward from the roster. A line of forwards has one center and two wingers (one left and one right). After the goaltender, the center is probably the most important player on the ice. He is responsible for winning face-offs throughout the game, which will determine team possession of the puck. He will also have to skate the most during a game; in addition to rushing up the ice in the offensive zone, he needs to provide coverage in the defensive zone.

The wingers need to generate chances in the offensive zone. They need to attack the net and play strong along the boards. In the defensive end of the rink, they are responsible for getting the puck out of the zone and for initiating a breakout if the puck comes to them along the boards.

Teams today either break their forwards into two categories (the top six and the bottom six) or simply roll four lines throughout the game. The top six are the first and second lines, comprised of skilled players who are more inclined to score goals. The bottom six—the third and fourth lines—may have a more defensive approach to their game.

Grouping lines into the top and bottom six results from a system of play in which the coach looks for beneficial matchups against the other team's lines throughout a game. The visiting team always has to put its line on the ice first after a whistle. The home team can then put whatever line it wants on the ice. For example, if the visiting team puts its top scoring line on the ice, then the home team may choose to put out its best defensive line. This is where hockey strategies can get very interesting. Coaches who prefer to match up lines will do whatever they can to get certain matchups during games. For those teams who roll through their lines, matching up isn't necessary because they just play their lines against whatever line the other team has on the ice.

The top line usually gets the most ice time of the forwards, with the second line right behind. Since these players may get more than 15 minutes of playing time, they won't need any additional conditioning. The only conditioning work they may need is a 10-minute postgame recovery ride on the stationary bike. Forwards who play on the third and fourth lines will usually play less than 20 minutes per game. With these players, conditioning will need to be added off the ice because they won't be playing as much unless they work their way up to the first or second line. Over the course of the season, these players can become deconditioned if they don't put in the extra off-ice conditioning work.

Here are immediate postgame exercise bike options for forwards who logged less than 15 minutes of total ice time during a game:

- 6-8 × 30-second sprints with 1-minute rest. Players sprint as hard as they can for 30 seconds at the highest resistance on the bike and then recover at the easiest resistance for 1 minute.
- 6-8 × 1-minute sprints with heart rate recovery to 130 bpm. For these sprints, players need to wear a heart rate monitor. They sprint for 1 minute at the highest resistance on the bike and then recover at the easiest resistance. When the heart rate lowers to 130 bpm, they sprint again.

CHARACTERISTICS OF FORWARD LINES IN HOCKEY

The forwards in hockey will usually consist of 4 lines of 3. Sometimes, if a coach decides to play 7 defenseman instead of 6, there could be 3 lines of 3 and 1 line of 4. Each line of forwards will have its own unique characteristics that may differ from any of the other 3 lines. Sometimes, coaches will roll their lines which is simply putting the next line on the ice when it is their turn to go and keep repeating that process all throughout the game. Other times, coaches may match up their lines with the opposing team's lines. For example, if the other team puts their top offensive line on the ice, then the home team coach (who gets the option of putting their line out last) may put on their top defensive line.

First Line

The top forward line on any hockey team is probably the three players who will play the most during the game. These players can expect to see 18 to 20-plus minutes of ice time in each 60-minute game. They will most likely be called on to score goals in key situations. As three of the more skilled guys on the team, they would probably be used in special-team situations such as the power play and the penalty kill. During the in-season phase, these players will need to spend more time recovering from games and won't train off the ice as much as their teammates. Although in-season strength and conditioning is still important for the first line, their ability to recover between games is crucial since they will be playing the most minutes over the season. Their conditioning should consist of some easy, steady-state riding on the stationary bike for 10 minutes postgame. This helps start the recovery process. Then they would do some strength training (if no game is scheduled for the next day), follow up with stretching, and then spend a few minutes in the cold tub.

Second Line

The second line of forwards usually sees 15 to 20 minutes of ice time per game. Although they won't play as much as the top line, they are expected to do the same as the top line. They must win face-offs, score goals, and play defense responsibly. Since they won't play as much as the top line, they will need more in-season off-ice training. Their postgame training should consist of some interval training on the bike, such as four to six sprints of 30 to 45 seconds on and 60 to 90 seconds off. This helps them keep their conditioning levels up for the minutes they didn't get during the game. Like the first line, they would also strength train (if not playing the next day), stretch, and cold plunge.

Third Line

The third-line players usually have less offensive skill than the first and second lines. Depending on whether the coach likes to match lines, the third line will most likely be a checking line responsible for playing against the other team's top line. They will also most likely be the top penalty killers. These players will see 12 to 18 minutes of ice time per game. The second and third lines have similar conditioning demands. Their postgame training should consist of some interval training on the bike, such as four to six sprints of 30 to 45 seconds on and 60 to 90 seconds off. This helps them keep their conditioning levels up for the minutes they didn't get during the game. Like the first line, they would also strength train (if not playing the next day), stretch, and cold plunge.

Fourth Line

The fourth line usually won't play as much as the other lines. They may play up to 12 minutes per game in all levels of hockey if the team matches up lines. These players provide energy during their shifts, which are brief but intense. The fourth line is usually called on to change the momentum of the game by being physical. Their conditioning off the ice needs to be increased dramatically during the season. Although they will most likely play less than anyone else, they need to be adequately conditioned to play more in case of injury or necessity during a game or if they are promoted to a higher line. These players can definitely get up to the 8- to 12-rep range for bike sprints postgame. This ensures their conditioning is up to speed throughout the season. They could also do more sets and reps in their strength training, followed by stretching and a cold tub.

DEFENSEMEN

There are two defensemen on the ice throughout the course of a game. Although their job is to provide defense in front of the goaltender, they are also responsible for sustaining pressure in the offensive zone by holding the blue line and making sure the puck isn't cleared out of the offensive zone by the opposing team's defenders. They can also be a big part of the offensive attack by getting shots on net from the blue line area (the point) or by rushing up the ice from the defensive zone.

Defensemen will have frequent shifts in the 45-second to 1-minute range. Although they will be skating more and working hard in the defensive zone of the ice when the other team is trying to score, they may not be working as hard in the offensive zone when their team is trying to score. The only exception is when an offensive defenseman joins the offensive zone play off the rush.

Usually six defensemen dress for a game, and they work in pairs. However, there are times when a team will play seven defensemen and 11 forwards (instead of 12). Like forwards, defensemen can be categorized by how they play and what they bring to the team.

Each pair of defensemen will play more than the lower pair. For example, the first pair (first and second defensemen) will play more than the second pair (third and fourth defensemen). The third pair (fifth and sixth defensemen) won't play as much as the first two.

The first pair is usually the team's top two defensive players. They must be both defensively responsible and able to bring an offensive presence. These players may play on the point during the power play while also being a key contributor in penalty-kill situations. They will play 18 to 30 minutes during the game. The second pair will have similar roles as the first but with slightly less ice time. They may see 15 to 20 minutes per game. The third pair will probably not play as much as the first two pairs. They may see around 10 to 12 minutes of ice time in total (sometimes less and sometimes more). These players will usually have a more stay-at-home, defense-first mind-set and may not have the offensive skill of the first two pairs.

Offensive-minded defensemen will be skating all over the ice and will probably play a lot of minutes. These players are going to approach their off-ice training similarly to the first-line forwards. Although the in-season strength and conditioning program is still very important, more emphasis is needed on rest and recovery. Their conditioning should consist of some easy, steady-state riding on the stationary bike for 10 minutes postgame. Then they would spend some time strength training (if no game is scheduled for the next day), stretching, and in the cold tub.

Players who are called on to try to shut down the other team's top line will get a lot of minutes, and they're going to be tough minutes. These players need to focus on recovering more than training off the ice as the season goes on.

As mentioned, the top pair will play the most, followed by the second pair and then the third. The top pairs should have minimal extra conditioning work on the stationary bikes. Their postgame conditioning should be nothing more than a 10-minute recovery flush ride to help kick-start the recovery process for the next game.

The third pair can put more work and time into their in-season off-ice training. Depending on how much they play during a game, they should also be performing bike sprints, strength training, stretching, and recovering immediately postgame. The postgame conditioning work for the fifth and sixth defensemen should consist of the following on the stationary bike:

- 6-8 × 45-second sprints with 1 minute and 15 seconds rest.
- 6-8 × 1-minute sprints with heart rate recovery to 130 bpm. For these sprints, players need to wear a heart rate monitor. They sprint for 1 minute at the highest resistance on the bike and then recover at the easiest resistance. When the heart rate lowers to 130 bpm, they sprint again.

GOALTENDER

The goaltender is the most important player on the ice. As the last line of defense, and her level of play during a game plays a huge factor in the result. There are two or three goaltenders (colleges will sometimes carry three) on the roster. They play the entire game, with the exception of when they skate to the bench when there is a delayed power play or when they are pulled for an extra attacker when the team is trying to tie up a game late in the third period.

Although they are on the ice for the entire game, goaltenders' conditioning demands are different from those of the forwards and defensemen. First, it is important to address the movement demands of the goaltender. The goaltender isn't a normal skater. Basically, he will stay in his crease for most of the game. He will be called on to do whatever it takes to stop the puck. From a movement perspective, a goalie must be able to go from standing to a position on his knees and back up again as well as move side to side as explosively as possible, all while wearing several pounds of equipment.

Five-on-five situations involve more back-and-forth play on the ice. The goaltender needs to be ready for whenever the puck is shot in his direction. During penalty-kill situations, he will get more work as the puck may be in the defensive zone for long periods. Penalty killing is very demanding, so the goaltender must be focused and well conditioned. When the team is on the power play, the goaltender must be ready at all times. He must retrieve the puck when the other team clears the zone and must be ready for the other team's shorthanded opportunities. There will also be times when the goaltender isn't doing much during the game.

Although they have totally different responsibilities, movement patterns, and conditioning demands on the ice, goalies still need to strength train and be in adequate condition throughout the season. It is the author's opinion that there are no reasons for goaltenders to do different exercises for their strength training program. Strong is strong and fast is fast no matter what. Goaltending-specific exercises in the weight room combined with on-ice drills in practices and then in game situations can result in overuse injuries.

In-season training from an off-ice perspective should emphasize recovery over training for the starting goaltender. If a team has a clearly established number one goaltender, then this player should be treated similarly to the first line of forwards and top pair of defensemen. Although strength and conditioning is important, there will be times when the number one goaltender needs to recover more, especially if he faced a lot of shots in the game. Goaltenders also need to pay attention to maintaining their hydration. It is not uncommon for a goaltender to lose up to 10 pounds (5 kg) during the course of a game. Hydration and body weight should be monitored at all times.

The starting goaltender will not have much to do after games from a conditioning perspective. If the team is strength training, then the goalie should strength train.

If they are not, then the goalie should do a recovery ride like the other players who play high minutes. The backup goaltender needs a longer conditioning session after the game, unless he put in a significant amount of work during the game-day workout. The backup should do a minimal ride of 30 minutes or so followed by strength training if the team is lifting. There are many different options to choose from for the backup goaltender:

- 30-minute preset fitness program on the bike. This is a great alternative to bike sprints.

- Cardiac output ride at a resistance that puts the heart rate in the 120- to 140-bpm range for 30 minutes. This consists of riding in manual mode and increasing resistance until the proper heart rate range is achieved.

- 6-8 × 1-minute sprints with heart rate recovery to 130 bpm. Use this option if the goalie wasn't on the ice at all that day and there isn't much time after the game. For these sprints, players need to wear a heart rate monitor. They sprint for 1 minute at the highest resistance on the bike and then recover at the easiest resistance. When the heart rate lowers to 130 bpm, they sprint again.

HEALTHY SCRATCHES, RED SHIRTS, AND INJURED PLAYERS

Not every player will dress for a game, and the players who don't play need to maintain their conditioning. The more games a player misses, the more he can get out of game condition. Healthy scratches need to be conditioned and ready to play the next game, similar to the backup goaltender. In some situations, scratched players will participate in the pregame warm-up. After the warm-up is the best time for them to work hard on the stationary bike. Ideally, they will condition and strength train immediately after the warm-up and be finished by the end of the first period of the game.

Healthy scratches will have usually done some hard on-ice conditioning earlier in the day at the game-day skate. But there are times when a healthy scratch may not have worked hard during the day, usually when there was no morning skate or if the player was scratched instead of another player in an attempt to match lines. For example, the other team might have dressed a player who is known as a fighter. The home team may choose to play a tougher player instead of a higher-skilled player to help the team match up better.

In the collegiate environment, a player may be redshirted (kept out of competition for a season). Although it isn't as common as in other sports such as football, redshirting in hockey does take place at the Division I level. Sometimes it will occur because of transfer rules in the NCAA. Players who sit out a season will have completely different conditioning programs. A higher-intensity program, similar to the off-season, is appropriate.

INJURY CONSIDERATIONS

Injuries are part of the game and will occur during the year. An injury can be short term or long term. A short-term injury such as a pulled groin or hip flexor can be treated by the team's athletic trainer. With the proper therapy, the player can return in a safe and quick manner. Other injuries such as shoulder separations, knee sprains, ankle sprains, minor fractures, and concussions will require the player to miss a considerable amount of time. Sometimes surgery is needed if an injury can't be fixed by traditional rehab, leading to a significant amount of time missed (10 to 12 weeks, minimum). Other longer-term injuries include ACL tears and fractures of larger bones such as the leg bones.

The strength and conditioning coach is one of the most important people involved in getting these players back on the ice. There is no reason a player can't continue to work on strength and conditioning. During the days leading up to the 2008 Super Bowl between the New England Patriots and the New York Giants, the NFL network aired a short piece on then Patriot strength and conditioning coach Mike Woicik. The story was about Coach Woicik's six Super Bowl rings and his work with the Patriots as well as with the Dallas Cowboys in the 1990s. It featured several current and former players who were coached by Woicik. Wide receiver Michael Irvin told a story of a conversation they had after Irvin suffered an ACL injury in 1989. Coach Woicik told him, "There are six parts of running: two ankles, two knees, and two hips. Although one of them isn't 100 percent, there is no [reason] why we can't keep you going." This is a unique part of being a strength and conditioning coach. Obviously, a coach hopes his programs will prevent injuries from happening, but he must be prepared for when athletes suffer an injury and be there for them every way he can be.

When an injury does occur, the thought process is that once the injury is rehabbed, the player should be able to return to action quickly. For this reason, it is important for a strength and conditioning coach to establish a good relationship with the athletic department or team's athletic training and medical staff. When there is trust, the other professionals will see that the continuation of the strength and conditioning program is important for the athlete. That way everyone is on board, working with each other while addressing the needs of the athlete and the team.

From the athlete's perspective, this may be the most challenging time in his career, especially if it's the first time he has suffered a long-term injury. The team needs to go about their daily business of trying to win games without the injured player. The strength and conditioning coach has to be very supportive and understanding while also being able to coach athletes through difficult times. It is not uncommon for the strength and conditioning coach to spend three or four hours a day, seven days a week, with an injured player. It's interesting to note that Michael Irvin thanked Mike Woicik publicly when he was recently inducted into the Pro Football Hall of Fame, calling him the best strength and conditioning coach in the National Football League.

Chapter 4

Pretraining

The pretraining period is the time spent in the weight room each session prior to the speed, power, and strength aspects of the off-season program. This can take up to an hour and focuses on many of the areas that can't be addressed during the in-season part of *Total Hockey Training*. The athlete can also spend more time on things that were not emphasized during the season.

PRETRAINING EXERCISES

Total Hockey Training suggests a pretraining period that consists of several components including soft tissue work, flexibility exercises, mobility exercises, resets, core activation, exercise band work, medicine ball work, plyometrics, speed and acceleration work, movement preparation, and sled work. Since this book has specific chapters on some of these components, those covered in this chapter include soft tissue work, mobility exercises, exercise bands, and movement preparation.

Soft Tissue Work

Soft tissue work helps athletes get to know their own bodies a little better. This is the time to find and address some areas in their muscles that might be hurting them. Some may not know where slight pain or discomfort is coming from until they begin with soft tissue work.

For soft tissue work in the hockey team setting, the foam roller is recommended. The foam roller should be used extensively throughout the entire year. Used on a daily basis, it can help help maintain muscle tissue quality. Soft tissue work should always be done when the player first arrives at the facility to begin training. This ensures that the player works on any tightness in the muscles and addresses trigger points, which can become common during the hockey season or the off-season program.

Foam rollers are available in two sizes—3 feet long and 6 inches wide (90 by 15 cm) or 1 foot long and 6 inches wide (45 by 15 cm). The smaller ones are great for traveling with because they can be put in the players' hockey bags, allowing for a team foam roller session at the rink or hotel. The more expensive foam rollers are firmer, while the less expensive kinds may get softer over time. A good foam roller is a wise investment.

Foam Roller Exercises

The player uses the foam roller and body weight to apply pressure to the muscle group. Some muscles may feel different from others because of their size or level of tenderness. As a general recommendation, 10 repetitions are prescribed of simply rolling the foam roller under the intended muscle. However, a tighter muscle group may require more reps.

Foam Roller: Hamstring

Foam Roller: Calf

Foam Roller: IT Band

Foam Roller: Rectus Femoris

Foam Roller: Pecs

Foam Roller: Lats

Foam Roller: Thoracic Spine

Foam Roller: Posterior Shoulder

Foam Roller: Glutes

Foam Roller: Hip Rotators

Foam Roller: Adductors

Mobility Exercises

Mobility exercises are for warming up the joints and restoring movement. The ankles, hips, and thoracic spine are important to focus on because hockey players are in a shortened position most of the time while playing the game. As a result, these areas can become stiff. Helping unlock these joints can help players achieve better performance.

Mobility exercises get the joints moving before other activities such as jumping, sprinting, and strength training take place. Movement can be classified into three planes—sagittal, frontal, and transverse. All three of these planes of motion should be addressed through mobility exercises. The sagittal plane involves movement from front to back or straight ahead. The frontal plane is movement from side to side or left to right. The transverse plane involves movement conducted with a rotational component or a combination of sagittal and frontal planes.

Quadruped Thoracic Spine Rotation

Setup

The athlete's knees and one elbow are on the ground, with the elbow under the shoulder and the hips back all the way until they are touching the heels. One hand is behind the back in a "chicken wing" position (see figure *a*).

Action

The athlete rotates the spine to the side with the hand behind the back (see figure *b*). The emphasis is on driving the elbow into the floor while rotating the other way. He inhales through the nose while trying to breathe through the diaphragm, not the chest, and exhales through the mouth during extension. Perform 10 repetitions on each side. Each repetition should be in the 2- to 3-second range.

Wall Ankle Mobilization

Setup

The athlete stands with the toes 3 inches (7.5 cm) from a wall.

Action

While keeping the heels flat on the floor, the athlete touches the knees to the wall and then returns to the starting position (see figures *a* and *b*). Perform 10 repetitions.

Split Squat

Setup

The athlete's front leg is forward as far as it can go, and the back leg is back as far as it can go, all in a straight line (see figure *a*).

Action

The athlete drops the back knee to the ground, touching the floor (see figure *b*), and returns to the starting position. Perform 5 repetitions on each side.

Lateral Squat

Setup

The athlete assumes an athletic position, with the chest up and eyes on the horizon (see figure *a*). The feet will be flat and both will be straight.

Action

The athlete squats to one side while keeping the other leg straight (see figure *b*). Perform 10 repetitions on each leg in an alternating fashion.

Transverse Plane Squat

Setup

The athlete's front foot is forward as far as it can go, and the back foot is at a 45-degree position in comparison to the front (see figure *a*). For example, if the left foot is in front, then the back foot is between 4 and 5 o'clock, with the toes facing that direction. If the right foot is in front, then the left foot is at 7 and 8 o'clock.

Action

The athlete squats to the back leg as though he is sitting on the heel (see figure *b*) and returns to the starting position. Perform 5 repetitions on each side.

Exercise Band Work

Exercise bands are an excellent tool for hockey players during the pretraining period. They are used extensively as a warm-up tool during the off-season program on lateral warm-up days, and they are used to strengthen the hip abductor muscles to stabilize both the hip and knee.

Exercise bands come in a number of resistance options. The easiest is yellow, followed by green and then blue, with black being the strongest. Younger and weaker players start with a yellow or green.

Monster Walk

Setup

The athlete assumes an athletic ready position, the feet a little wider than shoulder-width apart, with an exercise band secured around the ankles (see figure *a*).

Action

Keeping tension on the band, the athlete moves forward for 20 yards or meters and then backward for 20 yards (see figure *b* for an example of the forward walk). The chest is up and the butt is down throughout the entire set.

Exercise Band Lateral Shuffle

Setup

The athlete assumes a sideways-on athletic ready position, the feet a little wider than shoulder-width apart, with an exercise band secured around the ankles (see figure *a*).

Action

Keeping tension on the band, the athlete takes a big step to the right with the right foot while the left foot remains stable (see figure *b*). Then he quickly steps with the left foot while the right foot remains stable, maintaining the shoulder-width distance. The chest is up and the butt is down throughout the entire set. The athlete takes big steps for 20 yards or meters.

Movement Preparation

The movement preparation sequences are done throughout the off-season after the completion of core activation. They can also be done before practices and games throughout the hockey season. It is important to focus on these drills and to not just go through the motions in this aspect of the program. The main objectives of movement preparation are to increase core temperature so the muscular and nervous systems can function properly, to increase flexibility, and to prevent injuries.

The recommended distance for each movement preparation sequence is 20 yards or meters. Ideally, the exercises are done on a safe, even surface such as natural grass, artificial turf, a track, or a rubberized floor.

Linear Movement Prep

Linear movement prep prepares athletes for movements that take place in the sagittal plane (forward and backward). Plyometrics and speed exercises going straight ahead are performed on the same days as linear movement prep.

High-Knee Tuck

Setup

The athlete stands tall with feet shoulder-width apart (see figure *a*).

Action

The athlete pulls one knee into the chest as close as possible while keeping the other leg straight (see figure *b*). Repeat with the other leg and alternate while moving forward for 20 yards or meters.

Heel to Butt and Reach

Setup

The athlete stands tall with feet shoulder-width apart (see figure *a*).

Action

The athlete grabs one foot with the opposite hand and tries to touch the heel to the glute on the same side, while raising the free arm and keeping the knees together (see figure *b*). The stretch is felt in the quadriceps of the held leg. Alternate each leg while moving forward for 20 yards or meters.

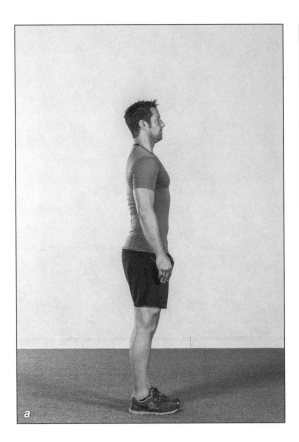

One-Leg Straight-Leg Deadlift

Setup

The athlete stands tall, feet shoulder-width apart. The arms are extended out to the sides so that the shoulder blades are squeezed together and the thumbs are up (see figure a).

Action

The athlete balances on one leg and bends at the waist, keeping the chest up and shoulder blades squeezed together, until a good stretch is felt in the hamstrings of the down leg (see figure b), and then returns to the starting position. The down leg will have a slight knee bend. Alternate each leg while moving forward for 20 yards or meters, and then repeat by moving backward for 20 yards.

Elbow to Instep Plus T-Spine Rotation Plus Hamstring Stretch

Setup

The athlete stands tall with feet shoulder-width apart.

Action

The athlete takes a big step forward with one leg and places the opposite-side hand on the ground even with the lead foot (see figure *a*). He touches the forearm of the arm on the lead-foot side to the ground and holds for a few seconds (see figure *b*).

He takes the same-side hand and reaches up and around while keeping an eye on the hand, holding the position for a few seconds (see figure *c*). He places the same-side hand on the outside of the foot and lifts the toe up toward the shin and straightens the lead leg (see figure *d*).

Repeat on the other side, and alternate each leg while moving forward for 20 yards or meters.

Reverse Lunge

Setup

The athlete stands tall with feet shoulder-width apart.

Action

The athlete clasps hands and reaches them overhead, then steps back with one leg as far as he can (see figure *a*) while reaching the arms in the opposite direction and keeping the back leg contracted (see figure *b*). Hold for a few seconds and then alternate each leg while moving backward for 20 yards or meters.

High-Knee Run

Setup

The athlete stands tall with feet shoulder-width apart.

Action

The athlete drives one knee up to the chest while alternating the knees (see figures *a* and *b*). Move forward at a moderate to fast pace for 20 yards or meters.

Heel-Ups

Setup

The athlete stands tall with feet shoulder-width apart.

Action

The athlete lifts the heels up to the hips while swinging the arms (see figure). Alternate each leg while moving forward at a moderate to fast pace for 20 yards or meters.

High-Knee Skips

Setup

The athlete stands tall with feet shoulder-width apart.

Action

The athlete skips and drives the knees up (see figures *a* and *b*). When the leg of the high knee hits the ground, the other leg's knee comes up. The emphasis is on exploding off of each foot to get up into the air. Alternate each leg while moving forward at a moderate to fast pace for 20 yards or meters.

Straight-Leg Skips

Setup

The athlete stands tall with feet shoulder-width apart.

Action

The athlete skips with straight legs, keeping the toes up toward the shins (see figures *a* and *b*). Alternate each leg while moving forward at a moderate to fast pace for 20 yards or meters.

Backward Open-Door Skip

Setup

The athlete stands tall with feet shoulder-width apart.

Action

The athlete skips backward and lifts one knee, rotating it to the outside while the other foot is on the ground, and repeats with the other leg (see figures *a* and *b*). Move at a moderate to fast pace for 20 yards or meters.

Backward Run

Setup

The athlete stands tall with feet shoulder-width apart.

Action

The athlete jogs backward while trying to reach the foot back as far as he can with each stride, reaching back with each leg and swinging the arms. Move at a moderate to fast pace for 20 yards or meters.

Forward Jog

Setup

The athlete stands tall with feet shoulder-width apart.

Action

The athlete jogs forward, taking big strides while swinging the arms. Move at a moderate to fast pace for 20 yards or meters.

Lateral Movement Prep

Lateral movement prep prepares athletes for movement in the frontal plane (side to side). Plyometrics and speed exercises going side to side are performed on the same days as linear movement prep.

Lateral Squat Walk

Setup

The athlete stands tall with feet shoulder-width apart.

Action

The athlete takes a big step to the right (see figure *a*) and while keeping the chest up, shifts his weight to the right. He sits back on the right heel while keeping the left leg straight and the left foot on the ground (see figure *b*). He brings the left foot over next to the right foot and then stands up straight. Repeat for 20 yards or meters and return in the opposite direction, performing the movement on the other leg.

IT Band Walk

Setup

The athlete stands tall with feet shoulder-width apart.

Action

The athlete keeps both legs straight and crosses the left foot over the right foot (see figure *a*). He shifts the right hip to the right and keeps both feet flat on the floor. He reaches his arms to the left side. Repeat for 20 yards or meters and return in the opposite direction, performing the movement on the other leg (see figure *b*).

Lateral Shuffle

Setup

The athlete assumes an athletic position with the chest up, hips back, and feet shoulder-width apart (see figure *a*).

Action

The athlete takes a big step to the right with the right foot while the left foot remains stable (see figure *b*). Then he quickly steps with the left foot while the right foot remains stable, maintaining the shoulder-width distance (see figure *c*). Repeat for 20 yards and return in the opposite direction.

Carioca

Setup

The athlete assumes an athletic position with the chest up, hips back, and feet shoulder-width apart (see figure *a*).

Action

The athlete crosses the left leg over the right and then shuffles the left foot behind the right foot, alternating the foot in front and then behind (see figures *b* and *c*). Move at a moderate pace for 20 yards or meters and return in the opposite direction, performing the movement with the right leg over the left.

Chapter 5

Core

Hockey is a fast-paced sport with frequent changes of direction and collisions. With so many games played by bigger and stronger players than in the past, injuries as a result of trauma or overuse are inevitable. Trauma injuries such as broken bones or those caused by a puck or opponent are certainly less preventable. However, overuse injuries can be reduced by combining core exercises with a proper strengthen and conditioning program.

The glutes (made up of the hip extensors and external rotators), hip abductors and adductors, hip flexors, abdominals, and lower back musculature make up a hockey player's core. These muscles need to be strong and able to engage at the correct time to prevent injuries. Core training should be done on a year-round basis for the purpose of preventing injuries.

CORE TRAINING EXERCISES

Total Hockey Training uses several methods for core training. They all train the core in different ways, but they overlap with one another and are of equal importance for proper core training.

Reflexive Core Stabilization

Before starting traditional core exercises such as flexion or extension of the trunk (or any other movement, for that matter), athletes should be able to demonstrate reflexive stabilization, which reduces the chance of muscular compensations during movement. Compensations occur when a muscle is weak, injured, tight, or sore, and another muscle that performs similar actions has to take over and overwork. In reflexive core stabilization, smaller stabilizer muscles including the transverse abdominis, multifidus, internal obliques, diaphragm, and pelvic floor muscles are trained to provide stability before bigger muscles are used in movement. This is important because faulty postures and the inability to maintain a proper lordosis (curve) in the lower back, which can be the result of weak abdominal and lumbar stability, have been shown to correlate with low back pain (Hodges and Richardson 1996; Christie, Kumar, and Warren 1995).

We were all born with the ability to move through a proper sequence of movement. When we were babies, our reflexive core was the first part of our bodies that worked to allow us to move. Automatically, our brain sent a signal to our core musculature before we rolled onto our bellies, before we lifted our heads, before we crawled, before we squatted, and so on. Somehow, most of us have lost the ability to move as we did when we were children. What has happened? For the most part, as a society, we have stopped moving. It's not hard to figure it out when you just look around. There is way more sitting and less moving.

As people move less over time, the ability to move like they once did can become lost. It's easy to forget what it was like to move when we were younger. However, athletes need to move to do their jobs. As a result, athletes become really good movement compensators. They figure out different movement strategies because they have lost the initial strategy that they learned automatically when they were younger. When you haven't done enough moving to sustain proper patterns, the result is tight and stiff muscles and joints due to overcompensation. Athletes need to get to the root of the problem by removing compensations and then moving in a better way.

A resource that explains this concept and defines a clear path for reestablishing proper movement patterns is *Becoming Bulletproof* by Tim Anderson and Mike McNiff (2011). In this book, the authors talk about how people can become better movers and activate the reflexive core through a series of exercises that resemble how people moved when they were babies. These exercises are called *resets*. By performing resets, athletes can activate the reflexive core before movement. The authors recommend performing resets throughout the day to combat daily habits and routines that involve sitting and moving with bad posture. This is a way to turn on the reflexive core before doing anything else in training sessions.

POSSIBLE MOVEMENT IMPAIRMENTS IN HOCKEY

Hockey players compete with their hips, knees, and spines flexed. The only time they may be upright on the ice is during the gliding phase of skating or between whistles when there is a stoppage of play. Players actually spend most of the game in flexion, whether playing, sitting on the bench, or sitting in their locker stalls during intermission.

They are also in flexion many other times during the day. Something to be taken into consideration is travel time. Bus travel in the minor leagues, juniors, and college can be up to 15 hours for one trip. Hockey players also spend an enormous amount of time on stationary bikes for numerous reasons including warm-up, conditioning, and postgame flush rides year-round. So between games, practices, training, and travel; hockey players are constantly sitting or skating with their joints in flexion.

From an injury prevention standpoint, the objective is to look at what can happen when athletes are flexed at the knee, hip, and spine for many hours throughout the day. The next step is coming up with strategies that try to eliminate problems that can occur because of muscle tightness or weakness from being in a shortened position. For the most part, these muscles include the hip flexors, abdominal muscles, groin muscles (adductors), and lower back muscles.

From previous evaluations and past experiences, some hockey players show some kind of lower crossed (see figure 5.1a) or upper crossed syndromes (see figure 5.1b). These syndromes were classified by neurologist Vladimir Janda of the Czech Republic to describe muscle imbalances in the upper body (upper crossed) or lower body (lower crossed) (Page, 2010, p. 84).

The muscles that are weak in the upper crossed syndrome are the neck flexors, rhomboids, and lower traps, while the tight muscles are the subscapularis, upper traps, levator scapulae, and pectorals. In the lower crossed syndrome, the weak muscles are the abdominals and gluteus max, while the tight muscles are the thoracic extensors, the lumbar extensors, and the hip flexors.

The main objective in a core program should be trying to eliminate these muscle imbalances and preventing them from happening. This is accomplished by lengthening the tight muscle groups and strengthening the weak ones. The core program strengthens the muscle groups that can become weak, along with other core muscles.

In addition to addressing these muscular imbalances and preventing the possible syndromes, it is important to ensure that a properly designed strength training program does not develop or contribute to muscle imbalances. A strength training program needs to balance chosen exercises.

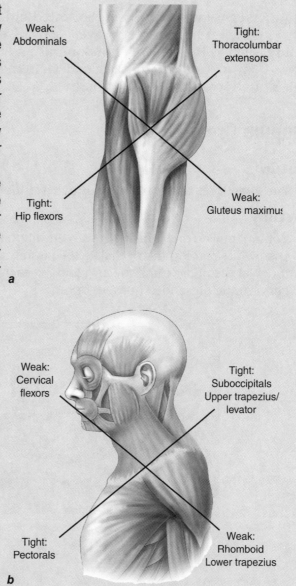

Figure 5.1 (a) Lower and (b) upper crossed syndromes.

When describing what she sees in people who regularly participate in physical activity, Shirley Sahrmann (2002) states that "Muscles frequently found to be weak are the lower trapezius, external oblique abdominal, gluteus maximus, and posterior gluteus medius. Even individuals who are active in sports demonstrate differences in the strength of synergistic muscles; one muscle can be notably weaker than its synergist" (p. 15). It is best to strengthen these muscles to prevent them from becoming weak and contributing to injury. A hockey player who doesn't participate in a structured core and strength and conditioning program has a good chance of experiencing weakness in the core muscles.

Cross Crawling

The cross crawling exercises were borrowed and implemented from *Becoming Bulletproof*. These exercises help hockey players activate or reset their inner abdominal musculature, such as the transverse abdominis and internal obliques, while engaging in a cross-body movement. This is beneficial to the hockey player because the movement takes place across the core and body.

Supine Cross Crawl

Setup

The athlete lies on his back with the hands behind the head.

Action

Without pulling on his head, the athlete alternately touches the elbow to the opposite knee while keeping the back flat (see figures *a* and *b*). The key is to ensure that they touch at the midline and the arm and leg each return to the proper starting position. Perform the prescribed number of reps.

Seated Cross Crawl

Setup

The athlete is in a seated position with the hands behind the head.

Action

The athlete alternately touches the elbow to the opposite knee (see figures *a* and *b*). The key is to ensure that they touch at the midline and that the arm and leg each return to the proper starting position. Perform the prescribed number of reps.

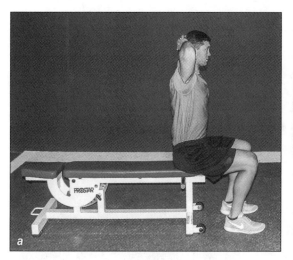

Standing Cross Crawl

Setup

The athlete is in a standing position with the hands behind the head (see figure *a*).

Action

The athlete alternately touches the elbow to the opposite knee (see figure *b*). The key is to ensure that they touch at the midline and that the arm and leg each return to the proper starting position. Perform the prescribed number of reps. A variation is to try this exercise with the eyes closed.

Rolling

Rolling is one of the first movements we learn as babies, from a position of lying on the back to being flat on the tummy and vice versa. This is a great exercise for awakening the reflexive core. This benefits hockey players by teaching them to engage the core before rolling, which they can transfer to other forms of movement (skating, passing, shooting, and so on).

Upper-Body Rolling

Setup

The athlete is in a supine position with the arms extended above the head and the legs as long as possible.

Action

The athlete rolls from his back to his stomach in one direction using the upper body only (see figure a). There should be no movement at all from the lower body. The initial movement involves lifting one arm up and reaching over the midline to create enough momentum to roll onto the stomach. When rolling from the stomach to the back, the initial movement

involves lifting one arm up and over to create enough momentum so that the athlete can roll onto the back (see figure b). Perform the prescribed number of reps in each direction for both the upper body and lower body.

Lower-Body Rolling

Setup

The athlete is in a supine position with the arms extended above the head and the legs as long as possible.

Action

The athlete rolls from his back to his abdomen in one direction using the lower body only. There is to be no movement at all from the upper body. The initial movement involves lifting one leg up and over the midline and the other leg to create enough momentum so that the athlete can roll onto the stomach (figure a). When rolling from the stomach to the back with the lower body only, one leg should be lifted up and crossed over the midline (figure b). Perform the prescribed number of reps in each direction for both the upper body and lower body.

Rocking

Rocking is a good way to use the reflexive core while also getting in some hip mobility work. This is another way a hockey player can engage the deep abdominal muscles before performing another movement.

Forearm Rocking

Setup

The athlete gets into a quadruped position with the forearms, knees, and toes on the ground (see figure *a*).

Action

With the eyes and head up toward the ceiling, the athlete rocks his hips back toward the heels (see figure *b*) and returns to the starting position. Perform the prescribed number of reps.

Straight-Arm Rocking

Setup

The athlete gets into a quadruped position with the hands, knees, and toes on the ground (see figure *a*).

Action

With the eyes and head up toward the ceiling, the athlete rocks his hips back toward the heels (see figure *b*) and returns to the starting position. Perform the prescribed number of reps.

Core Activation

Isolated muscle strengthening exercises are considered to be activation exercises. These are done immediately after resets to activate both the stabilizers (muscles that stabilize one joint so another joint can move) or prime movers (muscles that produce movement) in exercises and movement patterns that athletes will perform in the upcoming training session or game. The objective is for athletes to be able to do their jobs and prevent injuries.

It is important that hockey players address any muscles that can become weak. For example, the glutes are powerful hip extensors that can weaken because of the amount of time hockey players spend in hip flexion. Some coaches and trainers prescribe isolated muscle activation or strengthening work for the glutes. These exercises include glute bridges, one-leg glute bridges, and others that emphasize the quality of muscle contraction. However, some coaches and trainers think activation exercises are a fad and nothing but a waste of time. These same coaches often think that if their athletes are doing squats, lunges, one-leg squats, and split squats, then they are strengthening their glutes adequately.

Total Hockey Training prescribes glute activation exercises on a daily basis. All athletes should perform activation exercises, even if they have adequate posture and few injuries in the past. In my opinion, if physical therapists prescribe rehab exercises to treat injuries, why shouldn't healthy athletes do rehab exercises to prevent injuries from happening? Core activation exercises do not take a long time to perform and can help keep players healthy and on the ice.

Hip Extension

In the following exercises, athletes squeeze the glutes together to create the action of hip extension. The coaching cues include getting the athletes to brace the core, which prevents lumbar extension and drives the heels into the ground and lifts the hips up. The goal is to prevent what McGill (2011) refers to as glute amnesia, which occurs when the glutes are weak and an athlete needs to use her hamstrings, lower back, or both to create hip extension, which can be a recipe for lower back pain.

Glute Bridge

Setup

The athlete lies in a supine position with the arms at the sides and knees bent, with the feet together (see figure *a*).

Action

The athlete contracts the glutes and produces hip extension, so there is a straight line from knees to shoulders, and holds for 3 seconds (see figure *b*). The hamstrings will come into play, but the athlete keeps squeezing the glutes. Perform the prescribed number of reps.

One-Leg Glute Bridge

Setup

The athlete lies in a supine position with one knee held to the chest and the other foot flat on the ground with the knee bent (see figure *a*).

Action

The athlete contracts the glutes of the leg that is on the ground and produces hip extension, so there is a straight line from knee to shoulder, and holds for 3 seconds (see figure *b*). Perform the prescribed number of reps on each side.

Hands-Free One-Leg Glute Bridge

Setup

The athlete lies in a supine position with one knee close to the chest and the other foot flat on the ground with the knee bent (see figure *a*). A tennis ball is under the hip of the leg close to the chest.

Action

The athlete must hold the ball in place without using the hands and while contracting the glutes to produce hip extension, so there is a straight line from knee to shoulder, holding for 3 seconds (see figure *b*). Perform the prescribed number of reps on each side.

Medicine Ball One-Leg Glute Bridge

Setup

The athlete lies in a supine position with one foot on top of a medicine ball and the other leg on the ground (see figure *a*).

Action

The athlete contracts the glutes of the foot that is on the ball to produce hip extension, so there is a straight line from knee to shoulder, and holds for 3 seconds (see figure *b*). Perform the prescribed number of reps on each side.

Quadruped Bent-Knee Hip Extension

Setup

The athlete assumes a quadruped position on the hands and knees, with the hands under the shoulders and the knees under the hips (see figure *a*). The head is in a neutral position, neither up nor down. The athlete stabilizes the core before performing hip extension. This is accomplished by exhaling the breath so that core stability is attained before movement.

Action

While in a stable position, after exhaling, the athlete lifts one knee until the lower leg is perpendicular to the floor and holds for 3 seconds (see figure *b*). The only body part that moves is the leg being lifted. Perform the prescribed number of reps on each side.

Quadruped Straight-Leg Hip Extension

Setup

The athlete assumes a quadruped position on the hands and knees, with the hands under the shoulders and the knees under the hips (see figure *a*). The head is in a neutral position, neither up nor down. The athlete stabilizes the core before performing hip extension. This is accomplished by exhaling the breath so that core stability is attained before movement.

Action

While in a stable position, after exhaling, the athlete lifts one knee until the lower leg is perpendicular to the floor. Then he extends the leg so that the lower leg is parallel to the floor and holds for 3 seconds (see figure *b*). The only body part that moves is the leg being lifted. Perform the prescribed number of reps on each side.

Quadruped Alternating Arm–Leg Extension

Setup

The athlete assumes a quadruped position on the hands and knees, with the hands under the shoulders and the knees under the hips (see figure *a*). The head is in a neutral position, neither up nor down. The athlete stabilizes the core before performing hip extension. This is accomplished by exhaling the breath so that core stability is attained before movement.

Action

While in a stable position, after exhaling, the athlete lifts one knee until the lower leg is perpendicular to the floor. Then he extends the leg so that the lower leg is parallel to the floor, simultaneously reaching the opposite arm to a position that is straight and parallel to the floor, and holds for 3 seconds (see figure *b*). For example, if the right foot is extending, then the left arm will reach forward.

After the 3-second hold, the athlete moves the same arm's elbow and the same leg's knee under the body so they touch. He then goes back to the initial position and holds it for 3 seconds. Perform the prescribed number of reps on each side.

Hip Abduction

Hockey players do a lot of hip adduction work on the ice. Hip abduction exercises are prescribed to help balance strength in the hip joint. Several exercises in *Total Hockey Training* involve the hip abductors. However, this is activation, not necessarily strengthening.

Bent-Knee Side Bridge With Abduction

Setup

The athlete lies on his side with the knees bent and elbow on the floor.

Action

The athlete drives the hips up and holds this position just long enough to stabilize (see figure *a*). Then he abducts the top leg and holds it for 30 seconds (see figure *b*). Younger players shouldn't use any resistance—gravity will be sufficient. However, older and stronger players should use an exercise band above the knees. Perform the prescribed number of reps on each side.

Straight-Leg Abduction

Setup

The athlete lies on his side, keeping the bottom leg bent at 90 degrees and the top leg straight, in line with the hip.

Action

The athlete lifts the leg up while pointing the toe toward the ground (see figure). The core remains tight during the whole set. Perform the prescribed number of reps on each side.

Quadruped Bent-Knee Abduction

Setup

The athlete assumes a quadruped position on the hands and knees, with the hands under the shoulders and the knees under the hips (see figure *a*). The athlete keeps the core tight by exhaling until a stable core is maintained.

Action

The athlete abducts his leg out to the side (see figure *b*) and then returns to the starting position. No resistance is needed for younger athletes; older athletes will use an exercise band. Perform the prescribed number of reps on each side.

One-Leg Box Squat

Setup

The athlete stands on one leg next to a box or bench that is 14 to 24 inches (36 to 60 cm) in height (see figure *a*).

Action

While balancing on one leg, the athlete squats to the box or bench (see figure *b*), touches his glutes on the box, and then stands up. This is an advanced exercise for older players only; stronger players should use a band above the knees to facilitate the hip abductors. Perform the prescribed number of reps on each side.

Hip Flexion

Since the activation exercises feature extension and abduction, flexion exercises are also incorporated to activate the hip flexors. The deep hip flexors, including the psoas and iliacus, need to be flexible as well as strong. Other muscles important for hip flexion are the rectus femoris, tensor fasciae latae, sartorius, and some of the adductors.

Lying Hip Flexor With Band

Setup

The athlete lies on the floor in a supine position, with an exercise band secured around the ankles or feet (see figure *a*).

Action

The athlete exhales and then lifts one knee 90 degrees toward the head (see figure *b*). After holding this position for 3 seconds, he repeats on the other side. Perform the prescribed number of reps on each side.

Seated Hip Flexor With Overhead Reach

Setup

The athlete sits on a box with a straight torso and the knees above the hips (see figure *a*). The arms are reaching overhead.

Action

The athlete exhales and then lifts one knee up toward the head while keeping the spine stable (see figure *b*). After holding this position for 3 seconds, he repeats on the other side. Perform the prescribed number of reps on each side.

Standing Hip Flexor With Overhead Reach

Setup

The athlete stands with one foot on top of a box high enough so that the knee is above the hip (see figure *a*). The arms are reaching overhead.

Action

The athlete exhales and then lifts the knee of the leg that is on the box up toward the head while keeping the spine stable (see figure *b*). There is also an emphasis on extending the leg that is on the ground. After holding this position for 3 seconds, he repeats on the other side. Perform the prescribed number of reps on each side.

Mountain Climber

Setup

The athlete assumes a push-up position. One leg is straight and stationary on the ground; the other leg will be the working leg, with the foot on top of the slide board or Valslide (see figure *a*).

Action

The athlete exhales and then lifts the working-leg knee to a position above 90 degrees without any spinal movement (see figure *b*). There is also an emphasis on extending the leg that is on the ground. After holding this position for 3 seconds, he repeats on the other side. Perform the prescribed number of reps on each side.

GROIN ACTIVATION

The groin area is probably the most common place for soft tissue injury among hockey players. It is important that hockey players keep their groins healthy, especially at the beginning of the season when the volume of skating is high. With the core program, and the addition of foam rolling, flexibility work, and the strength and conditioning program, hockey players can be very proactive about preventing adductor and groin muscle injuries.

During the off-season, the adductors are strengthened in the strength training program through exercises such as lateral squats, front squats, one-leg squats, and straight-leg deadlifts. Using a slide board in the conditioning aspect of the program also helps prevent groin injuries. The slide board not only helps the athlete strengthen the muscles in the frontal plane but also produces a conditioning effect in a movement pattern that is much closer to skating than running or riding a stationary bike.

At the beginning of the competitive season, players need to be prepared for the rigorous demands of training camp, which consist of two to three hours on the ice daily plus preseason games. This schedule is tough to prepare for no matter how well the strength and conditioning program is designed. During this time, the program should include groin activation exercises, which are simply isolated adductor exercises in the supine position. The angle of the legs on the ground changes to give the athlete several variations of the same exercises. The athlete exhales and tightens the core before gently squeezing the ball to contract the adductors.

Combined with stretching and activation of the hip musculature, groin activation exercises can help prevent soft tissue injury.

Two great groin activation exercises are the short and long ball squeeze, where the athlete lies flat on the back with the knees bent and feet flat. The athlete exhales and then slightly squeezes a ball (about the size of a soccer ball) in between the knees for 3 seconds. After each hold, the athlete relaxes and then repeats the exercise for a prescribed number of reps. In the short ball squeeze, the knees are bent (see figure 5.2a and b); in the long ball squeeze, the knees are only slightly bent (see figure 5.3a and b).

Figure 5.2 Short ball squeeze.

Figure 5.3 Long ball squeeze.

Core Strength

According to Sahrmann (2002), "The most important aspect of abdominal muscle performance is obtaining the control that is necessary to (1) appropriately stabilize the spine, (2) maintain optimal alignment and movement relationships between the pelvis and spine, and (3) prevent excessive stress and compensatory motions of the pelvis during movements of the extremities" (p. 69). The core program is prescribed with those points in mind.

The hockey player must stabilize the core before doing other movements. The smaller muscle groups are trained so that the bigger muscles can do their job, which is stabilizing the spine under higher loads. Core strengthening and stabilization exercises are performed during the strength training portion of a training session.

Rollouts

Rollouts are included in the off-season program on days 1 and 3. They are performed during quad-sets to allow more rest for strength training exercises such as front squats and pull-ups. As the off-season progresses, rollouts progress to the stir-the-pot exercise. The goal is to promote stability in the trunk region while the arms or legs move the apparatus.

Stability Ball Rollout

Setup

The athlete assumes a position with the knees on the ground and the forearms on a stability ball (see figure a).

Action

The athlete rolls the ball forward while keeping the pelvis posteriorly rotated and the spine stable (see figure b). After reaching full hip extension, he returns to the starting position. Perform the prescribed number of reps.

Wheel Rollout

Setup

The athlete assumes a position with the knees on the ground and the hands on a wheel, such as a basic ab wheel or a Power Wheel (see figure *a*).

Action

The athlete rolls the wheel forward while keeping the pelvis posteriorly rotated and the spine stable (see figure *b*). After reaching full hip extension, he returns to the starting position. Perform the prescribed number of reps.

Stir the Pot

Setup

The athlete assumes a position with the knees on the ground and the forearms on a stability ball (see figure *a*).

Action

The athlete rolls the ball forward while keeping the pelvis posteriorly rotated and the spine stable (see figure *b*). After reaching full hip extension, he makes tight circles while keeping the spine stable and the core tight (see figure *c*). Perform the prescribed number of reps in each direction (clockwise and counterclockwise).

Straight-Leg Sit-Up

The straight-leg sit-up is a core exercise performed as part of the plate circuit during the preseason period.

Setup

The athlete lies on the back with the legs straight on the ground and the plate held across the chest (see figure *a*).

Action

The athlete performs a sit-up while trying to envision curling the trunk so that the upper body is perpendicular to the floor (see figure *b*). He then returns to the starting position. Perform the prescribed number of reps.

Chops and Lifts

Like other core stabilization exercises and progressions in *Total Hockey Training*, chops and lifts are exercises that are done for creating proper core stability before movement occurs. A cable column apparatus is necessary, although bands can work if a cable column is unavailable. The exercises progress from kneeling with two knees on the ground to standing with both feet on the ground.

Kneeling Cable Chop

Setup

The athlete kneels at a cable column in a tall position with both knees on the floor (see figure *a*). The exercise starts with the cable set at a high position.

Action

The athlete pulls the rope across and down toward the floor on the other side (see figure *b*). For example, if the cable column is to the left of the athlete, the right hand will be at the bottom of the rope and the left hand near the top. Most of the pulling is done by the right hand, while the pushing is done by the left hand. Perform the prescribed number of reps on each side.

Half-Kneeling Cable Chop

Setup

The athlete kneels at a cable column and assumes a tall position with the outside knee down (see figure *a*). The exercise starts with the cable set at a high position.

Action

The athlete pulls the rope across and down toward the floor on the other side (see figure *b*). For example, if the cable column is toward the left of the athlete, the right hand will be at the bottom of the rope and the left hand near the top. Most of the pulling is done by the right hand, while the pushing is done by the left hand. Perform the prescribed number of reps on each side.

Lunge Cable Chop

Setup

The athlete assumes a tall lunge stance at a cable column, with one foot in front of the other (see figure *a*). The leg that is closer to the cable column is in a forward position, while the outside foot is in the back position. The exercise starts with the cable set at a high position.

Action

The athlete pulls the rope across and down toward the floor on the other side (see figure *b*). For example, if the cable column is to the left of the athlete, the right hand will be at the bottom of the rope and the left hand near the top. Most of the pulling is done by the right hand, while the pushing is done by the left hand. Perform the prescribed number of reps on each side.

Standing Cable Chop

Setup

The athlete stands next to the cable column in an athletic stance (see figure *a*). The exercise starts with the cable set at a high position.

Action

The athlete pulls the rope across and down toward the floor on the other side (see figure *b*). For example, if the cable column is to the left of the athlete, the right hand will be at the bottom of the rope and the left hand near the top. Most of the pulling is done by the right hand, while the pushing is done by the left hand. Perform the prescribed number of reps on each side.

Kneeling Cable Lift

Setup

The athlete kneels at a cable column in a tall position with both knees on the floor (see figure). The exercise starts with the cable set at a low position.

Action

The athlete pulls the rope across and up toward the ceiling on the other side. For example, if the cable column is to the left of the athlete, the left hand will be at the bottom of the rope and the right hand near the top. Most of the pulling is done by the right hand, while the pushing is done by the left hand. Perform the prescribed number of reps on each side.

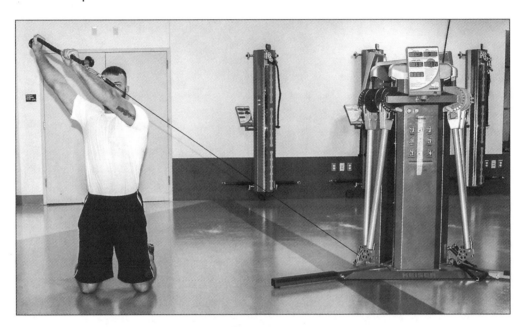

Half-Kneeling Cable Lift

Setup

The athlete kneels at a cable column and assumes a tall position with the knee closest to the cable column on the floor (see figure a). The exercise starts with the cable set at a low position.

Action

The athlete pulls the rope across and up toward the ceiling on the other side (see figure b). For example, if the cable column is to the right of the athlete, the right hand will be at the bottom of the rope and the left hand near the top. Most of the pulling is done by the left hand, while the pushing is done by the right hand. Perform the prescribed number of reps on each side.

Lunge Cable Lift

Setup

The athlete assumes a lunge stance at a cable column, with one foot in front of the other (see figure *a*). The leg that is closer to the cable column is in a back position, while the outside foot is in the forward position. The exercise starts with the cable set at a low position.

Action

The athlete pulls the rope across and up toward the ceiling on the other side (see figure *b*). For example, if the cable column is to the left of the athlete, the left hand will be at the bottom of the rope and the right hand near the top. Most of the pulling is done by the right hand, while the pushing is done by the left hand. Perform the prescribed number of reps on each side.

Standing Cable Lift

Setup

The athlete stands next to a cable column in an athletic stance (see figure *a*). The exercise starts with the cable set at a low position.

Action

The athlete pulls the rope across and up toward the ceiling on the other side (see figure *b*). For example, if the cable column is to the left of the athlete, the left hand will be at the bottom of the rope and the right hand near the top. Most of the pulling is done by the right hand, while the pushing is done by the left hand. Perform the prescribed number of reps on each side.

Get-Ups

The get-up is almost a hybrid exercise. When classifying this movement, it is considered a core strengthening exercise. However, an argument could be made that it is a total-body lift. This functional movement requires all the muscles in the body to work in a coordinated fashion while the core is strong and stable. It can also improve mobility in areas where hockey players tend to be stiff, such as the thoracic spine and hip flexors. The get-up works both sides of the body so that any differences in right and left sides can be addressed.

Although it appears to be a complicated exercise that is hard to teach—especially to a large group of athletes—the get-up can be broken down and taught in a safe manner over time. It is important to return to the starting position during each step. Athletes need proper body control and eccentric strength to complete the movement.

In the off-season program, get-up progressions are performed twice per week. Each three-week phase of the off-season program consists of one step of the exercise. The first step is in phase 1 (weeks 1 to 3), while a full get-up is performed in phase 4 (weeks 10 to 12). During the season, the same progressions are implemented in different phases. By the end of the season, the players should be performing full get-ups.

Get-Up: Step 1—Get Up to Hand

The athlete holds a kettlebell overhead with a straight arm; the opposite arm is on the floor at a 45-degree angle (see figure *a*). The leg on the kettlebell side is bent, with the foot flat on the floor. The opposite leg is straight, at a 45-degree angle parallel to the straight arm. The head is straight, with the eyes on the kettlebell. The emphasis is on movement from the abdominal muscles through the thoracic spine. The athlete drives the elbow of the straight arm into the ground and pauses (see figure *b*). Then he extends that arm and puts his hand on the floor (see figure *c*).

Get-Up: Step 2—Get Up to Hip Extension

This step is beneficial from a screening perspective. Hockey players with tight hip flexors and rectus femoris muscles will be unable to extend the hips. Those who need extra soft tissue work, stretching, or both for the hip flexors and rectus femoris can easily be identified during this phase of the get-up. This part of the get-up combined with all the glute bridging and hip flexor lengthening, is imperative for maintaining healthy hips.

The athlete holds a kettlebell overhead with a straight arm; the opposite arm is on the floor at a 45-degree angle. The leg on the kettlebell side is bent, with the foot flat on the floor. The opposite leg is straight, at a 45-degree angle parallel to the straight arm. The head is straight, with the eyes on the kettlebell. The emphasis is on movement from the abdominal muscles through the thoracic spine. The athlete drives the elbow of the straight arm into the ground and pauses. He extends that arm and puts his hand on the floor (see figure *a*). Then he drives the bent leg to a position of extended hips (see figure *b*).

Get-Up: Step 3—Get Up to Kneeling Position

This step requires coordination, balance, and stability throughout the body. The finishing position is a half-kneeling stance, which is used frequently throughout the training year.

The athlete holds a kettlebell overhead with a straight arm; the opposite arm is on the floor at a 45-degree angle. The leg on the kettlebell side is bent, with the foot flat on the floor. The opposite leg is straight, at a 45-degree angle parallel to the straight arm. The head is straight, with the eyes on the kettlebell. The emphasis is on movement from the abdominal muscles through the thoracic spine. The athlete drives the elbow of the straight arm into the ground and pauses. He extends that arm and puts his hand on the floor. He drives the bent leg to a position of extended hips. Then he moves the other leg from an extended position to a bent-knee position underneath the hips (see figure *a*). The end result is a half-kneeling position, with one knee on the ground and the opposite foot on the ground (see figure *b*).

Get-Up: Step 4—Full Get-Up

This is the last step of the get-up. By now the base has been established, and this is an easy progression.

The athlete holds a kettlebell overhead with a straight arm; the opposite arm is on the floor at a 45-degree angle. The leg on the kettlebell side is bent, with the foot flat on the floor. The opposite leg is straight, at a 45-degree angle parallel to the straight arm. The head is straight, with the eyes on the kettlebell. The emphasis is on movement from the abdominal muscles through the thoracic spine. The athlete drives the elbow of the straight arm into the ground and pauses. He extends that arm and puts his hand on the floor. He drives the bent leg to a position of extended hips. Then he moves the other leg from an extended position to a bent-knee position underneath the hips. The end result is a half-kneeling position, with one knee on the ground and the opposite foot on the ground. Now the athlete stands up out of the half-kneeling position while keeping the arm holding the kettlebell straight (see figure). The eyes can now look straight ahead.

Core Stabilization

Core stabilization improves musculature endurance in the trunk through exercises such as planks and side bridges. It is important to establish or reestablish trunk and lower back endurance. Endurance has a more protective value than does strength (Luoto et al. 1995). Plank and side bridge variations and progressions are performed in the core program.

Planks

A plank is a position that is held motionless for a set time. During the off-season program, planks progress from a basic hold in phase 1 to positions that add arm movement, leg movement, opposite arm and leg movement, and rowing.

Plank

Setup

The athlete lies facedown with the elbows on the ground in front of the shoulders. The head is in neutral position, looking neither up nor down toward the feet.

Action

The athlete exhales to create stability in the core and rises up from the floor (see figure). He attempts to contract every muscle possible to keep his body steady for 30 seconds. Perform the prescribed number of reps.

Plank With Arm Lift

Setup

The athlete lies facedown with the elbows on the ground in front of the shoulders. The head is in neutral position, looking neither up nor down toward the feet.

Action

The athlete exhales to create stability in the core and rises up from the floor (see figure *a*). Holding the plank position, he lifts one arm and holds for 3 seconds (see figure *b*), returns to the starting position, and repeats with the other arm. The key is having enough stability in the body so that the only body parts that are moving are the arms while moving up and down. Perform the prescribed number of reps on each side.

Plank With Leg Lift

Setup

The athlete lies facedown with the elbows on the ground in front of the shoulders. The head is in neutral position, looking neither up nor down toward the feet.

Action

The athlete exhales to create stability in the core and rises up from the floor (see figure *a*). Holding the plank position, the athlete creates a slight hip extension by lifting one foot off the ground toward the ceiling, holds for 3 seconds (see figure *b*), returns to the starting position, and repeats on the other leg. The leg lift requires the athlete to create core stability while moving a limb. Perform the prescribed number of reps on each side.

Plank With Alternating Arm and Leg Lift

Setup

The athlete lies facedown with the elbows on the ground in front of the shoulders. The head is in neutral position, looking neither up nor down toward the feet.

Action

The athlete exhales to create stability in the core and rises up from the floor (see figure *a*). Holding the plank position, the athlete simultaneously lifts one leg and the opposite arm and holds for 3 seconds (see figure *b*), returns to the starting position, and repeats with the other leg and arm. For example, if the right arm is lifted, then the left foot will be as well; if the left arm is lifted, then the right foot will be as well. The key is to have enough stability in the body so that the only body parts that are moving are the arms and legs while moving up and down. Perform the prescribed number of reps on each side.

Plank With Dumbbell Row

Setup

The athlete lies facedown with the arms straight under the shoulders, similar to a push-up position. The head is in neutral position, looking neither up nor down toward the feet. The hands are grasping dumbbells (the dumbbells should have flat edges).

Action

The athlete exhales to create stability in the core and rises up from the floor (see figure *a*). Holding the plank position, the athlete performs a dumbbell row (see figure *b*), returns to the starting position, and repeats with the other arm. Perform the prescribed number of reps on each side.

Side Bridges

The side bridge is used extensively as a core exercise in *Total Hockey Training*. Holding this position while engaging the core musculature provides the stability to keep the athlete from falling down. The deep abdominals are engaged by exhaling enough so that the rib cage descends. When this occurs, the athlete maintains that position and lifts the hips off the floor. During the off-season program, side bridges progress from a bent-knee side bridge to more difficult variations created by straightening the legs and then moving from one side to the other.

Bent-Knee Side Bridge

Setup

The athlete lies on one side and stacks the legs on top of one another with a bend in the knees so they are at a 90-degree angle (see figure *a*).

Action

The athlete lifts the hips off the floor, extending into a straight line all the way from the knees to the head (see figure *b*). He exhales and holds the position for 10 seconds and then relaxes the hips on the floor. He rests for a few seconds and then repeats. Perform the prescribed number of reps on each side.

Stacked-Leg Side Bridge

Setup

The athlete lies on one side and stacks the legs on top of one another, keeping them straight (see figure *a*).

Action

The athlete lifts the hips off the floor, extending into a straight line all the way from the feet to the head (see figure *b*). He exhales and holds the position for 10 seconds and then relaxes the hips on the floor. He rests for a few seconds and then repeats. Perform the prescribed number of reps on each side.

Straddle Side Bridge

Setup

The athlete lies on one side and crosses the top leg over the bottom leg, with both feet on the floor and kept straight.

Action

The athlete lifts the hips off the floor, extending into a straight line all the way from the feet to the head. He exhales and holds the position for 10 seconds (see figure). The hips do not touch the ground after each repetition. Instead, the athlete rotates from one forearm to the other while keeping the hips off the ground and rotating the feet so they change position. For example, when the athlete is lying on his left side, the right foot is in front. When he is lying on his right side, the left foot is in front. Perform the prescribed number of reps on each side.

Transitional Straddle Side Bridge

Setup

The athlete lies on one side and crosses the top leg over the bottom leg, with both feet on the floor and kept straight.

Action

The athlete lifts the hips off the floor, extending into a straight line all the way from the feet to the head (see figure a). He exhales and holds the position for 10 seconds, and then relaxes the hips on the floor. Then the athlete rotates from one forearm to the other while keeping the hips off the ground and rotating the feet so they change position (see figures b and c). For example, when the athlete is lying on the left side, the right foot is in front. When lying on the right side, the left foot is in front.

Core Power

A hockey shot is a rotational movement; whether it's a slap shot, wrist shot, or pass. Hockey players can use a medicine ball to train for power in these movements. Athletes perform plyometrics to increase power in their legs. The medicine ball allows the athletes to perform plyometrics for increasing power in the torso.

Athletes should throw the medicine ball as hard as possible, with the intention of putting a hole in the wall. Only use a concrete wall when throwing medicine balls. When selecting the proper ball size and weight, heavier balls generate more power for throwing against a wall. Performing these throws with a partner is not recommended because the speed the athlete is trying to accomplish will be too difficult for a partner to catch.

When throwing medicine balls, the focus isn't just on the forehand side. In fact, working the other side is important not only to improve backhand strength but also to prevent overuse injuries and potential asymmetries caused by working one side more than the other. Throws are also done from an overhead position and as chest passes in conjunction with the bench press.

Like many other exercises in *Total Hockey Training*, the progression is from kneeling to standing. The emphasis is on maintaining an upright posture and generating power in the hips. The athlete tries to generate as much power and speed as possible while keeping a stable torso.

During phase 1 of the off-season program, medicine ball work is done from a kneeling position. The following phases include half-kneeling, split positions, and standing.

Kneeling Front-Twist Toss

Setup

The athlete kneels in a tall position, holding a medicine ball.

Action

The athlete brings the ball to the side to generate power (see figure *a*) and throws the ball against the wall (see figure *b*). He catches it off the wall and then repeats. Perform the prescribed number of reps on each side.

 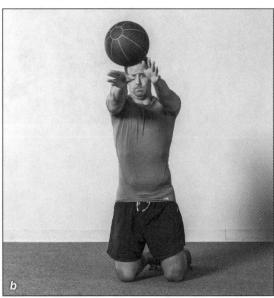

Kneeling Overhead Throw

Setup

The athlete kneels in a tall position, holding a medicine ball with both hands over the head (see figure *a*).

Action

The athlete throws the ball down toward the wall by generating power from the whole body (see figure *b*). He allows the ball to bounce once off the floor and then catches and repeats. Perform the prescribed number of reps.

Half-Kneeling Side-Twist Throw

Setup

The athlete kneels perpendicular to the wall. The inside knee is up, and the outside knee is on the floor. He holds the ball in both hands at hip level on the down-knee side (see figure *a*).

Action

While remaining in a tall position, the athlete twists and throws the ball against the wall (see figure *b*), catches it off the wall, and repeats. The emphasis is on remaining tall, generating power, and trying to put a hole in the wall. Perform the prescribed number of reps on each side.

Half-Kneeling Overhead Throw

Setup

The athlete kneels facing the wall. One knee is up, and the other knee is on the floor. He holds the ball overhead (see figure *a*).

Action

While remaining in a tall position, the athlete throws the ball down toward the wall (see figure *b*), lets it bounce off the floor once, and then catches it off the wall and repeats. The emphasis is on remaining tall, generating power, and trying to put a hole in the wall. Perform the prescribed number of reps on each side.

Split Side-Twist Throw

Setup

The athlete is perpendicular to the wall, with the inside foot forward and the outside foot backward. He holds the ball with both hands at the hip on the opposite side of the wall (see figure *a*).

Action

While remaining in a tall position, the athlete twists and throws the ball against the wall (see figure *b*), catches it off the wall, and repeats. Again, the emphasis is on remaining tall, generating power, and trying to put a hole in the wall. Perform the prescribed number of reps on each side.

Split Overhead Throw

Setup

The athlete is facing the wall straight ahead with the feet planted. He holds the ball overhead (see figure *a*).

Action

While remaining in a tall position, the athlete throws the ball down toward the wall (see figure *b*), lets it bounce off the floor once, and then catches it off the wall and repeats. The emphasis is on remaining tall, generating power, and trying to put a hole in the wall while preventing the lower back from going into extension. Perform the prescribed number of reps on each side.

Standing Side-Twist Throw

Setup

The athlete is perpendicular to the wall with the feet a little wider than shoulder-width apart, knees bent and hips back. He holds the ball with both hands at the hip on the opposite side of the wall (see figure *a*).

Action

The athlete rotates at chest level, the hips rotating simultaneously. He releases and throws the ball as hard as possible to the wall (see figure *b*) and then catches the ball and rotates into the next repetition. The objective is to think about putting a hole in the wall. Perform the prescribed number of reps on each side.

Standing Overhead Throw

Setup

The athlete is facing the wall with the knees bent and the hips back. He holds the medicine ball overhead (see figure *a*).

Action

The athlete throws the ball as hard as possible to the wall in a downward fashion (see figure *b*) while keeping the torso in a neutral position and not extending the back. He catches the ball off one bounce and then repeats. Perform the prescribed number of reps on each side.

Standing Chest Pass

Setup

The athlete is facing the wall in an athletic position. He holds the ball at chest level with both hands (see figure *a*).

Action

While remaining tall, the athlete pushes the medicine ball explosively off the chest toward the wall (see figure *b*). After the ball hits the wall, he catches it and let the arms bend slightly before explosively passing the ball off the wall again. Perform the prescribed number of reps.

Chapter 6

Strength and Power

The approach to strength training for hockey is very simple: The goal is to help players become stronger in order to prevent injuries and increase performance. Developing strength and power helps hockey players resist wear and tear over a full season. In team sports, the athletes' durability from game to game is sometimes what separates the good teams from the not-so-good teams. Having the best players play in every game gives a team the best chance for success.

Strength training is done on a year-round basis. Each component of the year will have a different emphasis on strength training. However, what remains consistent is trying to get stronger each time you participate in a strength training session.

During the off-season, strength training will take place over 4 days per week. Many exercises are prescribed and will consist of progressions being completed from the beginning of the off-season through the end. The volume (number of sets × number of reps), the intensity (the amount of weight on the bar, dumbbell, kettlebell, etc.), and exercise difficulty will change from phase to phase. During the pre-season, there is more of an emphasis on volume versus intensity. The objective is to get more strength training work completed in a shorter amount of time. In-season strength training will consist of a lower volume approach with an emphasis on trying to increase (in some cases, maintain) intensity. More basic exercises will be utilized so that the amount of time to train in the weight room is optimized.

FREE-WEIGHT TRAINING VERSUS MACHINE-BASED TRAINING

Machine-based strength training exercises provide stability and allow the exercise's range of motion to be done in a predetermined pattern. Compare an exercise such as the leg press with the front squat. In the front squat, the bar is racked properly on the shoulders in front of the body. The arms have to be in a position to hold the bar properly. Just standing with the bar on the shoulders in the racked position requires isometric contractions of several muscle groups to maintain stability As the athlete descends to a thighs-parallel position, additional demands on most of the muscle groups in the body keep the body stable and allow the leg muscles to work as efficiently as possible. This doesn't happen during the leg press. Several other devices are popular with some of today's hockey players. The leg extension, leg curl, multi-hip, and lat pull-down machines are all frowned upon in the *Total Hockey Training* program. The human body should be the machine that provides both the stability and strength.

STRENGTH TRAINING EXERCISES

In *Total Hockey Training*, strength training is categorized as follows: total body, lower body, posterior chain, and upper body.

Total-Body Strength and Power

Exercises such as Olympic lifts and kettlebell swings are done to develop total body strength and power. These exercises utilize a large amount of muscle groups to produce the movement. This is important for the hockey player because the sport of hockey is not played in body parts. The human body is designed for muscles to work together while participating in sports. The objective during these lifts is to get synchronization of the skeletal muscular system and the nervous system to produce these exercises.

Explosive Lifts

Traditional Olympic lifting variations are a way to improve total-body strength and power. Lifts such as the hang clean, hang snatch, and dumbbell snatch develop hip and leg power. These types of lifts implement some of the methods seen during Olympic weightlifting events. Olympic lifters are some of the most powerful athletes in the world, and hockey players can benefit from their methods. However, while Olympic lifters pull the barbell from the floor, in *Total Hockey Training*, hockey players will pull the barbell from above the knees, or the hang position. This technique makes the exercise safer and easier to learn as pulling the barbell from the floor is very technical and could put the athlete in a compromised position. In the hang position, the chest is up, the hips are back, and the shoulders are in front of the bar, with the wrists rolled under. All the athlete has to do is jump, shrug, and sit. It's pretty simple to do, but like any other exercise, it does take some coaching. Olympic lifts require supervision by someone who knows how to teach them effectively.

OPTIMIZING REST PERIODS

In *Total Hockey Training*, strength exercises are performed in pairs, tri-sets, or quad-sets.

Pairs

A *pair* is two exercises performed successively. The purpose of this is to get more work accomplished in a short amount of time. For example, during a traditional strength training session, a program may prescribe an exercise for 3 sets of 10 reps. In this situation, the athlete will perform the set, then rest for a few minutes, and then repeat the set. With pairing, the athlete can utilize the rest period between sets and perform another exercise while resting before the next set. The athlete performs 1 set of the first exercise, rests for 1 minute (unless it is a complex set), and then performs 1 set of the second exercise. He then rests for 1 or 2 minutes and starts the second set of the first exercise.

Tri-Sets

A *tri-set* is three exercises performed successively. The athlete performs 1 set of the first exercise, rests for 1 minute (unless it is a complex set), and then performs 1 set of the second exercise. He rests for 1 minute and then moves to the third exercise. After a 1- or 2-minute rest, he goes back to exercise 1.

Quad-Sets

A *quad-set* is four exercises performed successively. The athlete performs 1 set of the first exercise, rests for 1 minute (unless it is a complex set), and then performs 1 set of the second exercise. He rests for 1 minute and then moves to the third exercise, followed by a 1-minute rest before the fourth exercise. After a 1- or 2-minute rest, he goes back to exercise 1.

Hang Clean

Setup

The athlete stands with the feet shoulder-width apart. A barbell is slightly ahead of the athlete.

Action

- The athlete picks up the barbell properly from the floor or blocks (see figure *a*). Proper form cannot be neglected. The chest must be up, the back flat, the knees bent, and the arms long, with the barbell as close to the shins as possible. The athlete should think about driving the feet into the ground as he lifts the barbell off the floor or blocks.

- With the feet under the hips and shoulders back, the athlete bends the knees slightly while holding the barbell at shoulder width or slightly wider. He hinges the hips back until the barbell is right above the kneecaps (see figure *b*).

- With the wrists rolled over, chest up, and shoulders in front of the bar, the athlete jumps, shrugs, and sits in order to return the bar in the front squat, elbows-up position (see figure *c* and *d*).
- The athlete controls the bar and returns to the above-the-knee position as safely as possible.
- Perform the prescribed number of reps.

Hang Snatch

Setup

The athlete stands with the feet shoulder-width apart. A barbell is slightly ahead of the athlete.

Action

- The athlete picks up the barbell properly from the floor or blocks (see figure *a*). Proper form cannot be neglected. The chest must be up, the back flat, the knees bent, and the arms long, with the barbell as close to the shins as possible. The athlete should think about driving the feet into the ground as he lifts the barbell off the floor or blocks.

- With the feet under the hips and shoulders back, the athlete bends the knees slightly while holding the barbell at shoulder width or slightly wider. He hinges the hips back until the barbell is right above the kneecaps (see figure *b*).

- With the wrists rolled over, chest up, and shoulders in front of the bar, the athlete jumps, shrugs, and sits as he extends the arms straight overhead (see figure *c* and *d*).
- The athlete controls the bar and returns to the above-the-knee position as safely as possible.
- Perform the prescribed number of reps.

Dumbbell Snatch

Setup

The athlete stands with the feet shoulder-width apart. One dumbbell is slightly ahead of the athlete in between the feet.

Action

- The athlete picks up the dumbbell properly from the floor or blocks (see figure *a*). Proper form cannot be neglected.
- With the feet under the hips and shoulders back, the athlete bends the knees slightly while holding the dumbbell. He hinges the hips back until the dumbbell is in between the knees at a level right above the kneecaps The chest must be up, the back flat, the knees bent, and the arm long, with the dumbbell as close between the legs (see figure *b*).
- With the wrist rolled over, chest up, and shoulders in front of the dumbbell, the athlete jumps, shrugs, and sits as he extends the arm straight overhead (see figure *c*).
- The athlete controls the dumbbell and returns to the above-the-knee position as safely as possible.
- Perform the prescribed number of reps.

Barbell Complex

The barbell complex is a series of five separate exercises done for 6 repetitions in a circuit-like fashion (no rest between exercises) for 3 sets. This is prescribed during the preseason of *Total Hockey Training*. Players perform the complex with an empty barbell at first. As the preseason progresses, it is okay to add some weight to the barbell. Once the athlete picks the barbell off the floor, he doesn't return it to the floor until the last repetition of the last exercise is completed.

Setup

The athlete stands with the feet shoulder-width apart. A barbell is slightly ahead of the athlete.

Action

The five exercises in the barbell complex are executed as follows:

1. *Upright Row*

   • The athlete picks up the bar properly from the floor or blocks. Proper form cannot be neglected. The chest must be up, the back flat, the knees bent, and the arms long, with the barbell as close to the shins as possible. The athlete should think about driving the feet into the ground as he lifts the barbell off the floor or blocks to a position above the knees, with the hips back, chest up, and arms straight.

   • With the feet under the hips and shoulders back, the athlete bends the knees slightly while holding the barbell at shoulder width or slightly wider. He hinges the hips back until the barbell is right above the knees (see figure a).

   • The athlete pulls the barbell to chin level while straightening the body by extending the hips (see figure b) and then lowers it back to the position above the knees.

   • Perform 6 repetitions.

2. *Muscle Snatch*

- The athlete maintains the position of the barbell just above the knees, ensuring that the feet are under the hips, the shoulders are back, and he is holding the barbell at shoulder width or slightly wider (see figure *a*).
- With the wrists rolled over, chest up, and shoulders in front of the bar, the athlete pulls the bar up while keeping it close to the body, shrugs, and sits as he extends the arms straight overhead (see figure *b*).
- The athlete controls the bar and returns to the above-the-knee position as safely as possible.
- Perform 6 repetitions.

3. *Good Morning*

- The athlete maintains the shoulder-width foot position and brings the barbell behind the head and across the shoulders, with the hands holding the bar at a shoulder-width grip. The elbows should be under the bar (see figure *a*).
- With the knees slightly bent and the chest and eyes up, the athlete performs a hip hinge by pushing the hips back (see figure *b*). Once he feels a stretch in the hamstring muscles, he returns to the starting position.
- Perform 6 repetitions.

4. *Squat Plus Press*

- The athlete adjusts his position so that the feet are slightly wider than shoulder-width apart and slightly turned out to the sides (see figure *a*). The barbell remains behind the head on the shoulders, with the elbows under the bar.
- The athlete takes a deep breath and descends while keeping the hips back and his weight shifted on the heels, with the elbows directly under the bar and knees out over the toes—the knees should not collapse toward the middle (see figure *b*). When he achieves proper depth, he stands up while exhaling.
- After the squat repetition, the athlete presses the bar overhead until the arms are straight (see figure *c*).
- He lowers the barbell to the starting position and then starts the next repetition.
- Perform 6 repetitions.

5. *Bent-Over Row*

- The athlete bends over so that the upper body is parallel to the floor. The chest is up, the back is flat, and the hips are back. He holds the barbell under the chest with the arms straight.

- The athlete pulls the barbell up to the chest (see figure) and then lowers it under control. Proper positioning is important for this exercise to be successful. The only body parts that should be moving are the arms pulling the barbell.

- Perform 6 repetitions.

Swings

The kettlebell swing is a good choice for explosive lifting. It is a ballistic lift requiring the athlete to use maximum power of the posterior chain to accelerate the kettlebell with proper technique. Hockey players spend an enormous amount of time with their spines, hips, knees, and ankles in flexion. Whether they are playing the sport, sitting in the locker room, or traveling on the plane or the bus, hockey players are always in a shortened position. The swing helps them reach full hip extension more efficiently so they can lengthen the muscles that become shortened from prolonged flexion.

The swing is also an evaluation tool for those who have difficulty extending their hips. Players who can't seem to get their hips through at the end range of the swing can correct this with glute activation exercises. Glute activation combined with stretching out the hip flexors yields better results from the kettlebell swing.

When the swing is used as a power exercise, *Total Hockey Training* recommends 2 to 3 sets of 8 to 10 reps. It can also be used as a conditioning tool for players who are injured and not yet cleared to skate. An example is a player who has sustained an injury to a hand, wrist, or shoulder. Swings can be done with one arm or two. A heart rate monitor will ensure that rest periods are similar to what may be seen in a hockey game. Depending on the player and his role on the team, he can recover until he reaches a certain heart rate and then start his next set of swings.

Kettlebell Swing

Setup

The athlete stands with the feet shoulder-width apart. One kettlebell is slightly ahead of the athlete in between the feet.

Action

- The athlete picks up the kettlebell properly from the floor. Proper form cannot be neglected. The chest must be up, the back flat, the knees bent, and the arms long, the kettlebell held with both hands.
- With the feet under the hips and shoulders back, the athlete bends the knees while holding the kettlebell. He hinges the hips back until the kettlebell swings in between the knees (see figure *a*).
- With both hands on the kettlebell, he extends the glutes of both legs to a position of hip extension in which the kettlebell will feel as if it is floating forward through the air (see figure *b*).
- The athlete hinges the hips again and repeats.
- Perform the prescribed number of reps.

One-Arm Kettlebell Swing

Setup

The athlete stands with the feet shoulder-width apart. One kettlebell is slightly ahead of the athlete in between the feet.

Action

- The athlete picks up the kettlebell properly from the floor. Proper form cannot be neglected. The chest must be up, the back flat, the knees bent, and the arm long, the kettlebell held with one hand.
- With the feet under the hips and shoulders back, the athlete bends the knees while holding the kettlebell. He hinges the hips back until the kettlebell swings in between the knees (see figure *a*).
- He extends the glutes of both legs to a position of hip extension in which the kettlebell will feel as if it is floating forward through the air (see figure *b*).
- The athlete hinges the hips again and repeats.
- Perform the prescribed number of reps.

Double Kettlebell Swing

Setup

The athlete stands with the feet shoulder-width apart. Two kettlebells are next to each other and slightly ahead of the athlete in between the feet.

Action

- The athlete picks up the kettlebells properly from the floor. Proper form cannot be neglected. The chest must be up, the back flat, the knees bent, and the arms long, a kettlebell in each hand.
- With the feet under the hips and shoulders back, the athlete bends the knees while holding the kettlebells. He hinges the hips back until the kettlebells swing in between the knees (see figure *a*). It is important that both kettlebells be in sync without bumping into each other.
- He extends the glutes of both legs to a position of hip extension in which the kettlebells will feel as if they are floating forward through the air (see figure *b*).
- The athlete hinges the hips again and repeats.
- Perform the prescribed number of reps.

Lower Body Strength and Power

Developing leg strength and power should be the ultimate goal of any strength and conditioning program for hockey. Hockey players need to have stronger legs to improve performance, specifically on-ice speed. A stronger push of the skate blade into the ice will result in a more powerful skating stride. More important, stronger legs will help prevent injuries to the knees and hips, which are commonly injured in hockey.

Goblet Squat

The goblet squat is a great exercise to introduce double-leg squatting and should be found in any hockey player's strength and conditioning program. A kettlebell or dumbbell can be used. Goblet squats are tough to do incorrectly, which is a good thing in a team setting, and they are a safer way to get in some squatting work because they don't load the spine as much as the front squat.

Setup

The athlete stands with the feet shoulder-width apart holding a kettlebell (or dumbbell) with both hands (see figure *a*).

Action

While keeping the chest up and the implement held high, the athlete takes a deep breath and then descends until the elbows touch the knees (see figure *b*). He then ascends back to the starting position while exhaling. Perform the prescribed number of reps.

Front Squat

The primary exercise used for double-leg squatting is the front squat. I believe this is better than the traditional back squat from a technical standpoint. This is important when training a large number of athletes or a team and technical proficiency across the board is a must. The elbows are up, which results in a stable torso that helps the spine remain tall so flexion does not occur. The depth will look better even if there is a wide stance because the angle of the torso doesn't change in the descent. A feature of the front squat is that less weight is required. That will promote strength development without the need for inflated loads. Athletes who have been performing the regular back squat for a while should try switching to the front squat.

Setup

The athlete stands with the feet slightly wider than shoulder-width apart and slightly turned out to the sides (see figure *a*). He holds the barbell on the shoulders, with the elbows up.

Action

The athlete takes a deep breath and descends while keeping the hips back and his weight shifted on the heels, with the elbows up and knees out over the toes—the knees should not collapse toward the middle (see figure *b*). When he achieves proper depth, he stands up while exhaling. Perform the prescribed number of reps.

Plate Overhead Squat

The plate overhead squat is a preseason exercise in *Total Hockey Training*. It is part of a circuit that features a plate (a weight used with barbell training).

Setup

The athlete stands with the feet slightly wider than shoulder-width apart and slightly turned out to the sides (see figure *a*). He holds the plate above the head with the arms straight.

Action

The athlete takes a deep breath and descends while keeping the hips back and his weight shifted on the heels, with the arms straight and knees out over the toes—the knees should not collapse toward the middle (see figure *b*). When he achieves proper depth, he stands up while exhaling. Perform the prescribed number of reps.

Plate Overhead Squat Plus Triceps Extension

The plate overhead squat plus triceps extension is a preseason exercise in *Total Hockey Training*. It is part of a circuit that features a plate (a weight used with barbell training).

Setup

The athlete stands with the feet slightly wider than shoulder-width apart and slightly turned out to the sides. He holds the plate behind the head with the arms bent (see figure *a*).

Action

The athlete takes a deep breath and descends while keeping the hips back and his weight shifted on the heels, with the arms bent behind the head and knees out over the toes—the knees should not collapse toward the middle (see figure *b*). When he achieves proper depth, he stands up while exhaling (see figure *c*), straightening the arms so that the plate is overhead (see figure *d*). He then bends the arms and begins the next repetition. Perform the prescribed number of reps.

Trap Bar Deadlift

The trap bar deadlift is performed with a hexagon-shaped bar. Some bars have both high and low handles. The lower the handle, the more difficult the exercise. Regular-sized free weights should be used since the height of the weights will dictate how high the handles are off the floor. This is a safer version of a bilateral deadlift. It is a hybrid exercise that isn't a typical deadlift or squat but somewhere in between.

Setup

The athlete stands with the feet a little wider than shoulder-width apart in the center of a hexagon-shaped bar, with the hands holding the handles (see figure *a*).

Action

With the arms straight, chest up, and eyes on the horizon, the athlete squeezes the handles and lifts the bar off the floor. The emphasis should be on driving the feet through the floor. He stands up (see figure *b*), lowers the bar under control, and repeats. Perform the prescribed number of reps.

Lateral Squat

Setup

The athlete stands with the feet wider than shoulder-width apart in a wide yet comfortable position. He has the bar on his back, with the hands at shoulder width and the elbows under the bar.

Action

The athlete squats to one side while keeping the other leg straight (see figure). During the squat, he should feel a good stretch in the adductors of the opposite leg. Perform the prescribed number of reps in an alternating fashion.

Split Squat

Setup

The athlete stands in a split position with one foot in front and the other foot in back while remaining tall (see figure a). Athlete may hold a dumbbell (or kettlebell) in each hand.

Action

The athlete drops the back knee to touch the floor (see figure b), and returns to the starting position. The chest is up and the eyes are on the horizon. The front knee is situated above the front heel for the duration of the set. If the athlete simply drops the back knee, then there isn't a concern for the front leg if it's in the proper position. Perform the prescribed number of reps on each side.

Rear-Foot Elevated Split Squat

Setup

The athlete stands with the feet hip-width apart with his back to a 12- to 14-inch (30 to 35 cm) box. He may hold a dumbbell (or kettlebell) in each hand.

Action

The athlete takes a big step back with one foot and places it on top of the box (see figure *a*), drops the back knee to touch the floor (see figure *b*), and returns to the starting position. The chest is up and the eyes are on the horizon. The front knee is situated above the front heel for the duration of the set. If the athlete simply drops the back knee, then there isn't a concern for the front leg if it's in the proper position. Perform the prescribed number of reps on each side.

One-Leg Squat

Setup

The athlete stands on a box or platform with the feet hip-width apart and then balances on one leg (see figure a).

Action

While balancing on one leg, the athlete sits back on the heel of the down leg and simultaneously lifts the other leg, raising the arms parallel to the floor (see figure b). Once at proper below-parallel depth, the athlete stands up. This is a difficult exercise for younger players. It requires core stability, flexibility (especially in the hips and ankles), and strength. Perform the prescribed number of reps on each side.

One-Leg Skater Squat

Setup

The athlete stands with the feet hip-width apart and then balances on one leg, holding a dumbbell in each hand (see figure a).

Action

The athlete sits back on the down leg while dropping the raised leg's knee to the floor behind him (see figure b). The chest is up and the dumbbells are raised to parallel with the floor at the point where the knee touches the floor. Perform the prescribed number of reps on each side.

Front Split Squat

Setup

The athlete stands with the feet hip-width apart while holding a barbell on the shoulders, with the elbows up and toward the midline of the body.

Action

The athlete takes a big step back into a split stance (see figure *a*), drops the back knee to touch the floor (see figure *b*), and returns to the starting position. The chest is up and the eyes are on the horizon. The front knee is situated above the front heel for the duration of the set. If the athlete simply drops the back knee, then there isn't a concern for the front leg if it's in the proper position. Perform the prescribed number of reps on each side.

Slide-Board Split Squat

The slide-board split squat can be done with a regular slide board or a Valslide. This exercise is very much like the split squat and the rear-foot elevated split squat, with the exception that the back leg is moving, allowing the front knee to bend.

Setup

The athlete places one foot on the ground in front of the slide board and one foot on top of the slide board in a bootie (or on top of the Valslide if using it on carpet) (see figure *a*). Dumbbells, kettlebells, or a barbell across the upper back can be used for external resistance.

Action

The athlete slides the back foot back while maintaining balance (see figure *b*). While staying tall and keeping the chest up, he returns the back foot to the starting position. The athlete should think about using the glutes and hamstrings of the front leg to pull the back leg to the starting position. Perform the prescribed number of reps on each side.

Alternating Leg Lunge

The alternating leg lunge is performed during the leg circuit of the preseason period.

Setup

The athlete stands tall with the feet hip-width apart, with the hands next to the ears and the eyes and chest up (see figure *a*).

Action

The athlete steps (lunges) with one leg so that the stepping leg's knee is at 90 degrees and the back knee is almost touching the floor (see figure *b*). He pushes the front foot off the floor and returns to the starting position (see figure *c*). Perform the prescribed number of reps in an alternating fashion (see figure *d*).

Step-Up

The step-up is performed during the leg circuit of the preseason period.

Setup

The athlete stands behind a 24-inch (60 cm) box or a standard bench. One foot is flat on the box (or bench), with the knee bent at least 90 degrees. The athlete stands tall, with the hands next to the ears and the eyes and chest up (see figure *a*).

Action

The athlete steps up so that both legs are straight, but the foot that began on the floor does not touch the box or bench (see figure *b*). He returns to the starting position. Perform the prescribed number of reps before switching legs.

Posterior Chain Strength and Power

The posterior chain is a general term to describe the muscles in back of the body from the back to the knees. You can't see these muscles in the mirror, but they are very important for athletes—especially hockey players—so they are trained frequently in *Total Hockey Training*. Exercises include the back extension, the straight-leg deadlift, and leg curl progressions. Kettlebell swings could also be included in the posterior chain category, but since their concentric action is explosive, they are classified as explosive exercises.

Since the adductors and quadriceps tend to be overworked in hockey, hockey players need to strengthen their hamstrings and glutes to help promote muscular balance and joint integrity in the hips and knees. This is a must; especially for preventing injuries.

Back Extension

Setup

The athlete positions himself in a back extension apparatus or a glute–ham apparatus. The legs should be straight and the pads should be under the hips (see figure *a*). At the start, the upper body should simply be hanging over the pads.

Action

The athlete squeezes the hamstrings and glutes, pulling the upper body into a straight line parallel to the floor (see figure *b*). He holds this position for a second, lowers the upper body to the starting position, and repeats. Perform the prescribed number of reps.

One-Leg Straight Leg Deadlift

Setup

The athlete balances on one leg with a slight knee bend, holding a dumbbell (or kettlebell) in the opposite hand (see figure *a*). For example, if the left foot is on the ground, the dumbbell will be in the right hand.

Action

The athlete hinges at the hip while keeping the chest up and back flat. He lets the dumbbell slide down the front of the down leg until he feels a good stretch in the hamstrings of that leg (see figure *b*). Once he feels the stretch, he returns to the starting position while continuing to keep the other leg off the ground. Perform the prescribed number of reps on each side.

Two-Arm, One-Leg Straight-Leg Deadlift

Setup

The athlete balances on one leg with a slight knee bend, holding a dumbbell (or kettlebell) in each hand (see figure *a*).

Action

The athlete hinges at the hips while keeping the chest up and back flat. He lets the dumbbells slide down the front of the down leg until he feels a good stretch in the hamstrings of that leg (see figure *b*). Once he feels the stretch, he returns to the starting position while continuing to keep the other leg off the ground. Perform the prescribed number of reps on each side.

Two-Arm, Two-Leg Straight-Leg Deadlift

Setup

The athlete stands with the feet about hip-width apart and with a slight knee bend in both knees, holding a dumbbell (or kettlebell) in each hand (see figure *a*).

Action

The athlete hinges at the hips while keeping the chest up and back flat. He lets the dumbbells slide down the front of the legs until he feels a good stretch in the hamstrings of both legs (see figure *b*). Once he feels the stretch, he returns to the starting position. Perform the prescribed number of reps.

Ball Leg Curl

Setup

The athlete lies on the ground in the supine position, with the legs straight and heels on a stability ball (see figure *a*).

Action

The athlete drives the hips up to the ceiling and pulls the ball in close while keeping the feet on the ball (see figure *b*). While keeping the hips extended, he rolls the ball to the starting position. With patience, this can be progressed to a one-leg variation that is very difficult for those lacking strength. Perform the prescribed number of reps.

Slide-Board Leg Curl

Setup

The athlete lies on his back with the feet (in booties) on top of the slide board. (see figure *a*).

Action

With the legs straight and heels on the slide board, the athlete drives the hips up to the ceiling and pulls the legs in close while maintaining hip extension (see figure *b*). While keeping the hips extended, the legs are slid back to the starting position under control. If the athlete can't maintain hip extension, it is recommended that a concentric-only regression is used. This is simply not sliding the legs back to the starting position under control. Instead, the athlete will relax and drop the hips and then slide the legs back to the starting position without hip extension. With patience, this can be progressed to a one-leg variation that is very difficult for those lacking strength. Perform the prescribed number of reps.

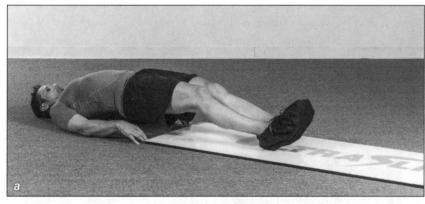

Upper Body Strength and Power

Although leg strength should be a priority for any hockey player, upper body strength can't be neglected. Hockey is a physical sport with body contact in all phases of the game. An upper body strength training program reduces the chances of injury and improves performance.

Pull-Ups

Hockey players need upper back strength. Pull-ups and their variations are a great way to get stronger quickly. Being unable to do pull-ups is an indicator of weak upper back strength. Athletes with weak upper backs are more prone to injury, especially at the shoulder joint. Strong shoulders are important for athletes in contact sports such as hockey. Athletes who don't (or in their minds, can't) do pull-ups often have shoulder injuries.

Pull-ups need to be done correctly in order to get the full benefit. To properly execute a pull-up, the athlete starts at full extension and proceeds to pull her chin up over the bar. She then lowers herself under control to full extension before doing the next rep.

All these variations can be done with or without load, depending on the strength of the athlete. Also, those who can't complete pull-ups on their own can use a band, common for younger players with inadequate strength.

Basic Pull-Up

Setup

The athlete stands at a bar secured high enough that he can hang freely. He uses an overhand grip that is wider than shoulder width and starts with the arms long (see figure *a*).

Action

The athlete pulls himself up until the chin is over the bar or higher than the hands while keeping the body straight (see figure *b*). Perform the prescribed number of reps.

Chin-Up

Setup

The athlete stands at a bar secured high enough that he can hang freely. He uses an underhand grip and starts with the arms long (see figure *a*).

Action

The athlete pulls himself up until the chin is over the bar or higher than the hands while keeping the body straight (see figure *b*). Perform the prescribed number of reps.

Parallel-Grip Pull-Up

Setup

The athlete stands at a pull-up bar with handles, secured high enough that he can hang freely. He grips the bar so that the hands are facing each other and starts with the arms long (see figure *a*).

Action

The athlete pulls himself up until the chin is over the bar or higher than the hands while keeping the body straight (see figure *b*). Perform the prescribed number of reps.

Mixed-Grip Pull-Up

Setup

The athlete stands at a bar secured high enough that he can hang freely. He grips the bar in an overhand grip with one hand and an underhand grip with the other (see figure *a*). The hands are wider than shoulder width, and the arms are long.

Action

The athlete pulls himself up until the chin is over the bar or higher than the hands while keeping the body straight (see figure *b*). This exercise is useful for hockey players because they can work on their weaker side in addition to how they grip their sticks. Perform the prescribed number of reps and then switch hand positions.

Rows

While pull-ups are in the vertical pulling category, rows are in the horizontal pulling category. Rows are a great exercise because they are directly antagonistic to the bench press, meaning they can correct muscle imbalances in athletes who bench press more frequently and do not do enough pulling exercises. Most young hockey players are in the category of too much pressing and not enough pulling.

Inverted Row

Setup

A bar is set up at bench press height. The athlete is in a supine position, gripping the bar in an overhand grip, with the legs straight and feet together (see figure *a*). The athlete will need to engage the glutes and abdominals to hold this position so that the body is a straight line from head to toe. To perform variations of this exercise, the athlete can use different grips. For those who find this exercise too easy, a bench can be placed on the ground in front of the barbell so that the feet can be placed on top which will increase the difficulty of the exercise. Inverted rows can also be done with a suspension training device, which allows the stabilizers to work harder before the big muscles such as the lats engage.

Action

With the feet on the ground or bench and the hips extended, the athlete pulls himself up until the chest touches the bar (see figure *b*) and then lowers himself under control to the starting position. Perform the prescribed number of reps.

Plate Upright Row

Setup

The athlete stands in an athletic position with the eyes and chest up. He holds the plate at hip level, both hands at the top of the plate (see figure *a*).

Action

The athlete pulls the plate to chin level (see figure *b*) and then lowers it back to hip level while remaining tall and upright. Perform the prescribed number of reps.

Dumbbell Row

Setup

With the chest up, back flat, and hips back, the athlete places one hand on a bench while the other hand grasps a dumbbell (see figure *a*).

Action

The athlete pulls the dumbbell to the hip of the same side (see figure *b*) and then lowers it under control. Proper positioning is important for this exercise to be successful. The only body part that should be moving is the arm pulling the dumbbell. Perform the prescribed number of reps on each side.

Plate Row

Setup

With the chest up, back flat, and hips back, the athlete grasps a weight plate (see figure *a*).

Action

The athlete pulls the plate to the hip of the same side (see figure *b*) and then lowers it under control. Proper positioning is important for this exercise to be successful. The only body part that should be moving is the arm pulling the plate. Perform the prescribed number of reps on each side.

Upper Back Dumbbell Row

Setup

With the chest up, back flat, and hips back, the athlete places one hand on a bench while the other hand grasps a dumbbell (see figure *a*).

Action

The athlete pulls the dumbbell up beside the chest, keeping the upper arm in close to the side (see figure *b*), and then lowers the dumbbell under control. Proper positioning is important for this exercise to be successful. The only body part that should be moving is the arm pulling the dumbbell. Perform the prescribed number of reps on each side.

One-Arm Cable Row

Setup

The athlete stands in an athletic position while facing a cable column with the chest up, hips back, and knees bent slightly, grasping the handle with one hand (see figure *a*). The handle should be set in the position closest to the floor.

Action

While staying tall and keeping the chest up, the athlete pulls the handle to the rib cage (see figure *b*) before returning to the starting position. Perform the prescribed number of reps on each side.

One-Arm, One-Leg Cable Row

Setup

The athlete stands on one leg while facing a cable column with the chest up, hips back, and knee bent slightly, grasping the handle on the same side as the raised leg (see figure a). The handle should be set in the position closest to the floor.

Action

The athlete pulls the handle toward the rib cage (see figure b). For example, if the left foot is off of the ground, he pulls the handle with the left hand to the left-side rib cage. Perform the prescribed number of reps on each side.

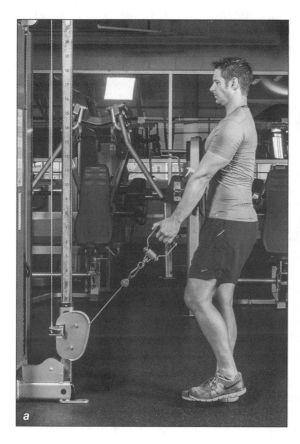

Presses

When someone thinks of upper body pressing exercises, the bench press immediately comes to mind. It is probably the most popular exercise in all weight rooms and gyms today. The next time you are in a large commercial gym, count how many flat bench press and incline benches there are in comparison to squat racks. Or on any given day, count how many people are bench pressing versus squatting.

The bench press is a great exercise for increasing upper body size and pushing strength, and it is easy to perform. Lying on your back and pressing a barbell off your chest to a locked-out position is not that difficult. However, the bench press works fewer muscle groups in comparison to other compound exercises. Further, it works the muscle groups you can see in the mirror every day. Some athletes are more interested in looking good at the beach than they are in increasing their performance in their sport. As a result, young athletes aren't doing the more difficult exercises in the weight room such as front squats, straight-leg deadlifts, and pull-ups. They aren't training the muscles that aren't in the mirror, such as the upper and lower back, the glutes, and hamstrings.

Total Hockey Training uses the bench press once per week during the off-season and once per week in-season. It is performed in conjunction with many other exercises for the upper body, including upper body pulling exercises, to prevent imbalances. Pull-ups, chin-ups, inverted rows, and dumbbell rows develop strength in the upper back and maintain upper body structural balance.

At the end of the day, if an athlete is not doing enough pulling exercises and the bench press is the number one exercise in his program, then he probably shouldn't be bench pressing. To find out if an athlete is doing enough pulling exercises, simply add up all the sets and reps of pulling and compare this to the total number of pressing sets and reps. If the athlete is pressing more than pulling, he could be heading for shoulder problems.

Horizontal Presses Horizontal pressing is a big part of a sound upper body strength training program. Pressing strength is important for players delivering checks, withstanding physical contact, and clearing opposing players away from the front of the net.

Other than the barbell, variations of the horizontal presses (with the exception of the push-up) include the following:

- *One-arm presses*, where one arm is used during the whole set. This variation is appropriate for those who have an injury to the opposite hand, arm, or shoulder.

- *Alternating-arm presses*, where both arms are used during the set, except each arm works independently from the other. While one arm is pressing, the other one will be in the starting position, maintaining stability.

Bench Press

Setup

The athlete lies faceup on a bench, arms straight overhead, and grasps a barbell in an overhand grip, hands slightly wider than shoulder-width apart (see figure *a*). The back of the head, shoulders, and butt are on the bench, and the feet stay on the floor at all times.

Action

The athlete lowers the barbell so it is touching the chest (see figure *b*) and then presses up, returning to the starting position. Perform the prescribed number of reps.

Incline Bench Press

Setup

The athlete lies faceup on a 45-degree incline bench, arms straight overhead, and grasps a barbell in an overhand grip, hands a little wider than shoulder-width apart (see figure *a*). The back of the head, shoulders, and butt are on the bench, and the feet stay on the floor at all times.

Action

The athlete lowers the barbell so it is touching the chest (see figure *b*) and then presses up, returning to the starting position. Perform the prescribed number of reps.

Dumbbell Bench Press

Setup

The athlete lies faceup on a bench and holds a dumbbell straight overhead in each hand (see figure *a*). The back of the head, shoulders, and butt are on the bench, and the feet stay on the floor at all times. Dumbbells allow for a greater range of motion than the barbell, thus strengthening stabilizers such as the rotator cuff muscles.

Action

The athlete lowers the dumbbells so they are both touching the chest (see figure *b*) and then presses up, returning to the starting position. Perform the prescribed number of reps.

One-Arm Dumbbell Bench Press

Setup

The athlete lies faceup on a bench and holds a dumbbell up so that it is perpendicular to the floor (see figure *a*). The back of the head, shoulders, and butt are on the bench, and the feet stay on the floor at all times.

Action

The athlete lowers the dumbbell so it touches the chest (see figure *b*) and then presses up, returning to the starting position. Perform the prescribed number of reps on each side.

Dumbbell Incline Press

Setup

The athlete lies faceup on a 45-degree incline bench and holds a dumbbell in each hand above the shoulders (see figure *a*). The back of the head, shoulders, and butt are on the bench, and the feet stay on the floor at all times.

Action

The athlete lowers the dumbbells so they are both touching the chest (see figure *b*) and presses up, returning to the starting position. Perform the prescribed number of reps.

Push-Up

Push-ups are an outstanding exercise, but they are often done improperly, especially with young hockey teams and players. What makes push-ups different from other horizontal pushing exercises is that the entire body is involved. Good core strength and stability are required to properly execute a push-up.

Setup

The athlete assumes a prone position, with the feet squeezed together, the glutes contracted, the core engaged, and the head in a neutral position. The hands should be underneath the shoulders, with the arms straight (see figure *a*).

Action

The athlete lowers the chest until the nose touches the floor while keeping the entire body in a plank position, with no lifting or sagging of the hips (see figure *b*). While maintaining a straight position, he presses up and returns to the starting position. Perform the prescribed number of reps.

Staggered Push-Up

Setup

The athlete assumes a prone position, with the feet squeezed together, the glutes contracted, the core engaged, and the head in a neutral position. One hand is at shoulder level, and the other hand is at hip level (see figure *a*).

Action

The athlete lowers the chest until the nose touches the floor while keeping the entire body in a plank position, with no lifting or sagging of the hips (see figure *b*). While maintaining a straight position, he presses up and returns to the starting position. Perform the prescribed number of reps.

Vertical Presses   Vertical pressing is a different variety of pressing. In horizontal pressing exercises, the athlete lies on a bench or remains in a prone position (push-up) while performing the movement. In vertical pressing, the athlete needs to remain tall in all the exercise variations. This provides a different training effect because the entire body is involved to provide stabilization before pressing.

Kneeling Dumbbell Curl and Press

Setup

The athlete is on both knees with a dumbbell in each hand, the arms long in front of the body (see figure a).

Action

With the glutes contracted and the core engaged, the athlete curls the dumbbells up to the shoulders (see figure b), turns the wrists (see figure c), and then presses the dumbbells overhead (see figure d). He lowers the dumbbells to the shoulders first (important) and then to full arm extension before the next repetition. Perform the prescribed number of reps.

Kneeling Kettlebell One-Arm Press

Setup

The athlete is on both knees holding a kettlebell at one shoulder, with the elbow slightly to the side (see figure *a*).

Action

While staying tall in a kneeling position, with the glutes contracted and the core engaged, the athlete presses the kettlebell overhead (see figure *b*) and then returns it to the racked position. It is important for the athlete to start from the comfortable racked position each time and to keep the kettlebell in line with the ear, not forward. Perform the prescribed number of reps on each side.

Half-Kneeling Kettlebell One-Arm Press

Setup

With one knee on the floor and the other foot in front, the athlete holds a kettlebell at the shoulder, with the elbow slightly to the side (see figure *a*). The kettlebell is on the same side as the knee that is on the ground.

Action

The athlete presses the kettlebell overhead (see figure *b*) and then returns it to the racked position. It is important for the athlete to start from the comfortable racked position each time and to keep the kettlebell in line with the ear, not forward. Perform the prescribed number of reps on each side.

Half-Kneeling Dumbbell Shoulder Press

Setup

With one knee on the floor and the other foot in front, the athlete holds a dumbbell in each hand at the shoulders (see figure a).

Action

The athlete presses the dumbbells overhead (see figure b) and then returns them to the starting position. The movement is up and back. Perform the prescribed number of reps.

Standing One-Arm Kettlebell Press

Setup

The athlete stands with a kettlebell at the shoulder (see figure *a*).

Action

With the glutes contracted and the core engaged, the athlete presses the kettlebell overhead (see figure *b*) and then returns it to the racked position. It is important for the athlete to start and return to the comfortable racked position and to keep the kettlebell in line with the ear, not forward. Perform the prescribed number of reps on each side.

Alternating-Arm Dumbbell Shoulder Press

The athlete stands with a dumbbell in each hand at the shoulders (see figure *a*).

Action

With the glutes contracted and the core engaged, using one arm at a time in an alternating fashion, the athlete presses each dumbbell overhead (see figure *b*) and then returns them to the starting position (see figure *c*). The movement is up and back (see figure *d*). Perform the prescribed number of reps.

Dumbbell Curl and Press

Setup

The athlete stands with a dumbbell in each hand at hip level, palms facing out (see figure *a*).

Action

With the glutes contracted and the core engaged, the athlete curls both dumbbells to shoulder level (see figure *b*). He rotates the hands (see figure *c*) and presses both dumbbells overhead until both arms are straight (see figure *d*). Then he lowers the dumbbells back to the shoulders and then back to the starting position before beginning the next repetition. Perform the prescribed number of reps.

Alternating-Arm Dumbbell Curl and Press

Setup

The athlete stands with a dumbbell in each hand at the shoulders (see figure *a*).

Action

With the glutes contracted and the core engaged, using one arm at a time in an alternating fashion, the athlete presses one dumbbell overhead (see figure *b*) and returns to the shoulder position while simultaneously extending the other arm and performing an arm curl (see figure *c*). At this point, both hands should be in the starting position. The athlete then performs the opposite exercise with each arm (see figure *d*). For example, if the left hand performed a press, it will now perform an arm curl while the right hand performs a press. Perform the prescribed number of reps on each side.

Dumbbell Triceps Extension

Setup

The athlete lies faceup on a bench while holding a dumbbell in each hand, with the arms straight overhead (see figure *a*).

Action

The athlete bends both arms at the elbows while keeping the upper arms in a stable position (see figure *b*). Once a good stretch is felt in the triceps, the athlete extends the arms back to the starting position. Perform the prescribed number of reps.

Dumbbell Pullover

Setup

The athlete lies faceup on a bench while holding a dumbbell in each hand, with the arms straight overhead (see figure *a*).

Action

The athlete bends both arms at the elbows while also flexing at the shoulders so that both arms are bent slightly and allowed to lower behind the head (see figure *b*). Once the athlete feels a good stretch in the lats, he extends the arms back to the starting position. Perform the prescribed number of reps.

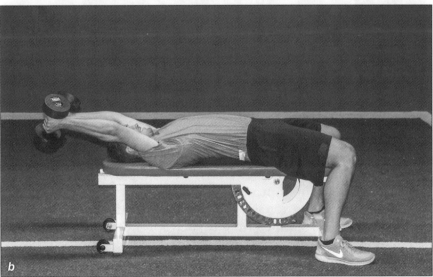

Plate Steering Wheel

The plate steering wheel is a preseason exercise in *Total Hockey Training*. It is part of a circuit that features a plate.

Setup

The athlete stands with the feet slightly wider than shoulder-width apart and slightly turned out to the sides. He holds the plate directly in front with the arms straight.

Action

The strength and conditioning coach directs this exercise because it is done for time. While keeping the arms straight, the athlete turns the plate like a car steering wheel for the determined amount of time (see figures *a* and *b*).

Walks and Carries Walks and carries are considered to be upper body exercises since the implements are held in the hands. Hockey players benefit not only from training the grip but also from improving rotator cuff strength, core strength and stability, and leg strength. These exercises are done during the off-season on days 2 and 4. The goal is to carry the dumbbell or kettlebell for a certain distance. *Total Hockey Training* recommends 80 yards or meters.

Suitcase Carry

Setup

The athlete stands with a dumbbell or kettlebell in one hand, like a suitcase (see figure). The implement should be heavy enough to be very challenging. A light implement would defeat the purpose of the exercise.

Action

The athlete walks for 40 yards or meters in a straight line. He then switches hands and returns to the starting position. He tries to remain as straight as possible. The athlete tries to work up to a weight that is 50 percent of his body weight.

Farmer's Walk

Setup

The athlete stands with a dumbbell or kettlebell in each hand (see figure). The implements should be heavy enough to be very challenging. A light implement would defeat the purpose of the exercise.

Action

The athlete walks for 40 yards or meters in a straight line and then returns to the starting position. He tries to remain as straight as possible. The athlete tries to work up to a weight in each hand that is 50 percent of his body weight.

Bottom's Up Kettlebell Walk

Setup

The athlete stands with a kettlebell upside down in one hand (see figure). He uses a weight that is significantly lighter than for the suitcase carry or farmer's walk.

Action

The athlete walks for 40 yards or meters in a straight line and then switches hands and returns. The emphasis is on squeezing the kettlebell handle and holding the elbow at 90 degrees in front of the body.

Cross Walk

Setup

The athlete stands with an upside-down kettlebell in one hand and a dumbbell in the other (see figure). The dumbbell should be heavy enough to be very challenging, but the kettlebell can be light.

Action

The athlete walks for 40 yards or meters in a straight line while squeezing the handles and remaining upright.

Y, T, W, L   This circuit is considered prehab because the exercises are common in the rehabilitation of shoulder injuries. In *Total Hockey Training*, all exercises are executed with the purpose of injury prevention and performance enhancement. These exercises build rotator cuff strength and endurance while also stabilizing the scapulae.

Y

The athlete lies across a table or a stability ball, with the arms hanging off the edge (see figure *a*). The arms remain straight throughout the exercise, with the thumbs up at a 45-degree angle. Using the upper back musculature, the athlete lifts the arms so they are parallel to the floor—the arms and the athlete's body now resemble a letter Y (see figure *b*); he returns to the starting position. Perform the prescribed number of reps.

T

The athlete lies across a table or a stability ball, with the arms hanging off the edge and touching each other (see figure *a*). The arms remain straight throughout the exercise, with the thumbs out to the sides. Using the upper back musculature, the athlete lifts the arms out to each side so they are parallel to the floor—the arms and the athlete's body now resemble the letter T (see figure *b*); he returns to the starting position. Perform the prescribed number of reps.

W

The athlete lies across a table or a stability ball, with the arms hanging off the edge and the elbows touching each other (see figure *a*). The arms remain bent throughout the exercise, with the hands flat. Using the upper back musculature, the athlete lifts the arms out to each side so they are parallel to the floor—the arms and the athlete's body now resemble the letter W (see figure *b*); he returns to the starting position. Perform the prescribed number of reps.

L

The athlete lies across a table or a stability ball, with the arms held out to the sides and the elbows bent (see figure *a*). The arms remain bent throughout the exercise, with the hands flat. Using the upper back musculature and shoulder joints, the athlete rotates the elbows so that the arms move from a position of thumbs down to a position of thumbs up to resemble the letter L (see figure *b*); he returns to the starting position. Perform the prescribed number of reps.

Chapter 7

Acceleration and Speed

The game of hockey is all about speed, and most of today's players can skate fast. Really talented hockey players with average speed likely have above-average skills in another area of the game. They may possess an offensive touch in front of the net or they may be a defenseman with rock-solid defensive skills and a bullet shot from the point on the power play. There are few players who can survive without speed. Young players at all levels need to develop their on-ice speed so they can play at a quicker pace, while older players need to maintain their speed and power on the ice as best they can.

Hockey speed can be developed with a sound lower body plyometric program, short-burst off-ice sprinting (acceleration work), and a good strength and conditioning program with an emphasis on lower body strength. Plyometrics and speed drills should make up a large component of the off-season program for a young hockey player.

ACCELERATION AND SPEED TRAINING EXERCISES

There are several components of acceleration and speed training in *Total Hockey Training*, including plyometrics, acceleration work, and sled training.

Plyometrics

Plyometrics are short, explosive muscular contractions that are used to improve speed. When combined with a lower body strength training program, plyometric exercises can also increase power. By performing jumps, hops, and bounds in a progressive, systematic fashion, hockey players can teach their brains to instruct the muscles to contract faster so that they can be more explosive.

In *Total Hockey Training*, plyometrics will be primarily performed in the off-season and pre-season. During the in-season phase, plyometrics will not be performed because optimizing the time spent in the weight room is critical. Also, the goal of the plyometric and speed program are to enhance off-ice speed and power so that the on-ice product is faster. In-season, the time spent on power and speed development needs to be done on the ice in practices. During the off-season, a basic plyometric progression starts with jumps and hops that emphasize a stable landing using an athletic stance so that players become accustomed to a deep-knee position, which is imperative for skating acceleration and turning ability. Teaching the body how to absorb force and land properly helps prevent overuse injuries such as patellar tendinitis. Athletes need to learn how to put the brakes on and decelerate before accelerating.

Here's how plyometrics are progressed through the four phases of the off-season:

Phase 1 Plyometrics

During phase 1 of the off-season, the emphasis for plyometrics is on the landing of all the jumps and bounds. Learning how to land and decelerate helps athletes gain eccentric strength and provides a foundation for the higher-impact plyometric exercises found in later phases. Players may find some of the plyometrics too easy, but it is important not to skip this phase.

Phase 2 Plyometrics

During phase 2 of the off-season, plyometrics progress from jumping onto boxes to jumping over hurdles in a more horizontal manner. As in phase 1, the landing mechanics are emphasized. Since the sport of hockey has significant horizontal and 45-degree components, it is important to add drills for improving power in those directions.

Phase 3 Plyometrics

During phase 3 of the off-season, plyometrics progress by adding a mini-hop between repetitions. These mini-hops help the athletes transition from landing properly to safely applying force to the ground in an explosive manner. Note that for safety reasons, the Heiden hop in phase 3 remains a continuous action, with no mini-bounce.

Phase 4 Plyometrics

During phase 4 of the off-season, plyometrics progress to jumps where there is minimal contact with the ground. Landing safely and immediately exploding for the next repetition is the emphasis during this phase. This is probably what other professionals would refer to as true plyometrics. However, hockey players need a good foundation of learning how to jump and land properly, so the previous phases are important.

During the off-season program, plyometrics are either linear (straight ahead) or lateral (side to side). Linear plyometrics, acceleration, and speed drills are performed on days 1 and 3. Each drill is done in a straight-ahead fashion. Days 2 and 4 consist of lateral drills that emphasize movement from right to left and vice versa. The goal is to be prepared to move explosively in either direction.

Plyometrics are done after the warm-up period and before acceleration and speed training. They are also done during the training session of phase 2 and as part of the circuit training sessions in the preseason. The idea is to apply the benefits of the plyometric exercise to the speed drill that follows. The sets and reps take a low-volume approach of one exercise for 3 or 4 sets of 5 reps on double-leg jumps, while single-leg hops and bounds are done for 3 or 4 sets of 5 reps each leg. This will be consistent through the off-season.

Box Jump

Setup

The athlete assumes an athletic stance approximately 6 to 12 inches (15 to 30 cm) from a box (see figure *a*). A box with a height of 24 to 30 inches (60 to 76 cm) is recommended.

Action

The athlete jumps onto the box with both feet while swinging the arms from back to front (see figures *b* and *c*). He should land with both feet softly on the box (with no movement of the knees toward the middle), pause, and then step down easily. Do not move to a higher box until all reps and sets are done easily and softly; if the landing is not soft and quiet, then simply use a smaller box. Perform the prescribed number of reps.

One-Leg Lateral Box Hop With Stabilization

Setup

The athlete assumes an athletic stance approximately 6 to 12 inches (15 to 30 cm) perpendicular to a box (see figure a). A box height of 12 inches (30 cm) is recommended.

Action

The athlete jumps onto the box with one foot (see figure b). He should land with the foot softly on the box (with no movement of the knee toward the middle), pause, and then step down easily. Do not move to a higher box until all reps and sets are done easily and softly; if the landing is not soft and quiet, then simply use a smaller box. Perform the prescribed number of reps on each side.

One-Leg Box Hop With Stabilization

Setup

The athlete assumes an athletic stance approximately 6 to 12 inches (15 to 30 cm) behind a box (see figure a). A box height of 12 inches (30 cm) is recommended.

Action

The athlete jumps onto the box with one foot (see figure b). He should land with the foot softly on the box (with no movement of the knee toward the middle), pause, and then step down easily. Do not move to a higher box until all reps and sets are done easily and softly; if the landing is not soft and quiet, then simply use a smaller box. Perform the prescribed number of reps on each side.

Heiden Hop With Stabilization

Setup

The athlete assumes an athletic stance.

Action

Named after a drill that former Olympic speedskater Eric Heiden performed while training, the Heiden hop is a plyometric drill performed in the frontal plane. The athlete hops from one foot to the other in a side-to-side fashion (see figures *a–c*). The emphasis is on getting as much height and distance as possible and then landing softly and under control. The athlete needs to make a conscious effort to stabilize the foot when landing. Perform the prescribed number of reps.

Squat Jump

Setup

The athlete assumes an athletic stance with the hands next to the ears and the chest up.

Action

The athlete dips down into a quarter squat (see figure *a*) and then jumps into the air with both feet while keeping the hands next to the ears (see figure *b*). He should land with both feet and rebound into the next repetition. Perform the prescribed number of reps.

Angle Bound With Stabilization

Setup

The athlete assumes an athletic position (see figure *a*).

Action

The athlete bounds at a 45-degree angle to the left (see figure *b*) and lands on the left foot in an athletic position while facing forward, with a conscious effort to stabilize the foot when landing (see figure *c*). He repeats the same movement to the right. Perform the prescribed number of reps.

Heiden Hop

Setup

The athlete assumes an athletic stance (see figure *a*).

Action

Named after a drill that former Olympic speedskater Eric Heiden performed while training, the Heiden hop is a plyometric drill in the frontal plane. The athlete hops from one foot to the other in a side-to-side fashion, with as much height and distance as possible, and then lands softly and under control, but in a continuous manner without pause (see figures *b* and *c*). The athlete tries to act like a bouncy ball. Perform the prescribed number of reps.

Hurdle Jump With Stabilization

Setup

Five hurdles are set up 3 feet (1 m) apart. The athlete assumes an athletic position facing the hurdles.

Action

The athlete jumps over the five hurdles in successive fashion (see figures *a* and *b*), with an emphasis on stabilizing upon landing on the ground before going over the next hurdle. Perform the prescribed number of reps.

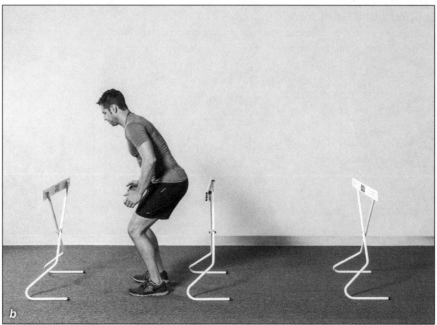

One-Leg Lateral–Medial Hurdle Hop With Stabilization

Setup

Five mini hurdles are set up 18 to 24 inches (46 to 60 cm) apart. The athlete assumes an athletic position laterally, or sideways, to the hurdles and balances on one leg.

Action

The athlete hops over the five hurdles in successive fashion, landing on the same foot (see figures *a* and *b*), with an emphasis on stabilizing upon landing on the ground before going over the next hurdle. Perform the prescribed number of reps on each side.

One-Leg Hurdle Hop With Stabilization

Setup

Five mini hurdles are set up 18 to 24 inches (46 to 60 cm) apart. The athlete assumes an athletic position facing the hurdles and balances on one leg.

Action

The athlete hops over the five hurdles in successive fashion, landing on the same foot (see figures *a* and *b*), with an emphasis on stabilizing upon landing on the ground before going over the next hurdle. Perform the prescribed number of reps on each side.

Hurdle Jump With Bounce

Setup

Five hurdles are set up 3 feet (1 m) apart. The athlete assumes an athletic position facing the hurdles.

Action

The athlete jumps over the five hurdles in successive fashion, with an emphasis on landing on the ground softly and rebounding quickly. After each landing, he performs a mini-jump (a 1- to 2-inch jump) and lands again before hopping over the next hurdle (see figures a-c). Perform the prescribed number of reps.

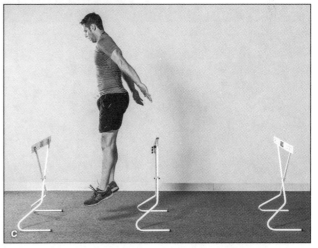

One-Leg Lateral Hurdle Hop With Bounce

Setup

Five mini hurdles are set up 18 to 24 inches (46 to 60 cm) apart. The athlete assumes an athletic position laterally, or sideways, to the hurdles and balances on one leg (see figure *a*).

Action

The athlete hops over the five hurdles in successive fashion, landing on the same foot, with an emphasis on landing on the ground softly and then rebounding quickly (see figures *b* and *c*). After each landing, he performs a mini-jump (a 1- to 2-inch jump) and lands again before hopping over the next hurdle (see figure *d*). Perform the prescribed number of reps on each side.

One-Leg Hurdle Hop With Bounce

Setup

Five mini hurdles are set up 18 to 24 inches (46 to 60 cm) apart. The athlete assumes an athletic position facing the hurdles and balances on one leg (see figure *a*).

Action

The athlete hops over the five hurdles in successive fashion, on the same foot, with an emphasis on landing on the ground softly and then rebounding quickly (see figures *b* and *c*). After each landing, he performs a mini-jump (a 1- to 2-inch jump) and lands again before hopping over the next hurdle (see figure *d*). Perform the prescribed number of reps on each side.

Hurdle Jump

Setup

Five hurdles are set up 18 to 24 inches (46 to 60 cm) apart. The athlete assumes an athletic position facing the hurdles.

Action

The athlete jumps over the five hurdles in successive fashion, with an emphasis on landing with minimal ground contact and rebounding quickly before jumping over the next hurdle (see figures a–c). Perform the prescribed number of reps.

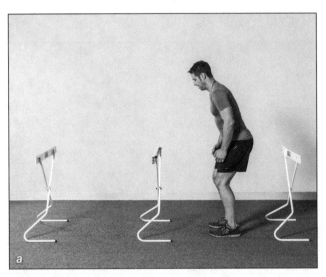

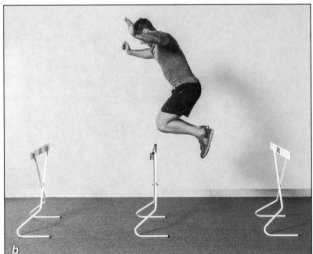

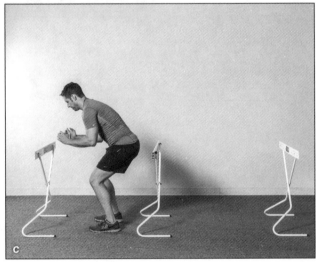

One-Leg Lateral Hurdle Hop

Setup

Five mini hurdles are set up 18 to 24 inches (46 to 60 cm) apart. The athlete assumes an athletic position laterally, or sideways, to the hurdles and balances on one leg.

Action

The athlete hops over the five hurdles, in successive fashion, with an emphasis on landing with minimal ground contact and rebounding quickly before hopping over the next hurdle (see figures *a–c*). Perform the prescribed number of reps on each side.

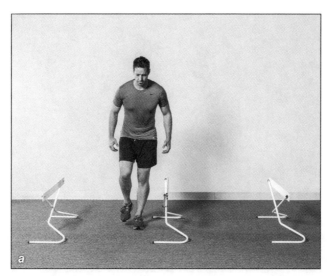

One-Leg Hurdle Hop

Setup

Five mini hurdles are set up 18 to 24 inches (46 to 60 cm) apart. The athlete assumes an athletic position facing the hurdles and balances on one leg.

Action

The athlete hops over the five hurdles in successive fashion, landing on the same foot, with an emphasis on landing with minimal ground contact and rebounding quickly before hopping over the next hurdle (see figures a–c). Perform the prescribed number of reps on each side.

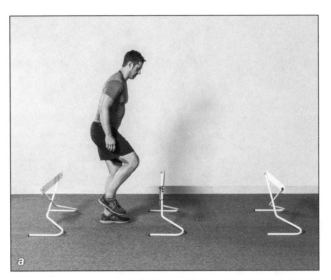

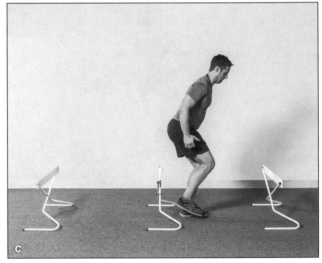

Angle Bound

Setup

The athlete assumes an athletic position.

Action

The athlete bounds to the right at a 45-degree angle and lands on the right foot while facing forward. He immediately jumps off that foot at another 45-degree angle (see figure) to land on the left foot while still facing forward. There is emphasis on distance, height, and minimal contact time with the foot on the ground. Perform the prescribed number of reps.

Acceleration and Speed

Hockey is a game of stops, starts, and frequent changes of direction. The game's fastest and most agile players are able to accelerate, decelerate, and then stop and quickly accelerate again. Acceleration is the ability to go from a dead stop to a sprint in as little time as possible.

Although players rarely get up to their top-end speed, the ability to accelerate faster than others is a characteristic of the quickest athletes. Strength and conditioning coach Mike Boyle and hockey exercise physiologist Jack Blatherwick are among those who have promoted the need for hockey players to develop acceleration.

It's important to think about what characteristics the faster players in hockey have in common. They are all built like a track sprinter or a football running back—big and strong quads, glutes, and hips. There is no reason why hockey players shouldn't train like sprinters.

In *Total Hockey Training*, acceleration and speed drills will be performed in the off-season only. During the pre-season and in-season phases, they will not be performed because the player is on the ice most of the time. During the pre-season and in-season, the time spent on acceleration and speed needs to be done during drills prescribed by the hockey coach in practices. The goals of the off-season acceleration and speed program is to help players develop power and acceleration and, most important, transfer it to the ice. The program enhances the multidirectional and chaotic pattern of hockey to prepare athletes to move faster in any direction. The focus should be on the first three to five steps, which should be done as fast as possible. Similar to the plyometric exercises, acceleration drills are either linear (straight ahead) or lateral (side to side). Linear speed drills are performed on days 1 and 3, and days 2 and 4 consist of lateral drills that emphasize sprinting out of a position and changing directions.

Acceleration drills are always done before any strength training or conditioning exercises. Also, athletes need to be fresh and well recovered while performing acceleration drills. These are not conditioning drills. In speed drills, the athlete is trying to go as hard as she possibly can. The muscles and the nervous system need to recover fully after each repetition.

Linear Speed

Linear speed is straight-ahead speed. The shortest distance from one location on the ice to another is a straight line. Therefore, hockey players need to incorporate linear speed drills into their off-season programs. These acceleration drills help players exert force into the ice and improve their straight-ahead speed.

Here's how linear speed is progressed through the four phases of the off-season:

Phase 1 Linear Speed

During phase 1 of the off-season, the emphasis is on trying to push hard into the ground so the athlete can increase speed. Linear speed drills help the athlete feel what it is like to be fast.

Phase 2 Linear Speed

During phase 2 of the off-season, the same linear speed drills are performed. However, they are performed as a superset with sled pulls to get a load contrast. This is similar to the complex method done with plyometrics and strength training that is also done during this phase.

Phase 3 Linear Speed

During phase 3 of the off-season, linear speed drills transition to those that train the athlete's reaction ability and require a partner. When the partner drops a tennis ball, the sprinter needs to react and then sprint as fast as possible.

Phase 4 Linear Speed

In phase 4 of the off-season, linear speed drills are more competitive. Creating competiveness within the off-season program is important because athletes will push each other, bringing more out of each athlete. It's amazing how competitive young hockey players can be.

Lean, Fall, and Run

Setup

The athlete assumes a tall stance (see figure *a*).

Action

At the start, the athlete remains tall and falls forward to a position just short of falling over (see figure *b*). When he reaches this point, he plants with his foot to push off and sprints straight ahead for three to five hard steps (see figure *c*). Do 3 repetitions with each foot in front, alternating the planted foot each time.

90-Degree Lean, Fall, and Run

Setup

The athletes assumes a position bent at the waist (see figure *a*).

Action

The athlete falls forward to a position just short of falling over. When he reaches this point, he plants with his foot to push off and sprints straight ahead for three to five hard steps (see figures *b* and *c*). Do 3 repetitions with each foot in front, alternating the planted foot each time.

Ball Drop

Setup

Two partners face each other from 5 yards or meters away. One partner holds a ball, and the working partner assumes an athletic stance. The partner holding the ball starts the drill.

Action

The partner drops the ball, and the working partner sprints and attempts to catch the ball before it hits the ground twice (see figure). The distance between the players should be at least 5 yards when they first attempt this drill; the distance of the partner and the height of the ball from the ground dictate the difficulty of the drill.

Push-Up Start

Setup

Two athletes start on the ground in a push-up position. One athlete is designated to start the drill.

Action

The designated athlete starts the drill by getting up and sprinting as fast as possible. The other athlete's objective is to chase down the first athlete and tag him before the athletes can sprint 20 yards or meters. This is the longest distance the athletes will sprint in the off-season program.

To increase the difficulty of this drill, each athlete can wear a juke belt. The athlete who starts the drill wants to break away from the chasing athlete, while the chasing athlete doesn't want the lead athlete to break away.

Lateral Speed

Since hockey features repeated changes of direction, lateral speed development is also important. Lateral speed drills are performed twice per week during the off-season on the days linear speed isn't being trained. Being able to change directions quickly and run in a straight line can help hockey players increase lateral speed on the ice. Like linear acceleration drills, the focus is on the first three to five steps.

Crossovers are one of the key skills that hockey players continually work on. The crossover step is an important component of skating at all levels, a movement necessary for turning, stopping, and changing direction. Hockey players often describe the crossover as "blasting off." Since it is such an important aspect of skating, strength and conditioning coaches should develop progressions and strategies to improve this skill.

From a coaching and technical standpoint, players need to shift their weight and lean in the direction they want to go. This is very similar to the lean, fall, and run acceleration drill. The farther athletes lean, the better the drill is for them. In the crossover acceleration drills, a body lean is incorporated on the side of the direction the athlete wants to go. For example, if the athlete wants to move to the left, he will lean to the left and shift his weight to the outside of the left foot. When he reaches the tipping point, he then crosses the right foot over the left and pushes off of the right foot.

Here's how lateral speed is progressed through the four phases of the off-season:

Phase 1 Lateral Speed

During the off-season, drills are incorporated so that the athlete has to prevent themselves from falling by pushing off the ground hard to go the other way in the crossover step. Phase 1 lateral speed drills are performed to help the athlete feel what it is like to be fast.

Phase 2 Lateral Speed

During the off-season, phase 2 lateral speed drills are performed in conjunction with sled pulls to get a load contrast. The heavy sled pull will help the athlete run faster, while the fast sprint will help the athlete pull the sled quicker.

Phase 3 Lateral Speed

During the off-season, phase 3 lateral speed drills are performed to help the athlete react to an external stimulus that will help the athlete run as soon as the stimulus is added to the repetition in the drill.

Phase 4 Lateral Speed

During the off-season, phase 4 lateral speed drills involve a partner to increase competitiveness and so that athletes can react to each other's movements. This gets the athletes a little out of their own comfort zones and pushes them to work harder and faster.

Lean, Fall, Crossover, and Run

Setup

The athlete begins in an athletic stance (see figure *a*).

Action

In a lateral fashion, the athlete leans to the side and then crosses over with the outside leg (see figure *b*), turns, and sprints (see figure *c*). The emphasis is on getting a good push, taking three fast steps, and then coasting. The idea is to use the foot that is crossing over to explode and change directions. For example, if the athlete is leaning to the right, the left foot will cross over and help the athlete sprint to the right. Do 3 crossovers and sprints on each leg.

One-Leg Bent-Knee Crossover and Run

Setup

The athlete stands on one leg with the chest up, hips back, and eyes up. The athlete runs to the side of the foot that is on the ground. For example, if the athlete's right foot is on the ground, he will cross the left foot over the right and then run to the right.

Action

In a lateral fashion, the athlete leans to the side and then crosses over the outside leg (the foot and leg that are on the ground), turns, and sprints (see figures *a* and *b*). The emphasis is on getting a good push, taking three fast steps, and then coasting. The idea is to use the foot that is crossing over to explode and change directions. For example, if the athlete is leaning to the right, the left foot will cross over and help the athlete sprint to the right. Do 3 crossovers and sprints on each leg.

Lateral Crossover Ball Drop

Setup

Two partners face each other from 5 yards or meters away. One partner holds a ball, and the working partner assumes an athletic stance perpendicular to the partner with the ball. The partner holding the ball will start the drill.

Action

The partner drops the ball, and the working athlete crosses over, sprints, and attempts to catch the ball before it hits the ground twice. The distance between the players should be at least 5 yards when they first attempt this drill; the distance of the partner and the height of the ball from the ground dictates the difficulty of the drill.

Partner Agility Mirror Drill

Setup

Two athletes assume an athletic position, facing each other and straddling a line. There is another line 5 yards or meters to the right and also 5 yards or meters to the left.

Action

One athlete starts the drill without warning. He begins a sprint in one direction toward one of the lines, touches it and turns to sprint in the other direction to the far line, touches it and then turns to sprint through the original starting line. The partner must react to the starting athlete's movement and try to beat him through the starting position.

Sled Work

Pushing and pulling sleds can increase speed and strength. During the off-season, sled work is performed after plyometric and speed drills and also during a complex with acceleration drills during phase 2. Sled drills need to be performed with adequate rest in between sets. They are not conditioning drills; they are drills to help improve strength and power. The heart rate will climb during these drills. Therefore the athlete shouldn't begin his next repetition until he is fully recovered.

Similar to the plyometric and speed drills, sled work is arranged in a linear and lateral fashion. Linear sled pulls and pushes are done on days 1 and 3, while the lateral crossover sled work is on days 2 and 4.

Here's how sled work is progressed through the four phases of the off-season:

Phase 1 and 2 Sled Work

During the off-season, sled work in phases 1 and 2 help the athlete move in a straight direction while pulling resistance. The concept is to reinforce sprinting mechanics against heavy load while trying to push the foot hard into the ground with each step. This will give the athlete more powerful steps in sprinting and also skating.

Phase 3 Sled Work

During the off-season, sled work for phase 3 progresses to pushing the sled. The athlete is pushing against resistance while trying to maintain sprint mechanics. This is another way to train the athlete to produce a hard step into the floor, with the intention of producing more powerful steps while sprinting and more explosive pushing on the ice.

Phase 4 Sled Work

During the off-season, phase 4 has no sled work because heavy sled work can be extremely stressful on the nervous system. When the plyometric program shifts toward being more elastic, the sled pulls and pushes are stopped.

Resisted March

Setup

A sled is attached to the athlete with a harness. The sled is behind the athlete.

Action

With the sled attached, the athlete walks slowly in a straight line for 25 yards or meters (see figure). The load

must be heavy enough that the athlete must lean forward to move the sled. It is important that the load is not too heavy or too light. Perform 6 repetitions of 25 yards.

Lateral Resisted Crossover

Setup

A sled is attached with a harness to the side of the athlete (see figure *a*).

Action

This is a lateral drill where the emphasis is on the crossover step. The athlete drags the sled for 25 yards or meters by crossing over laterally, emphasizing a hard step with the foot that is crossing over (see figures *b* and *c*). Like the resisted march, the load has to be just right so the athlete can perform the crossover but not be able to jog with it.

Sled Push

Setup

The athlete gets behind a sled much heavier than the load in other sled drills.

Action

The athlete gets into a comfortable and effective position and pushes the sled for 25 yards or meters (see figure).

Chapter 8

Flexibility

Static stretching, where a stretch is held for 30 seconds, has always been very popular among hockey players. Athletes in all sports—some of the best athletes and teams in the world—spend hours stretching every day, before, during, and after activity. *Total Hockey Training* recommends stretching daily.

THOUGHTS ON STRETCHING

There is a common belief that static stretching decreases power, as some studies have shown decreases in power after stretching statically (Hough, Ross, and Howatson 2009). Although static stretching alone led to a demonstrated decrease in power, there was a positive improvement in power as a result of a dynamic warm-up. Over an extended time without static stretching, the muscles used in hockey can become short and tight. If the muscles are too tight, overuse injuries, such as muscle strains and pulls, can occur. Stretching on a consistent basis helps the muscles maintain their length and their ability to do their job.

A dynamic warm-up is always recommended before activity whether it is an off-season training session, in-season practice, or a game. The dynamic warm-up not only warms up the muscles and joints but it also addresses flexibility. Static stretching before activity without a proper dynamic warm-up is never recommended.

Hockey players skate with the knees, hips, and spine bent, so the hip adductors and hip flexors have a greater chance of becoming overworked and being injured. When players are not on the ice, they're sitting on the bench waiting for their next shift or they're sitting in their locker room stalls during intermission. These athletes are always in flexion. The movements performed in hockey, combined with prolonged sitting, can contribute to the shortening of the muscles in the body. To prevent this from happening, some simple daily stretching exercises need to be implemented into the program.

OPTIMAL TIMES FOR STRETCHING

In *Total Hockey Training*, there are three different times when stretching is recommended: before training, during training, and after training. Again, the belief is that the benefits of stretching happen over time, not immediately after stretching. The reality is that stretching can contribute to helping hockey players feel better.

Stretching Before Training

During the off-season, static stretching is recommended immediately after the foam rolling period, discussed in chapter 4. The foam roller has worked the soft tissue, and now it is time to lengthen the muscles that have just been rolled. This process makes sense from a perspective of removing knots and other soft tissue restrictions before stretching. If the restrictions are not removed, then the muscle can't be lengthened fully during the specific stretches. The quads, hip flexors, hip rotators, hamstrings, lats, pecs, and calves can all be stretched.

Stretching During Training

Active isolated stretching, founded and endorsed by massage therapist Aaron Mattes, is done within strength training sessions. This is recommended for two reasons: (1) to allow for a longer rest period between strength training exercises and (2) to incorporate antagonistic muscle relaxation, with the belief that it will enhance the muscle being used in the next strength training exercise. These types of stretches are included in pairs, tri-sets, and quad-sets with strength training exercises. For example, if the upper back muscles are stressed in an exercise such as the chin-up, then active isolated stretches for the chest muscles are prescribed between sets. One repetition will consist of the stretch being held for 6 seconds followed by a brief 1- to 2-second rest, and then being repeated two more times. The athlete tries to stretch a little farther each time. While the stretch is being held, the opposite muscle group is being activated. In the case of stretching the pectorals (chest), the upper-back musculature is activated.

Stretching After Training

After training, the stretching protocol is similar to the pretraining session after foam rolling. The stretch is held for 20 to 30 seconds. This is another opportunity to stretch groins and hip flexors, as well as other muscle groups that traditionally become tight in hockey players, such as the IT bands, quads, hamstrings, and pectorals. Static stretching is done primarily after practices and games because stretching after activity helps bring the muscles back to a lengthened state after being used in the game or practice. It is also a traditional way to cool down the body after an intense game, practice, or training session.

STATIC STRETCHES

In hockey, the following stretches have been shown to help players over time. These are traditional, bang-for-your-buck stretches that players can do on a daily basis to help combat the daily movement patterns of hockey.

In *Total Hockey Training*, the idea is to relax when stretching. The athlete can help the body further relax by focusing on breathing. Ideally, the athlete will breathe in through the nose with the mouth closed, and exhale through the mouth while the stretch is held. Also, the ability to breathe in to the diaphragm versus the chest is important and is accomplished by concentrating on not allowing the chest and shoulders to rise. This will allow the athlete to relax more and allow for further flexibility during each stretch.

Hip Flexor Stretch

Setup

The athlete kneels on one knee; the other knee is bent. He is as tall as possible, keeping the head up and eyes straight on the horizon (see figure *a*).

Action

The athlete inhales and then breathes out while contracting the gluteus maximus muscle of the leg with the knee on the ground. He leans into the front leg at hip level only (see figure *b*). He should feel a stretch on the front of the hip. Next, he reaches the same-side arm up and over the head, which allows for a deeper stretch.

Squat Stretch

Setup

The athlete squats so that the hips are below the knees. His hands are clasped together, with elbows touching the inside of the knees (see figure). The eyes and chest are up. He focuses on keeping his weight shifted on the heels of the feet.

Action

The athlete pushes the knees out to the side with the elbows. He holds this position while trying to relax into the stretch for 30 seconds.

Quad Stretch

Setup

The athlete kneels on one knee; the other knee is bent. He is as tall as possible, keeping the head up and eyes straight on the horizon (see figure *a*). This is also a stretch for the hip flexor.

Action

The athlete inhales and then breathes out while grabbing the foot that is on the floor behind him (see figure *b*). Initially, he may be able to just touch the foot, but as he gets better over time, he will be able to grab the foot and lightly pull on it.

Hamstring Stretch

Setup

The athlete puts one foot up on a bench or a table while keeping both legs straight (see figure *a*).

Action

While remaining as tall as possible, the athlete inhales and then breathes out while contracting the rectus femoris muscle (quad). Keeping the upper body tall, he leans forward until he feels a stretch in the hamstring muscle (see figure *b*).

Adductor Stretch

Setup

The athlete stands with both feet as wide as comfortably possible, chest up, hands behind the head, and eyes on the horizon (see figure *a*).

Action

The athlete breathes in and then breathes out while squatting to one side, keeping the chest up and the other leg straight (see figure *b*).

Hip External Rotator Stretch

Setup

The athlete sits on the ground with one leg in front and the other leg behind. The front leg is bent 90 degrees at the knee and faces toward the middle (see figure).

Action

While keeping the chest and eyes up, the athlete breathes in and then breathes out while leaning forward so that the sternum touches the front knee.

Hip Internal Rotator Stretch

Setup

The athlete lies across a stability ball, with the upper back, shoulders, and head on the ball and the hips extended with the feet shoulder-width apart (see figure *a*).

Action

The athlete breathes in and then breathes out while trying to touch the knees together (see figure *b*). The hips should remain extended throughout the entire stretch.

Quadratus Lumborum Stretch

Setup

The athlete lies over a stability ball on one side, with the top leg forward and the bottom leg reaching behind (see figure *a*).

Action

The athlete breathes in and then breathes out as he reaches the arm over the head. For example, if the athlete is lying on the left side, then his right foot is forward and left foot back. He reaches his right arm overhead while leaning over the ball on the left side, which will stretch out the left quadratus lumborum (see figure *b*). After he stretches one side, he repeats on the other side.

Calf Stretch

Setup

The athlete stands on a box or a platform (see figure *a*), allowing the heel to drop while keeping the ball of the foot on the platform (see figure *b*).

Action

To stretch the gastrocnemius, the athlete keeps the knees straight. To stretch the soleus muscle, he bends the knees.

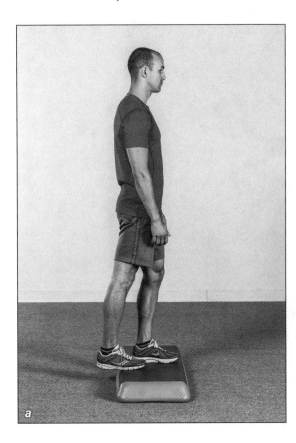

Lat Stretch

Setup

The athlete grabs onto a squat rack, a pole, or a band with one arm. The head and spine are in a neutral position (see figure *a*).

Action

The athlete breathes in and then breathes out as he keeps the arm straight and shifts the hips back so that he feels a stretch in the latissimus dorsi (see figure *b*). He repeats on the other side.

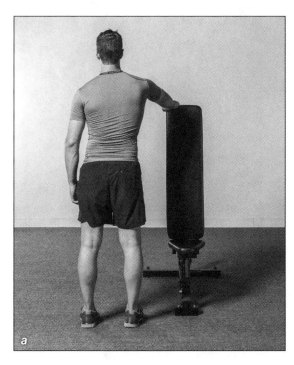
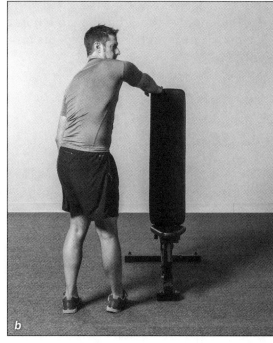

Chest Stretch

Setup

The athlete stands tall inside a doorway or a squat rack.

Action

The athlete bends one arm at the elbow, with the upper arm parallel to the ground and the forearm perpendicular to the ground. The athlete breathes in and then breathes out as he leans forward while remaining tall (see figure). He should feel a stretch in the pectoralis major muscle. He repeats on the other side.

Chapter 9

Conditioning

Hockey players want to be just as fast and as powerful late in a game as they were at the beginning of the game, so devising a proper conditioning protocol is a critical area for a strength and conditioning coach. Although the coach's job is to help hockey players become stronger and faster, conditioning is also part of the job description. A proper conditioning program is an ongoing process.

IMPLEMENTING A CONDITIONING PROGRAM

Conditioning for hockey has come a long way since off-ice methods were first implemented. There was a time when professional hockey players did next to nothing during the off-season in terms of training. Players would use the then four- to six-week training camps as the time to get in proper condition for the season. It wasn't until the 1980s that hockey started to embrace off-ice training and testing protocols to help players improve. Exercise physiologists were consulted and asked to provide proper fitness protocols at a time when none existed. At first, the training was primarily aerobic, with long, steady-state rides on exercise bikes. The intention was to improve $\dot{V}O_2max$. As a result, $\dot{V}O_2max$ became the universal method of assessing hockey conditioning for many years and is still used by many hockey teams and organizations at the professional and amateur levels.

Today, a strength and conditioning coach needs to understand how to design and implement conditioning sessions on a year-round basis. Conditioning programs should follow the principle of specificity to mimic the energy demands of hockey: Players need to train like they play. A shift lasts anywhere from 20 seconds to more than 80 seconds, depending on the player's position and the situation on the ice. Players sit and recover for a few minutes, and the cycle repeats for the rest of the game, which also has two intermission periods (usually 15 to 18 minutes). During the third period, especially if the team is trailing by a goal or trying to protect a lead, the higher-skilled players will usually play more minutes. Therefore, these players may be on the ice for longer shifts, and they may be off the ice for less time. This is universal in hockey, regardless of the level. The only difference is the total time of the game—60 minutes at the higher levels of hockey and 36 minutes or so at the lower levels.

The conditioning program needs to be implemented at the beginning of the off-season. As the preseason starts, the program transitions from primarily off-ice conditioning to more on-ice conditioning. Although the goal of the off-season conditioning program is to become a highly fit player, conditioning doesn't stop when the regular season begins. The regular season is the time for players to maintain their conditioning so they can play at the highest level possible.

CONDITIONING DRILLS

There are recommended conditioning drills for each part of the season—off-season, preseason, and in-season.

Off-Season Conditioning Drills

During the off-season, all conditioning methods are off-ice, or dryland. The beginning of this period is easier compared with later in the off-season. It is the time for players to get reacquainted with a more time-consuming and demanding training regimen without the use of sticks, skates, and pucks. It is also when running needs to be reintroduced at all levels of hockey. Running allows hockey players to extend their hips with their feet on the ground, which is important since they primarily train in skates with a flexed posture during the season. Their muscles need to be able to apply force through the ground and get to a lengthened state. This will help combat the in-season shortened hip flexion position that occurs over and over again with a large volume of skating.

Conditioning progresses from lower volume in terms of repetitions and distance covered to higher volume which consists of more reps and distance covered. The athletes adapt to the stresses that the conditioning program imposes on the body. By the end of the off-season, players will be well conditioned for the start of the preseason phase, which consists of on-ice and off-ice training.

Off-season conditioning methods in *Total Hockey Training* include tempo running, slide-board intervals, and running shuttles.

Tempo Runs

Tempo running is a method of conditioning used throughout the off-season. It has been advocated by track and field and strength and conditioning coaches such as Charlie Francis, Al Vermeil, and Mike Boyle. Charlie Francis used tempo running with his track sprinters as a method of increasing work capacity and recovery. It builds the aerobic system without long, steady-state work to help enhance recovery for when the high-end anaerobic work is started.

Setup

The athlete starts in an athletic stance in a corner of the back of the end zone of a football or soccer field.

Action

The athlete runs down the sideline until he reaches the opposite goal line or corner of the soccer field to complete 1 repetition. He walks across the goal line to the opposite sideline and then runs down the sideline to the back of the other end zone or corner of the soccer field to complete the next repetition. From there, he walks across the end zone until he reaches the opposite corner and starts the next repetition. Perform the prescribed number of reps.

Tempo running is at a good pace, neither jogging nor sprinting but somewhere in between, in the range of 75 to 85 percent of maximum speed. This drill can be successfully implemented in a group setting by having the athletes run down the sideline in single file and walk through the end zone in the same format.

Protocol

Tempo running should be done one or two times per week throughout the off-season. There are two days of tempo running at the beginning, with a transition to one day when shuttle runs are introduced a few weeks into the program. These consist of running 110 yards or meters.

Slide-Board Conditioning

Hockey players need to be able to play in multiple directions. The slide board is a tool that helps athletes condition in the frontal plane, or side to side. Off-season training conditions the muscles used in skating, such as the hip adductors and abductors, to help the players prepare for a return to the ice. Being efficient on the slide board during the off-season can help a hockey player improve her conditioning while also mimicking the demands of skating as closely as possible.

Although the slide board is used for lateral conditioning during the off-season, it should rarely be used during the in-season phase with healthy players. Once the players return to the ice, the slide boards should be put away until the following off-season. (The exception is when the slide board is used in an in-season rehab setting for a player with an injury such as a groin or hip flexor strain.) Also, if a player decides he wants to resume skating during the off-season, the volume of slide-board conditioning should be dropped. The risk of overuse injuries should be minimized before the start of the preseason.

Setup

The athlete assumes a low center of gravity by sustaining a deep knee bend (see figure a).

Action

The athlete is always in an athletic stance. He glides from side to side, eyes on the horizon, with the knees bent, hips back, and chest up. The emphasis is on the push-off (see figure b) and then the gliding phase of each slide-board repetition, all while staying low. Perform for the prescribed amount of time.

Protocol

Previously mentioned strength and conditioning coach Mike Boyle is a pioneer in regard to the slide board and its implementation into a strength and conditioning program. His work has been instrumental in guiding the slide-board programming process. Players use the slide board on Tuesdays and Fridays during phases 2 to 4 of the off-season program. During work intervals, the objective is to try to work as hard as possible once technique is established. The slide-board program starts with 30-second intervals and progresses to 45 seconds (defensemen) as the off-season goes along.

Shuttles

Shuttle runs are another great way to condition the body for the energy system demands of hockey. The runs are tough since they are close to 100 percent maximum sprinting speed. Although the times of a shuttle run and an actual hockey shift are similar, an on-ice shift includes periods of gliding and also may contain stoppages of play. Gliding does not occur during a shuttle run. What is also great about shuttle runs is the frequency of changing direction. This develops eccentric strength when the athlete decelerates before he turns and changes directions.

Setup

The athlete starts in an athletic stance on the end line of a football field.

Action

The athlete sprints to the 25-yard line and then changes direction and runs back to the starting line. He completes the run three times so that 150 yards total is achieved. The objective is to finish in less than 30 seconds. Perform the prescribed number of reps. The rest period is 1 minute and 30 seconds.

For 300-yard shuttles, the athlete runs 50 yards down and back instead of 25 yards (or he could still use the 25-yard distance but run down and back six times). He tries to accomplish this in less than 1 minute. He rests for 3 minutes at the beginning and then progresses to 2 minutes' rest.

Protocol

Shuttle runs start with a distance of 150 yards or meters. The 300-yard shuttles are done in the third and fourth phases of the off-season.

Preseason Conditioning Drills

Hockey players need to get back on the ice in the preseason. Conditioning also takes place primarily on the ice, although off-ice conditioning that complements the on-ice work is recommended. Running should be discontinued so that players can adapt to the specific demands of skating—the pounding of running would interfere with their recovery from skating drills. The transition to the exercise bike can begin. Although not recommended during the off-season, the exercise bike is used during the preseason and in-season periods to further enhance conditioning.

During the preseason, most hockey teams come together and operate practices on their own. In high school and collegiate hockey, this is considered "captains' practice," where practices are operated without the coaches. The team leaders are responsible for planning and organizing the practice sessions. At the professional level, it is not uncommon for teams to organize practices on their own from mid-August through early September, the time when players report back to the cities in which their teams are located. This is close to the time frame in junior hockey settings as well.

Whether it is at the collegiate (limited responsibility), junior, or professional level, a team's strength and conditioning coach can implement a progressive on-ice conditioning program. Like the off-season program, it should have less volume at the beginning and more volume and intensity near the end. A general assessment of the players' current skating capability is helpful. Some will have already begun skating a few weeks before, while others might be on the ice for the first time during this phase. In general, it is safer to assume that each player is just getting back on the ice or hasn't done any serious on-ice conditioning work. As a result, drills that include many stops and starts should be avoided at the beginning. Performing stopping and starting drills at the beginning of the preseason can be very stressful and can result in injury. The phase should start with flow drills that consist of more straight-ahead skating plus turning to change directions. Then, after a few sessions, the more demanding stopping and starting drills can begin.

Here are some conditioning drills that the strength and conditioning coach can implement during the preseason, with an emphasis on flow drills at the beginning and progressing to more intense drills with frequent changes of direction. These would be performed after all team hockey drills have been completed.

4x3 Laps

Setup

Divide the skaters into two groups. One group is at the red line, while the other group is near the middle of the ice, waiting until it's time for them to go. With a large group of players, bring the nets out toward the middle of the ice a few feet.

Action

At the whistle, the group at the red line performs three laps around the ice. The next group starts once the first group crosses the red line. The focus should be on maintaining a low center of gravity and having long strides, with an emphasis on pushing off hard and gliding. The players change directions after each set of 3 laps so that both directions are worked equally. Complete 4 sets with a 1:1 work–rest ratio.

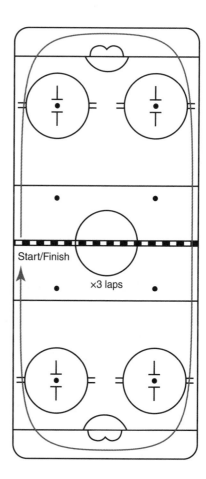

Partner Laps

Setup

Divide the skaters into two groups. One group is at the red line, while the other group is near the middle of the ice, waiting until it's time for them to go.

Action

One group performs one lap, and then the next group goes. Then the first group performs two laps, and then the next group goes. This continues for the prescribed number of laps. The players change directions after each set of laps so that both directions are worked equally, or they perform the laps in the same direction while climbing up and then skate in the opposite direction while going down. Although the drill calls for the players to skate up to four laps and then back down, the coach can decide on whatever number of laps he wants.

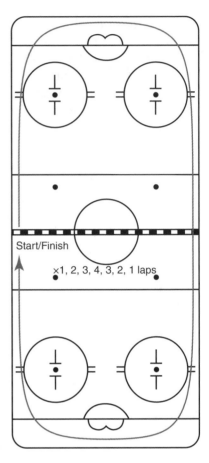

Start/Finish

×1, 2, 3, 4, 3, 2, 1 laps

Mountains

Setup

The players line up on the goal line across the ice. This drill can be performed with large groups, with small groups, or individually. A very large number of players can be divided into two groups.

Action

At the coach's whistle, the players skate to the near blue line and return to the goal line; they skate to the red line and return to the goal line; they skate to the opposite blue line and return to the goal line; then they skate all the way down to the opposite goal line and return. The next group then performs the drill, if applicable. A work–rest ratio of 1:1, 1:2, or 1:3 is recommended, depending on what the coach wants to accomplish or where the players are in their overall conditioning.

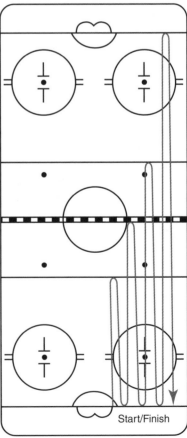

Start/Finish

Protocol

Mountains can be done with either tight turns or stops and starts. Tight turns are easier and are recommended earlier in the preseason, with a progression to stopping and starting, which happens more frequently in game situations.

Another great thing about mountains is the many variation options. For example, the players can do full mountains or they can do part of the drill, such as blue line and back plus far blue line and back, or red line and back plus far goal line and back. Like all conditioning drills, the coach's imagination and how hard he wants to push the team are the limiting factors. Begin with 2 repetitions and progress by 1 rep each week. Mountains are difficult, especially at the end of a preseason practice, so it's important not to overdo it.

Widths

Setup

The players line up along the boards in one to three groups, depending on the number of players participating.

Action

When the coach blows the whistle, the first group skates to the opposite boards and then back as quickly as possible. This is 1 repetition. Then the second group performs 1 repetition. If there is a third group, those players go. The first group then performs 2 repetitions, followed by the other groups. Perform the desired number of repetitions.

Protocol

Widths are another difficult on-ice conditioning drill that can also be done with tight turns or stopping and starting. Instead of going up and down the ice in a vertical fashion as for mountains, the players skate across the width of the ice horizontally.

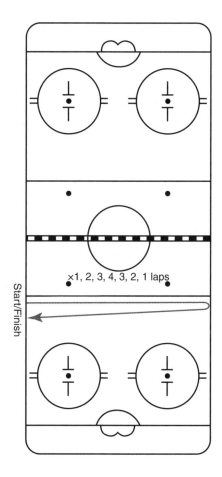

Four Dots

Setup

This drill is best for a smaller number of players, done one player at a time. Four of the face-off dots are used, making a square.

Action

Starting on one dot, the player does the following:

- Skates to the second dot and returns to the first dot, using tight turns or stopping and starting
- Skates around the second dot all the way to the third dot
- Skates back to the second dot
- Skates to the fourth dot
- Skates back to the third dot
- Skates back to the original dot and then to the fourth dot
- Skates through the first dot
- Perform the desired number of repetitions in both directions.

Protocol

This is a tough drill that should be performed only a few times. The ice will become pretty rough from multiple players and repetitions. Feel free to use the other dots on the ice. Use a 1:1, 1:2, or 1:3 work–rest ratio.

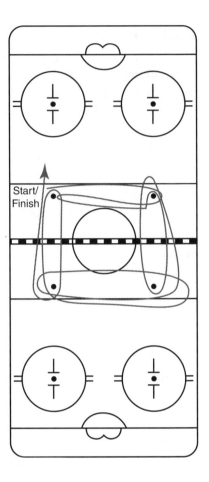

Blue Line, Red Line Drills

Setup

The players form two groups and line up on each blue line, facing each other. Half the team goes at a time.

Action

The coach describes the drill before blowing the whistle. For example, the coach may say, "Red line back, blue line back." At the whistle, one group skates to the red line and back and then to the opposite blue line and back as quickly as possible. Then the other group does the same on the coach's whistle. There are many other possible drills, such as blue line back, red line back; blue line back × 4; and red line back × 4. Perform the desired number of repetitions.

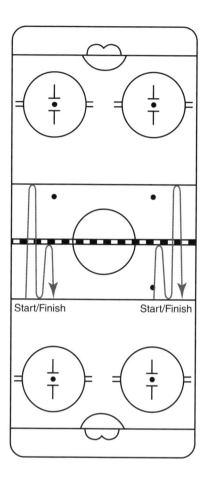

Stationary Bike Training

Although the on-ice conditioning is very demanding in the preseason, off-ice work should be implemented that complements the on-ice work, including anaerobic work on the stationary bike (if available). The stationary bike is a useful tool during preseason and in-season phases. Unlike strength training, which is performed before practice in a circuit-like fashion, off-ice bike conditioning should be done postpractice.

Stationary bike work needs to be difficult during the preseason. The work should be interval based to closely mimic shift demands in hockey. Interval training involves periods of work followed by periods of rest repeated for a given number of repetitions. The best part about interval training is that the work and rest periods can be manipulated so there are different training effects. All the conditioning work done in the off-season involved interval-based training (which hockey pretty much is). The only difference now is that the bike allows for more speed and power to be achieved with the legs alone.

Here are some preseason exercise bike rides:

:30/1:00-1:30 Rest

For these intervals, after a good 3- to 5-minute warm-up on the bike, the player sprints as hard as he can for 30 seconds. The level of resistance is the determining factor in how hard the sprint will be. The bike should be set at manual resistance, and the warm-up should be around level 10 to 12 at 80 rpm. Most exercise bikes will go up to level 20, 21, or 25. The higher levels should be used during the sprinting portion of the ride. When the sprint is finished, the level on the bike should be dropped to 10 or below so the athlete can recover before the next sprint.

The heart rate should be elevated at the end of the sprint. If the coach has access to enough heart rate monitors for the entire group, another rest option is to recover until the heart rate drops to below 130 or 120 bpm (depending on what the coach decides) before sprinting again. This allows the more fit players to begin their next sprint if they have recovered before other players. It also gives the less fit players optimal recovery time before sprinting again. Perform the desired number of repetitions.

1:00/2:00-3:00 Rest

These are obviously going to be harder than the 30-second sprints. The extra 30 seconds makes a big difference and will give players the stamina to perform at the end of a long shift. The heart rate response and the demand on the legs are going to be greater as well. Like the 30-second sprints, the heart rate monitor can be used on an individual basis. Perform the desired number of repetitions.

Tabata Method

Tabata is a very high-end anaerobic method that became popular after a study showed that 8 sets of 20-second high-intensity sprints (170 percent $\dot{V}O_2$max) with 10 seconds' rest was superior to long, steady work for the improvement of $\dot{V}O_2$max (Tabata). Basically, after a 3- to 5-minute warm up, the athlete sprints at the highest resistance on the bike for 20 seconds, recovers for 10, and then repeats seven more times. It is 4 minutes of work, but it should feel a lot longer than that, especially if the player works really hard. This ride has a negative work–rest ratio, which is unlike any other interval training method or hockey itself.

In-Season Conditioning Drills

In general, in-season conditioning is primarily on the ice. The whole team will be in better condition during the in-season period than they were during the preseason as a byproduct of daily participation in practices and games. Sufficient recovery after practices and games is imperative to combat the physical stresses of training and competing. For the most part, the team will not need extra off-ice conditioning during the season unless the exercise bike is used in place of an on-ice practice. This could occur as a result of the head coach's decision to do something else that day instead of skating or as a result of facility logistics where ice may not be available. When the strength and conditioning coach evaluates each player's individual role on the team, extra off-ice work may need to be prescribed based on how much time each player logs in games.

During the in-season phase, off-ice conditioning can be individualized according to the specific demands of players' roles on the team. For example, a first-line forward who is on the power-play and penalty-kill units will not have the same conditioning prescription as a fourth-line player who plays 5 to 8 minutes a game. This could be programmed from both on-ice and off-ice perspectives.

The most important factor to analyze is how much ice time a player gets. Unless a team simply rolls three or four lines throughout the course of the game, the top players on any team will play more minutes (i.e., the first line will play more than the fourth line). This difference in minutes played occurs at all levels of hockey. Power-play and penalty-kill situations always disrupt the flow of line rolling because more offensive-minded players always play more on the power play, while the more defensive-minded players assume roles on the penalty kill. The best players can do both successfully, and their minutes played will be much higher than the rest of the team.

As the season progresses, the players' roles will become defined. The strength and conditioning coach should be able to recognize each player's situation and design conditioning programs accordingly. The coach will need to make adjustments for times when players don't play as a result of injury or being a healthy scratch. Any changes in the conditioning program need to be made clear to the affected players.

The conditioning demands of the team will be equal in practices. It is not uncommon for the entire team to perform the same drills in a practice session and then finish off with a conditioning skate. Game days are when the players who don't play as much need to optimize their time by working on off-ice conditioning. If a player hasn't been playing a lot of minutes, then extra work should be put in on the bike postgame. Players who are healthy scratches should condition on the bike during the game, especially if they participated in the pregame warm-up (mainly at the professional and major junior levels). Injured players are a different situation. Their conditioning needs to be designed on an individual basis depending on the injury, where they are in the rehabilitation process, and what they can or can't do as far as conditioning methods go.

15-Plus Minutes Played

These players should ride the bike as a postgame flush. The resistance should be low to medium intensity, and they will ride at a steady pace for 10 to 20 minutes. This type of ride helps the players cool down after the game while also kick-starting the recovery process. Combined with stretching and the cold tub, this is a good postgame protocol for those who play many minutes.

10 to 15 Minutes Played

These players should participate in a bike program that gets them close to the energy demand of the players with more ice time. For example, if the top forward on the team played 25 minutes, then players who played only 15 should do a minimum of 10 minutes of interval training.

Methods of interval training used here are similar to preseason exercise bike rides, with less time during the rest period. Players could do four to six 30-second sprints with 1 minute's rest, or four 1-minute sprints with 2 minutes' rest. As with other conditioning methods, this would be up to the strength and conditioning coach.

Less Than 10 Minutes Played

Those with less than 10 minutes of ice time require a longer period on the bike postgame. For example, if a player played 6 minutes while the top player played 25, then he should put in 19 minutes of work. In this case, 8 to 12 30-second sprints with 1 minute off or 4 to 6 1-minute sprints with 2 minutes' rest may be the norm.

Healthy Scratched

Healthy scratches and backup goaltenders need to put in a large amount of work. As mentioned before, a healthy scratch does conditioning work during the game immediately after the warm-up, while backup goaltenders must do their conditioning postgame. Scratched players need to be handled on an individual basis. They may be scratched for the first time in their career, or it could be another in a large number of successive games they haven't suited up for. Their conditioning should be 20 to 30 minutes, such as 10 to 14 30-second sprints or 6 to 8 1-minute sprints.

The season is very long, and some players will find themselves doing a lot of postgame biking. The strength and conditioning coach should keep things fresh by changing the exercise bike work every now and then. Prescribing a variety of bike rides keeps the athletes from adapting to the same routines over and over again. The Tabata method can be used frequently, and an occasional long, steady-state ride can be incorporated.

The heart rate monitor can also be used to further individualize bike conditioning sessions. Instead of following general recovery recommendations, the players could recover to a specific heart rate before beginning the next interval. The strength and conditioning coach would determine how much rest is required. For example, a heart rate of 130 bpm would be considered an incomplete recovery, while a heart rate of 110 bpm would be considered complete. This requires minimal coaching because the heart rate monitor would dictate the training session.

Chapter 10

Off-Season Training Programs

The off-season training period follows the competitive season. It is called the off-season because no team-related on-ice activities are scheduled during this time, which ranges between 9 and 16 weeks depending on the level of play. For example, a team who has played in the Stanley Cup finals may have a 9-week off-season, while a high school team or a junior team that didn't qualify for the playoffs in their respective leagues may have 16 weeks.

The off-season is a crucial time for improving the physical characteristics that are important in hockey, such as strength, speed, and conditioning. Since players are not attending practices and games, they can devote more time to intense training, allowing for tremendous improvements while they take a break from the rink.

DESIGNING AN OFF-SEASON STRENGTH AND CONDITIONING PROGRAM FOR HOCKEY

During the off-season program, *Total Hockey Training* addresses mobility, flexibility, core strength and stability, power, acceleration, strength, and conditioning in a progressive, systematic fashion. The initial exercises are basic, with an emphasis on technique from the players' perspective, because it is important to establish a foundation before the players participate in more technical exercises and drills. The off-season also lets players become familiar with any exercises that will be done on a year-round basis. For example, an exercise found in the off-season can also be used during the in-season period.

The goal of the program is stronger, faster, and better conditioned hockey players. Methods for improving strength, speed, and conditioning are applicable to all positions. It is okay for a goaltender to perform the same off-season program as a forward. Strength, speed, and conditioning are universal—especially in the off-season. Position-specific training can be added in the preseason and in-season phases when the players are on the ice.

The players train four days per week, ideally on Monday, Tuesday, Thursday, and Friday, with Wednesdays and Saturdays as recovery days. The recovery days emphasize foam rolling and stretching, and possibly some low-intensity aerobic conditioning.

Sundays are always off days. Each training day consists of a proper warm-up, core activation, plyometrics, acceleration exercises, explosive lifting, and conditioning. The sessions should take anywhere from 90 minutes to two hours to complete. This lets players devote a small part of the day to working on their strength and conditioning while also giving them ample time to enjoy the off-season.

Follow the prescribed sets and repetitions for each exercise and drill as outlined in the program. Be patient and stick with the program as prescribed. As far as strength training goes, let the number of repetitions that need to be completed dictate the load on the bar or in the athlete's hands. For example, if the prescription for a front squat is 3×8, this means the athlete does 3 sets of 8 repetitions. In this situation, use a weight that allows 8 good reps but not 9 or 10. The key is to use the appropriate weight and try to increase the load from week to week. This needs to be done for each exercise so that resistance can be added progressively. This is the proper application of strength training and will help the players get stronger. Again, stick with the sets and repetitions prescribed, and try to add load over time, emphasizing proper form on each exercise. Patience is important.

SAMPLE OFF-SEASON TRAINING PROGRAMS

The following tables contain 12 weeks of sample off-season training programs that bring together everything that has been discussed in *Total Hockey Training*. These sample programs are for any player at any level.

Table 10.1 Off-Season Training Program: Monday, Week 1

Foam rolling		Pg. 26	5 min
Static stretching		Pg. 198	5 min
Resets			
Supine cross crawl		Pg. 50	10 reps each side
Rolling (supine and prone)		Pg. 52	3 reps each side lower; 3 reps each side upper
Forearm rocking		Pg. 53	30 reps; on forearms
Core activation			
Glute bridge		Pg. 55	10 reps
Bent-knee side bridge with abduction		Pg. 61	30 sec each side
Lying hip flexor with band		Pg. 64	5 reps with 10-sec hold each side
Mobility			
Quadruped thoracic spine rotation		Pg. 29	10 reps each side
Wall ankle mobilization		Pg. 30	10 reps each (front, right, left)
Split squat		Pg. 30	5 reps each side
Lateral squat		Pg. 31	5 reps each side
Transverse plane squat		Pg. 32	5 reps each side
Movement preparation			
Linear movement prep		Pg. 34	20 yd each
Plyometric training			
Box jump		Pg. 173	4 x 5
Speed training			
Lean, fall, and run		Pg. 188	4 x 10 yd
90-degree lean, fall, and run		Pg. 189	4 x 10 yd
Sled training			
Resisted march		Pg. 195	6 x 25 yd
Strength training			
Tri-set	Kettlebell swing	Pg. 116	3 x 10
	Hip flexor stretch	Pg. 199	2 x 20 sec each side
	Quadruped bent-knee hip extension	Pg. 58	2 x 5 each side
Quad-set	Front squat	Pg. 120	3 x 8
	Chin-up	Pg. 137	3 x 8
	Stability ball rollout	Pg. 70	3 x 8
	Chest stretch	Pg. 206	2 x 20 sec
Quad-set	Split squat	Pg. 124	3 x 8 each side
	Dumbbell row	Pg. 142	3 x 8 each side
	Get up to hand	Pg. 82	2 x 5 each side
	Hamstring stretch	Pg. 200	2 x 20 sec each side
Conditioning			
Tempo run		Pg. 208	10 x 110 yd

Table 10.2   Off-Season Training Program: Tuesday, Week 1

		Pg. 26	5 min
Foam rolling		Pg. 26	5 min
Static stretching		Pg. 198	5 min
Resets			
Supine cross crawl		Pg. 50	10 reps each side
Rolling (supine and prone)		Pg. 52	3 reps each side lower; 3 reps each side upper
Forearm rocking		Pg. 53	30 reps; on forearms
Core activation			
Glute bridge		Pg. 55	10 reps
Bent-knee side bridge with abduction		Pg. 61	30 sec each side
Lying hip flexor with band		Pg. 64	5 reps with 10-sec hold each side
Mobility			
Quadruped thoracic spine rotation		Pg. 29	10 reps each side
Wall ankle mobilization		Pg. 30	10 reps each (front, right, left)
Split squat		Pg. 30	5 reps each side
Lateral squat		Pg. 31	5 reps each side
Transverse plane squat		Pg. 32	5 reps each side
Exercise band work			
Monster walk		Pg. 33	15 yd each
Exercise band lateral shuffle		Pg. 34	15 yd each
Movement preparation			
Lateral movement prep		Pg. 44	20 yd each
Plyometric training			
One-leg lateral box hop with stabilization		Pg. 174	4 x 5 each leg
Speed training			
Lean, fall, crossover, and run		Pg. 191	3 x 25 yd each side
One-leg bent-knee crossover and run		Pg. 192	3 x 25 yd each side
Sled training			
Lateral resisted crossover		Pg. 195	3 x 25 yd each
Medicine ball work			
Kneeling front-twist toss		Pg. 94	3 x 10 each side
Kneeling overhead throw		Pg. 95	3 x 10
Strength training			
Tri-set	Hang clean	Pg. 106	3 x 10
	Squat stretch	Pg. 199	2 x 20 sec each side
	Plank	Pg. 86	2 x 5 each side
Quad-set	One-arm dumbbell bench press	Pg. 150	3 x 8
	Two-arm, two-leg straight-leg deadlift	Pg. 133	3 x 8
	Bent-knee side bridge	Pg. 90	5 x 10 sec each side
	Quad stretch	Pg. 200	2 x 20 sec
Tri-set	Kneeling dumbbell curl and press	Pg. 154	3 x 8
	Ball leg curl	Pg. 134	3 x 8
	Kneeling cable chop	Pg. 74	3 x 10 each side
Pairs	Y, T, W, L	Pg. 167	3 x 8 each
	Suitcase carry	Pg. 165	3 x 40 yd each side
Conditioning			
Slide-board conditioning		Pg. 209	8 x 30 sec with 90-sec rest

Table 10.3 Off-Season Training Program: Thursday, Week 1

		Pg.	
Foam rolling		Pg. 26	5 min
Static stretching		Pg. 198	5 min
Resets			
Supine cross crawl		Pg. 50	10 reps each side
Rolling (supine and prone)		Pg. 52	3 reps each side lower; 3 reps each side upper
Forearm rocking		Pg. 53	30 reps; on forearms
Core activation			
Glute bridge		Pg. 55	10 reps
Bent-knee side bridge with abduction		Pg. 61	30 sec each side
Lying hip flexor with band		Pg. 64	5 reps with 10-sec hold each side
Mobility			
Quadruped thoracic spine rotation		Pg. 29	10 reps each side
Wall ankle mobilization		Pg. 30	10 reps each (front, right, left)
Split squat		Pg. 30	5 reps each side
Lateral squat		Pg. 31	5 reps each side
Transverse plane squat		Pg. 32	5 reps each side
Movement preparation			
Linear movement prep		Pg. 34	20 yd each
Plyometric training			
One-leg box hop with stabilization		Pg. 174	4 x 5 each leg
Speed training			
Lean, fall, and run		Pg. 188	4 x 10 yd
90-degree lean, fall, and run		Pg. 189	4 x 10 yd
Sled training			
Resisted march		Pg. 195	6 x 25 yd
Strength training			
Tri-set	Dumbbell snatch	Pg. 110	3 x 5 each side
	Hip flexor stretch	Pg. 199	2 x 20 sec each side
	Quadruped bent-knee hip extension	Pg. 58	2 x 5 each side
Quad-set	Front squat (25% lighter than Monday)	Pg. 120	3 x 8
	Parallel-grip pull-up	Pg. 138	3 x 8
	Stability ball rollout	Pg. 70	2 x 10
	Chest stretch	Pg. 206	2 x 20 sec each side
Quad-set	Rear-foot elevated split squat	Pg. 125	3 x 8 each side
	Inverted row	Pg. 140	3 x 8
	Get up to hand	Pg. 82	3 x 5 each side
	Hamstring stretch	Pg. 200	2 x 20 sec each side
Conditioning			
Tempo run		Pg. 208	10 x 110 yd

Table 10.4   Off-Season Training Program: Friday, Week 1

Foam rolling		Pg. 26	5 min
Static stretching		Pg. 198	5 min
Resets			
Supine cross crawl		Pg. 50	10 reps each side
Rolling (supine and prone)		Pg. 52	3 reps each side lower; 3 reps each side upper
Forearm rocking		Pg. 53	30 reps; on forearms
Core activation			
Glute bridge		Pg. 55	10 reps
Bent-knee side bridge with abduction		Pg. 61	30 sec each side
Lying hip flexor with band		Pg. 64	5 reps with 10-sec hold each side
Mobility			
Quadruped thoracic spine rotation		Pg. 29	10 reps each side
Wall ankle mobilization		Pg. 30	10 reps (front, right, left)
Split squat		Pg. 30	5 reps each leg
Lateral squat		Pg. 31	5 reps each leg
Transverse plane squat		Pg. 32	5 reps each leg
Exercise band work			
Monster walk		Pg. 33	15 yd each
Exercise band lateral shuffle		Pg. 34	15 yd each
Movement preparation			
Linear movement prep		Pg. 34	20 yd each
Plyometric training			
Heiden hop with stabilization		Pg. 175	4 x 5 each leg
Speed training			
Lean, fall, crossover and run		Pg. 191	3 x 25 yd each side
One-leg bent-knee crossover and run		Pg. 192	3 x 25 yd each side
Sled training			
Lateral resisted crossover		Pg. 195	3 x 25 yd each side
Medicine ball work			
Kneeling front-twist toss		Pg. 94	3 x 10 each side
Kneeling overhead throw		Pg. 95	3 x 10
Strength training			
Tri-set	Hang clean	Pg. 106	5 x 5
	Squat stretch	Pg. 199	2 x 20 sec
	Plank	Pg. 86	2 x 30 sec
Quad-set	Dumbbell incline press (alternate arms)	Pg. 151	3 x 8 each side
	One-leg straight-leg deadlift	Pg. 132	3 x 8 each side
	Bent-knee side bridge	Pg. 90	3 x 5 with 10-sec hold each side
	Lat stretch	Pg. 205	2 x 20 sec each side
Tri-set	Push-up (weighted)	Pg. 152	5 x 10
	Ball leg curl	Pg. 134	5 x 8
	Kneeling cable lift	Pg. 78	5 x 10 each side
Pairs	Y, T, W, L	Pg. 167	3 x 8 each
	Suitcase carry	Pg. 165	3 x 40 yd each side
Conditioning			
Slide-board conditioning		Pg. 209	9 x 30 sec with 90-sec rest

Table 10.5 Off-Season Training Program: Monday, Week 2

Foam rolling		Pg. 26	5 min
Static stretching		Pg. 198	5 min
Resets			
Supine cross crawl		Pg. 50	10 reps each side
Rolling (supine and prone)		Pg. 52	3 reps each side lower; 3 reps each side upper
Forearm rocking		Pg. 53	30 reps; on forearms
Core activation			
Glute bridge		Pg. 55	10 reps
Bent-knee side bridge with abduction		Pg. 61	30 sec each side
Lying hip flexor with band		Pg. 64	5 reps with 10-sec hold each side
Mobility			
Quadruped thoracic spine rotation		Pg. 29	10 reps each side
Wall ankle mobilization		Pg. 30	10 reps (front, right, left)
Split squat		Pg. 30	5 reps each leg
Lateral squat		Pg. 31	5 reps each leg
Transverse plane squat		Pg. 32	5 reps each leg
Movement preparation			
Linear movement prep		Pg. 34	20 yd each
Plyometric training			
Box jump		Pg. 173	4 x 5
Speed training			
Lean, fall, and run		Pg. 188	4 x 10 yd
90-degree lean, fall, and run		Pg. 189	4 x 10 yd
Sled training			
Resisted march		Pg. 195	6 x 25 yd
Strength training			
Tri-set	Kettlebell swing	Pg. 116	3 x 12
	Hip flexor stretch	Pg. 199	2 x 20 sec each side
	Quadruped bent-knee hip extension	Pg. 58	2 x 8 each side
Quad-set	Front squat	Pg. 120	3 x 8
	Chin-up (weighted)	Pg. 137	3 x 8
	Stability ball rollout	Pg. 70	2 x 12
	Chest stretch	Pg. 206	2 x 20 sec
Quad-set	Split squat	Pg. 124	3 x 10 each side
	Dumbbell row	Pg. 142	3 x 10 each side
	Get up to hand	Pg. 82	3 x 5 each side
	Hamstring stretch	Pg. 200	2 x 20 sec
Conditioning			
Tempo run		Pg. 208	11 x 110 yd

Table 10.6   Off-Season Training Program: Tuesday, Week 2

Foam rolling		Pg. 26	5 min
Static stretching		Pg. 198	5 min
Resets			
Supine cross crawl		Pg. 50	10 reps each side
Rolling (supine and prone)		Pg. 52	3 reps each side lower; 3 reps each side upper
Forearm rocking		Pg. 53	30 reps; on forearms
Core activation			
Glute bridge		Pg. 55	10 reps
Bent-knee side bridge with abduction		Pg. 61	30 sec each side
Lying hip flexor with band		Pg. 64	5 reps with 10-sec hold each side
Mobility			
Quadruped thoracic spine rotation		Pg. 29	10 reps each side
Wall ankle mobilization		Pg. 30	10 reps (front, right, left)
Split squat		Pg. 30	5 reps each leg
Lateral squat		Pg. 31	5 reps each leg
Transverse plane squat		Pg. 32	5 reps each leg
Exercise band work			
Monster walk		Pg. 33	15 yd each
Exercise band lateral shuffle		Pg. 34	15 yd each
Movement preparation			
Linear movement prep		Pg. 34	20 yd each
Plyometric training			
One-leg lateral box hop with stabilization		Pg. 174	4 x 5 each leg
Speed training			
Lean, fall, crossover, and run		Pg. 191	3 x 25 yd each side
One-leg bent-knee crossover and run		Pg. 192	3 x 25 yd each side
Sled training			
Lateral resisted crossover		Pg. 195	3 x 25 yd each side
Medicine ball work			
Kneeling front-twist toss		Pg. 94	3 x 10 each side
Kneeling overhead throw		Pg. 95	3 x 10
Strength training			
Tri-set	Hang clean	Pg. 106	3 x 5
	Squat stretch	Pg. 199	2 x 20 sec
	Plank	Pg. 86	2 x 30 sec
Quad-set	One-arm dumbbell bench press	Pg. 150	3 x 10 each side
	Two-arm, two-leg straight-leg deadlift	Pg. 133	3 x 8
	Bent-knee side bridge	Pg. 90	3 x 5 with 10-sec hold each side
	Quad stretch	Pg. 200	2 x 20 sec
Tri-set	Kneeling dumbbell curl and press	Pg. 154	3 x 8
	Ball leg curl	Pg. 134	3 x 10
	Kneeling cable chop	Pg. 74	3 x 10 each side
Pairs	Y, T, W, L	Pg. 167	3 x 8 each
	Suitcase carry	Pg. 165	3 x 40 yd each side
Conditioning			
Slide-board conditioning		Pg. 209	10 x 30 sec with 90-sec rest

Table 10.7   Off-Season Training Program: Thursday, Week 2

Foam rolling	Pg. 26	5 min
Static stretching	Pg. 198	5 min
Resets		
Supine cross crawl	Pg. 50	10 reps each side
Rolling (supine and prone)	Pg. 52	3 reps each side lower; 3 reps each side upper
Forearm rocking	Pg. 53	30 reps; on forearms
Core activation		
Glute bridge	Pg. 55	10 reps
Bent-knee side bridge with abduction	Pg. 61	30 sec each side
Lying hip flexor with band	Pg. 64	5 reps with 10-sec hold each side
Mobility		
Quadruped thoracic spine rotation	Pg. 29	10 reps each side
Wall ankle mobilization	Pg. 30	10 reps (front, right, left)
Split squat	Pg. 30	5 reps each leg
Lateral squat	Pg. 31	5 reps each leg
Transverse plane squat	Pg. 32	5 reps each leg
Movement preparation		
Linear movement prep	Pg. 34	20 yd each
Plyometric training		
One-leg box hop with stabilization	Pg. 174	4 x 5 each side
Speed training		
Lean, fall, and run	Pg. 188	4 x 10 yd
90-degree lean, fall, and run	Pg. 189	4 x 10 yd
Sled training		
Resisted march	Pg. 195	6 x 25 yd
Strength training			
Tri-set	Dumbbell snatch	Pg. 110	3 x 5 each side
	Hip flexor stretch	Pg. 199	2 x 20 sec each side
	Quadruped bent-knee hip extension	Pg. 58	2 x 8 each side
Quad-set	Front squat	Pg. 120	3 x 8
	Parallel-grip pull-up	Pg. 138	3 x 8
	Stability ball rollout	Pg. 70	2 x 12
	Chest stretch	Pg. 206	2 x 20 sec
Quad-set	Rear-foot elevated split squat	Pg. 125	3 x 10 each side
	Inverted row	Pg. 140	3 x 8
	Get up to hand	Pg. 82	3 x 5 each side
	Hamstring stretch	Pg. 200	2 x 20 sec
Conditioning			
Tempo run	Pg. 208	12 x 110 yd	

Table 10.8 Off-Season Training Program: Friday, Week 2

Foam rolling		Pg. 26	5 min
Static stretching		Pg. 198	5 min
Resets			
Supine cross crawl		Pg. 50	10 reps each side
Rolling (supine and prone)		Pg. 52	3 reps each side lower; 3 reps each side upper
Forearm rocking		Pg. 53	30 reps; on forearms
Core activation			
Glute bridge		Pg. 55	10 reps
Bent-knee side bridge with abduction		Pg. 61	30 sec each side
Lying hip flexor with band		Pg. 64	5 reps with 10-sec hold each side
Mobility			
Quadruped thoracic spine rotation		Pg. 29	10 reps each side
Wall ankle mobilization		Pg. 30	10 reps (front, right, left)
Split squat		Pg. 30	5 reps each leg
Lateral squat		Pg. 31	5 reps each leg
Transverse plane squat		Pg. 32	5 reps each leg
Exercise band work			
Monster walk		Pg. 33	15 yd each
Exercise band lateral shuffle		Pg. 34	15 yd each
Movement preparation			
Linear movement prep		Pg. 34	20 yd each
Plyometric training			
Heiden hop with stabilization		Pg. 175	4 x 5 each leg
Speed training			
Lean, fall, crossover, and run		Pg. 191	3 x 25 yd each side
One-leg bent-knee crossover and run		Pg. 192	3 x 25 yd each side
Sled training			
Lateral resisted crossover		Pg. 195	3 x 25 yd each side
Medicine ball work			
Kneeling front-twist toss		Pg. 94	3 x 10 each side
Kneeling overhead throw		Pg. 95	3 x 10
Strength training			
Tri-set	Hang clean	Pg. 106	3 x 5
	Squat stretch	Pg. 199	2 x 20 sec
	Plank	Pg. 86	2 x 30 sec
Quad-set	Dumbbell incline press (alternate arms)	Pg. 151	3 x 10 each side
	One-leg straight-leg deadlift	Pg. 132	3 x 8 each side
	Bent-knee side bridge	Pg. 90	3 x 5 with 10-sec hold
	Lat stretch	Pg. 205	2 x 20 sec
Tri-set	Push-up (weighted)	Pg. 152	3 x 12
	Ball leg curl	Pg. 134	3 x 10
	Kneeling cable lift	Pg. 78	3 x 10 each side
Pairs	Y, T, W, L	Pg. 167	3 x 8 each
	Suitcase carry	Pg. 165	3 x 40 yd each side
Conditioning			
Slide-board conditioning		Pg. 209	11 x 30 sec with 90-sec rest

Table 10.9   Off-Season Training Program: Monday, Week 3

Foam rolling		Pg. 26	5 min
Static stretching		Pg. 198	5 min
Resets			
Supine cross crawl		Pg. 50	10 reps each side
Rolling (supine and prone)		Pg. 52	3 reps each side lower; 3 reps each side upper
Forearm rocking		Pg. 53	30 reps; on forearms
Core activation			
Glute bridge		Pg. 55	10 reps
Bent-knee side bridge with abduction		Pg. 61	30 sec each side
Lying hip flexor with band		Pg. 64	5 reps with 10-sec hold each side
Mobility			
Quadruped thoracic spine rotation		Pg. 29	10 reps each side
Wall ankle mobilization		Pg. 30	10 reps (front, right, left)
Split squat		Pg. 30	5 reps each leg
Lateral squat		Pg. 31	5 reps each leg
Transverse plane squat		Pg. 32	5 reps each leg
Movement preparation			
Linear movement prep		Pg. 34	20 yd each
Plyometric training			
Box jump		Pg. 173	4 x 5
Speed training			
Lean, fall, and run		Pg. 188	4 x 10 yd
90-degree lean, fall, and run		Pg. 189	4 x 10 yd
Sled training			
Resisted march		Pg. 195	6 x 25 yd
Strength training			
Tri-set	Kettlebell swing	Pg. 116	3 x 15
	Hip flexor stretch	Pg. 199	2 x 20 sec each side
	Quadruped bent-knee hip extension	Pg. 58	2 x 10 each side
Quad-set	Front squat	Pg. 120	3 x 8
	Chin-up (weighted)	Pg. 137	3 x 8
	Stability ball rollout	Pg. 70	2 x 15
	Chest stretch	Pg. 206	2 x 20 sec
Quad-set	Split squat	Pg. 124	3 x 12 each side
	Dumbbell row	Pg. 142	3 x 12 each side
	Get up to hand	Pg. 82	2 x 5 each side
	Hamstring stretch	Pg. 200	2 x 20 sec each side
Conditioning			
Tempo run		Pg. 208	13 x 110 yd

Table 10.10 Off-Season Training Program: Tuesday, Week 3

Foam rolling		Pg. 26	5 min
Static stretching		Pg. 198	5 min
Resets			
Supine cross crawl		Pg. 50	10 reps each side
Rolling (supine and prone)		Pg. 52	3 reps each side lower; 3 reps each side upper
Straight-arm rocking		Pg. 54	30 reps; on forearms
Core activation			
Glute bridge		Pg. 55	10 reps
Bent-knee side bridge with abduction		Pg. 61	30 sec each side
Lying hip flexor with band		Pg. 64	5 reps with 10-sec hold each side
Mobility			
Quadruped thoracic spine rotation		Pg. 29	10 reps each side
Wall ankle mobilization		Pg. 30	10 reps (front, right, left)
Split squat		Pg. 30	5 reps each leg
Lateral squat		Pg. 31	5 reps each leg
Transverse plane squat		Pg. 32	5 reps each leg
Exercise band work			
Monster walk		Pg. 33	15 yd each
Exercise band lateral shuffle		Pg. 34	15 yd each
Movement preparation			
Linear movement prep		Pg. 34	20 yd each
Plyometric training			
One-leg lateral box hop with stabilization		Pg. 174	4 x 5 each leg
Speed training			
Lean, fall, crossover, and run		Pg. 191	3 x 25 yd
One-leg bent-knee crossover and run		Pg. 192	3 x 25 yd
Sled training			
Lateral resisted crossover		Pg. 195	3 x 25 yd each
Medicine ball work			
Kneeling front-twist toss		Pg. 94	3 x 10 each side
Kneeling overhead throw		Pg. 95	3 x 10
Strength training			
Tri-set	Hang clean	Pg. 106	3 x 5
	Squat stretch	Pg. 199	2 x 20 sec
	Plank	Pg. 86	2 x 30 sec
Quad-set	One-arm dumbbell bench press	Pg. 150	3 x 12 each side
	Two-arm two-leg straight-leg deadlift	Pg. 133	3 x 8
	Bent-knee side bridge	Pg. 90	3 x 5 with 10-sec hold
	Quad stretch	Pg. 200	2 x 20 sec each side
Tri-set	Kneeling dumbbell curl and press	Pg. 154	3 x 8
	Ball leg curl	Pg. 134	3 x 12
	Kneeling cablechop	Pg. 74	3 x 10 each side
Pairs	Y, T, W, L	Pg. 167	3 x 10 each
	Suitcase carry	Pg. 165	3 x 40 yd each side
Conditioning			
Slide-board conditioning		Pg. 209	12 x 30 sec with 90-sec rest

Table 10.11 Off-Season Training Program: Thursday, Week 3

Foam rolling		Pg. 26	5 min
Static stretching		Pg. 198	5 min
Resets			
Supine cross crawl		Pg. 50	10 reps each side
Rolling (supine and prone)		Pg. 52	3 reps each side lower; 3 reps each side upper
Forearm rocking		Pg. 53	30 reps; on forearms
Core activation			
Glute bridge		Pg. 55	10 reps
Bent-knee side bridge with abduction		Pg. 61	30 sec each side
Lying hip flexor with band		Pg. 64	5 reps with 10-sec hold each side
Mobility			
Quadruped thoracic spine rotation		Pg. 29	10 reps each side
Wall ankle mobilization		Pg. 30	10 reps each (front, right, left)
Split squat		Pg. 30	5 reps each leg
Lateral squat		Pg. 31	5 reps each leg
Transverse plane squat		Pg. 32	5 reps each leg
Movement preparation			
Linear movement prep		Pg. 34	20 yd each
Plyometric training			
Box jump		Pg. 173	4 x 5
Speed training			
Lean, fall, and run		Pg. 188	4 x 10 yd
90-degree lean, fall, and run		Pg. 189	4 x 10 yd
Sled training			
Resisted march		Pg. 195	6 x 25 yd
Strength training			
Tri-set	Dumbbell snatch	Pg. 110	3 x 5 each side
	Hip flexor stretch	Pg. 199	2 x 20 sec each side
	Quadruped bent-knee hip extension	Pg. 58	2 x 10 each side
Quad-set	Front squat (25% lighter than Monday)	Pg. 120	3 x 8
	Parallel-grip pull-up (weighted)	Pg. 138	3 x 8
	Stability ball rollout	Pg. 70	2 x 15
	Chest stretch	Pg. 206	2 x 20 sec
Quad-set	Rear-foot elevated split squat	Pg. 125	3 x 12 each side
	Inverted row	Pg. 140	3 x 8
	Get up to hand	Pg. 82	2 x 5 each side
	Hamstring stretch	Pg. 200	2 x 20 sec each side
Conditioning			
Tempo run		Pg. 208	14 x 110 yd

Table 10.12 Off-Season Training Program: Friday, Week 3

Foam rolling		Pg. 26	5 min
Static stretching		Pg. 198	5 min
Resets			
Supine cross crawl		Pg. 50	10 reps each side
Rolling (supine and prone)		Pg. 52	3 reps each side lower; 3 reps each side upper
Forearm rocking		Pg. 53	30 reps; on forearms
Core activation			
Glute bridge		Pg. 55	10 reps
Bent-knee side bridge with abduction		Pg. 61	30 sec each side
Lying hip flexor with band		Pg. 64	5 reps with 10-sec hold each side
Mobility			
Quadruped thoracic spine rotation		Pg. 29	10 reps each side
Wall ankle mobilization		Pg. 30	10 reps (front, right, left)
Split squat		Pg. 30	5 reps each leg
Lateral squat		Pg. 31	5 reps each leg
Transverse plane squat		Pg. 32	5 reps each leg
Exercise band work			
Monster walk		Pg. 33	15 yd each
Exercise band lateral shuffle		Pg. 34	15 yd each
Movement preparation			
Linear movement prep		Pg. 34	20 yd each
Plyometric training			
Heiden hop with stabilization		Pg. 175	4 x 5 each leg
Complex training: speed and sled			
Lateral resisted crossover + lean, fall, crossover, and run		Pg. 195, 191	25 yd + 25 yd x 3 each side
Medicine ball work			
Half-kneeling side-twist throw		Pg. 96	3 x 10 each side
Half-kneeling overhead throw		Pg. 97	3 x 6 each side
Strength training			
Tri-set	Hang clean	Pg. 106	3 x 3
	Squat stretch	Pg. 199	2 x 20 sec each side
	Plank with arm lift	Pg. 86	2 x 5 each side
Quad-set	Bench press + standing chest pass (medicine ball) superset	Pg. 147, 102	3 x 5 + 10
	One-leg straight-leg deadlift	Pg. 132	3 x 6 each side
	Side bridge	Pg. 90	3 x 5 with side 10-sec hold
	Quad stretch	Pg. 200	2 x 20 sec each side
Tri-set	Half-kneeling dumbbell shoulder press	Pg. 157	3 x 6 each side
	Ball leg curl	Pg. 134	3 x 8
	Half-kneeling cable chop	Pg. 75	3 x 10 each side
Pairs	Dumbbell pullover	Pg. 163	3 x 8
	Farmer's walk	Pg. 165	3 x 40 yd
Conditioning			
Slide-board conditioning		Pg. 209	10 x 30 sec with 90-sec rest

Table 10.13   Off-Season Training Program: Monday, Week 4

Foam rolling		Pg. 26	5 min
Static stretching		Pg. 198	5 min
Resets			
Seated cross crawl		Pg. 51	10 reps each side
Rolling (supine and prone)		Pg. 52	3 reps each side lower; 3 reps each side upper
Forearm rocking		Pg. 53	30 reps; on forearms
Core activation			
One-leg glute bridge		Pg. 56	10 reps each side
Straight-leg abduction		Pg. 61	10 sec each side
Seated hip flexor with overhead reach		Pg. 65	10 reps each side with 3-sec hold
Mobility			
Quadruped thoracic spine rotation		Pg. 29	10 reps each side
Wall ankle mobilization		Pg. 30	10 reps (front, right, left)
Split squat		Pg. 30	5 reps each leg
Lateral squat		Pg. 31	5 reps each leg
Transverse plane squat		Pg. 32	5 reps each leg
Movement preparation			
Linear movement prep		Pg. 34	20 yd each
Plyometric training			
Hurdle jump with stabilization		Pg. 178	4 x 5
Complex training: speed and sled			
Lean, fall, and run + resisted march		Pg. 188, 195	25 yd + 25 yd x 6
Strength training			
Tri-set	Double kettlebell swing	Pg. 118	3 x 8
	Hip flexor stretch	Pg. 199	2 x 20 sec each side
	Quadruped straight-leg hip extension	Pg. 59	2 x 5 each side
Quad-set	Front squat + hurdle jump with stabilization superset	Pg. 120, 178	3 x 5
	Pull-up (weighted)	Pg. 136	3 x 5
	Stir the pot	Pg. 72	2 x 8 each side
	Chest stretch	Pg. 206	2 x 20 sec
Quad-set	One-leg box squat	Pg. 63	3 x 6 each side
	Dumbbell row	Pg. 142	3 x 6 each side
	Get up to hip extension	Pg. 83	2 x 5 each side
	Hamstring stretch	Pg. 200	2 x 20 sec
Conditioning			
Tempo run		Pg. 208	13 x 110 yd

Table 10.14 Off-Season Training Program: Tuesday, Week 4

Foam rolling		Pg. 26	5 min
Static stretching		Pg. 198	5 min
Resets			
Seated cross crawl		Pg. 51	10 reps each side
Rolling (supine and prone)		Pg. 52	3 reps each side lower; 3 reps each side upper
Forearm rocking		Pg. 53	30 reps; on forearms
Core activation			
One-leg glute bridge		Pg. 56	10 reps each side
Straight-leg abduction		Pg. 61	10 reps each side
Seated hip flexor with overhead reach		Pg. 65	10 reps each side with 10-sec hold
Mobility			
Quadruped thoracic spine rotation		Pg. 29	10 reps each side
Wall ankle mobilization		Pg. 30	10 reps (front, right, left)
Split squat		Pg. 30	5 reps each leg
Lateral squat		Pg. 31	5 reps each leg
Transverse plane squat		Pg. 32	5 reps each leg
Exercise band work			
Monster walk		Pg. 33	15 yd each
Exercise band lateral shuffle		Pg. 34	15 yd each
Movement preparation			
Linear movement prep		Pg. 34	20 yd each
Plyometric training			
One-leg lateral–medial hurdle hop with stabilization		Pg. 179	4 x 5 each leg
Speed training			
Lean, fall, crossover, and run		Pg. 191	3 x 25 yd each side
One-leg bent-knee crossover and run		Pg. 192	3 x 25 yd each side
Sled training			
Lateral resisted crossover		Pg. 195	3 x 25 yd each side
Medicine ball work			
Kneeling front-twist toss		Pg. 94	3 x 10 each side
Kneeling overhead throw		Pg. 95	3 x 10
Strength training			
Tri-set	Hang clean	Pg. 106	3 x 5
	Squat stretch	Pg. 199	2 x 20 sec
	Plank	Pg. 86	2 x 30 sec
Quad-set	One-arm dumbbell bench press	Pg. 150	3 x 10 each side
	Two-arm, two-leg straight-leg deadlift	Pg. 133	3 x 8
	Bent-knee side bridge	Pg. 90	3 x 5 with 10-sec hold each side
	Quad stretch	Pg. 200	2 x 20 sec
Tri-set	Kneeling dumbbell curl and press	Pg. 154	3 x 8
	Ball leg curl	Pg. 134	3 x 10
	Kneeling cable chop	Pg. 74	3 x 10 each side
Pairs	Y, T, W, L	Pg. 167	3 x 8 each
	Suitcase carry	Pg. 165	3 x 40 yd each side
Conditioning			
Slide-board conditioning		Pg. 209	10 x 30 sec with 90-sec rest

Table 10.15 Off-Season Training Program: Thursday, Week 4

Foam rolling		Pg. 26	5 min
Static stretching		Pg. 198	5 min
Resets			
Seated cross crawl		Pg. 51	10 reps each side
Rolling (supine and prone)		Pg. 52	3 reps each side lower; 3 reps each side upper
Forearm rocking		Pg. 53	30 reps; on forearms
Core activation			
One-leg glute bridge		Pg. 56	10 reps each side
Straight-leg abduction		Pg. 61	10 reps each side
Seated hip flexor with overhead reach		Pg. 65	10 reps each side with 3-sec hold
Mobility			
Quadruped thoracic spine rotation		Pg. 29	10 reps each side
Wall ankle mobilization		Pg. 30	10 reps each (front, right, left)
Split squat		Pg. 30	5 reps each leg
Lateral squat		Pg. 31	5 reps each leg
Transverse plane squat		Pg. 32	5 reps each leg
Movement preparation			
Linear movement prep		Pg. 34	20 yd each
Plyometric training			
One-leg lateral box hop with stabilization		Pg. 174	4 x 5 each side
Complex training: speed and sled			
Lean, fall, and run + resisted march		Pg. 188, 195	25 yd + 25 yd x 6
Strength training			
Tri-set	Dumbbell snatch	Pg. 110	3 x 3 each side
	Hip flexor stretch	Pg. 199	2 x 20 sec each side
	Quadruped straight-leg hip extension	Pg. 59	2 x 5 each side
Quad-set	Front split squat + one-leg hurdle hop with stabilization superset	Pg. 127, 180	3 x 6 + 5
	Mixed-grip pull-up	Pg. 139	3 x 6
	Stir the pot	Pg. 72	2 x 8 each side
	Chest stretch	Pg. 206	2 x 20 sec
Quad-set	Rear-foot elevated split squat	Pg. 125	3 x 8 each side
	Upper back dumbbell row	Pg. 143	3 x 8 each side
	Get up to hip extension	Pg. 83	2 x 5 each side
	Hamstring stretch	Pg. 200	2 x 20 sec each side
Conditioning			
Tempo run		Pg. 208	6 x 150 yd (perform in less than 30 sec with 90-sec rest)

Table 10.16 Off-Season Training Program: Friday, Week 4

Foam rolling		Pg. 26	5 min
Static stretching		Pg. 198	5 min
Resets			
Seated cross crawl		Pg. 51	10 reps each side
Rolling (supine and prone)		Pg. 52	3 reps each side lower; 3 reps each side upper
Forearm rocking		Pg. 53	30 reps; on forearms
Core activation			
One-leg glute bridge		Pg. 56	10 reps each side
Straight-leg abduction		Pg. 61	10 reps each side
Seated hip flexor with overhead reach		Pg. 65	10 reps each side with 3-sec hold
Mobility			
Quadruped thoracic spine rotation		Pg. 29	10 reps each side
Wall ankle mobilization		Pg. 30	10 reps (front, right, left)
Split squat		Pg. 30	5 reps each leg
Lateral squat		Pg. 31	5 reps each leg
Transverse plane squat		Pg. 32	5 reps each leg
Exercise band work			
Monster walk		Pg. 33	15 yd each
Exercise band lateral shuffle		Pg. 34	15 yd each
Movement preparation			
Linear movement prep		Pg. 34	20 yd each
Plyometric training			
Angle bound with stabilization		Pg. 176	4 x 5 each leg
Complex training: speed and sled			
Lateral resisted crossover + lean, fall, crossover, and run		Pg. 195, 191	25 yd + 25 yd x 3 each side
Medicine ball work			
Half-kneeling side-twist throw		Pg. 96	3 x 10 each side
Half-kneeling overhead throw		Pg. 97	3 x 6 each side
Strength training			
Tri-set	Hang clean (light weight)	Pg. 106	3 x 5
	Squat stretch	Pg. 199	2 x 20 sec each side
	Plank with arm lift	Pg. 86	2 x 5 each side
Quad-set	Incline bench press + standing chest pass (medicine ball) superset	Pg. 148, 102	3 x 5 + 10
	One-leg skater squat	Pg. 126	3 x 6 each side
	Side bridge	Pg. 90	3 x 5 with side 10-sec hold
	Quad stretch	Pg. 200	2 x 20 sec each side
Tri-set	Half-kneeling dumbbell shoulder press	Pg. 157	3 x 6 each side
	Ball leg curl	Pg. 134	3 x 8
	Half-kneeling cable chop	Pg. 75	3 x 10 each side
Pairs	Dumbbell pullover	Pg. 163	3 x 8
	Farmer's walk	Pg. 165	3 x 40 yd
Conditioning			
Slide-board conditioning		Pg. 209	10 x 30 sec with 90-sec rest

Table 10.17 Off-Season Training Program: Monday, Week 5

Foam rolling		Pg. 26	5 min
Static stretching		Pg. 198	5 min
Resets			
Seated cross crawl		Pg. 51	10 reps each side
Rolling (supine and prone)		Pg. 52	3 reps each side lower; 3 reps each side upper
Forearm rocking		Pg. 53	30 reps; on forearms
Core activation			
One-leg glute bridge		Pg. 56	10 reps each side
Straight-leg abduction		Pg. 61	10 reps each side
Seated hip flexor with overhead reach		Pg. 65	10 reps each side with 3-sec hold
Mobility			
Quadruped thoracic spine rotation		Pg. 29	10 reps each side
Wall ankle mobilization		Pg. 30	10 reps (front, right, left)
Split squat		Pg. 30	5 reps each leg
Lateral squat		Pg. 31	5 reps each leg
Transverse plane squat		Pg. 32	5 reps each leg
Movement preparation			
Linear movement prep		Pg. 34	20 yd each
Plyometric training			
Hurdle jump with stabilization		Pg. 178	4 x 5
Complex training: speed and sled			
Lean, fall, and run + resisted march		Pg. 188, 195	25 yd + 25 yd x 6
Strength training			
Tri-set	Double kettlebell swing	Pg. 118	3 x 10 each side
	Hip flexor stretch	Pg. 199	2 x 20 sec each side
	Quadruped straight-leg hip extension	Pg. 59	2 x 8 each side
Quad-set	Front squat + hurdle jump with stabilization superset	Pg. 120, 178	4 x 5 + 5
	Pull-up (weighted)	Pg. 136	3 x 5
	Stir the pot	Pg. 72	2 x 10 each side
	Chest stretch	Pg. 206	2 x 20 sec
Quad-set	One-leg box squat	Pg. 63	3 x 6 each side
	Dumbbell row	Pg. 142	3 x 6 each side
	Get up to hip extension	Pg. 83	2 x 5 each side
	Hamstring stretch	Pg. 200	2 x 20 sec each side
Conditioning			
Tempo run		Pg. 208	15 x 110 yd

Table 10.18 Off-Season Training Program: Tuesday, Week 5

Exercise	Pg.	Prescription
Foam rolling	Pg. 26	5 min
Static stretching	Pg. 198	5 min
Resets		
Seated cross crawl	Pg. 52	10 reps each side
Rolling (supine and prone)	Pg. 52	3 reps each side lower; 3 reps each side upper
Straight-arm rocking	Pg. 54	
Core activation		
One-leg glute bridge	Pg. 56	10 reps each side
Straight-leg abduction	Pg. 61	10 reps each side
Seated hip flexor with overhead reach	Pg. 65	10 reps each side with 3-sec hold
Mobility		
Quadruped thoracic spine rotation	Pg. 29	10 each side
Wall ankle mobilization	Pg. 30	10 reps each (front, right, left)
Split squat	Pg. 30	5 reps each side
Lateral squat	Pg. 31	5 reps each side
Transverse plane squat	Pg. 32	5 reps each side
Exercise band work		
Monster walk	Pg. 33	15 yd each
Exercise band lateral shuffle	Pg. 34	15 yd each
Movement preparation		
Linear movement prep	Pg. 34	20 yd each
Plyometric training		
One-leg lateral–medial hurdle hop with stabilization	Pg. 179	4 x 5 each side
Speed training		
Lean, fall, crossover and run	Pg. 191	3 x 25 yd each side
One-leg bent-knee crossover and run	Pg. 192	3 x 25 yd each side
Complex training: speed and sled		
Lateral resisted crossover + lean, fall, crossover, and run	Pg. 195, 191	25 yd + 25 yd x 3 each side
Medicine ball work		
Half-kneeling side-twist throw	Pg. 96	3 x 10 each side
Half-kneeling overhead throw	Pg. 97	3 x 8 each side
Strength training			
Tri-set	Hang clean	Pg. 106	4 x 3
	Squat stretch	Pg. 199	2 x 20 sec each side
	Plank with arm lift	Pg. 86	2 x 8 each side
Quad-set	Bench press + standing chest pass (medicine ball) superset	Pg. 147, 102	4 x 5 + 10
	One-leg straight-leg deadlift	Pg. 132	3 x6 each side
	Side bridge	Pg. 90	2 x 5 each side with 10-sec hold
	Quad stretch	Pg. 200	2 x 5 each side with 10-sec hold
Tri-set	Half-kneeling dumbbell shoulder press	Pg. 157	3 x 6 each side
	Ball leg curl	Pg. 134	3 x 10
	Half-kneeling cable chop	Pg. 75	3 x 10 each side
Pairs	Dumbbell pullover	Pg. 163	3 x 8
	Farmer's walk	Pg. 165	3 x 40 yd
Conditioning			
Slide-board conditioning		Pg. 209	14 x 30 sec with 90-sec rest

Table 10.19   Off-Season Training Program: Thursday, Week 5

Foam rolling		Pg. 26	5 min
Static stretching		Pg. 198	5 min
Resets			
Seated cross crawl		Pg. 51	10 reps each side
Rolling (supine and prone)		Pg. 52	3 reps each side lower; 3 reps each side upper
Forearm rocking		Pg. 53	30 reps; on forearms
Core activation			
One-leg glute bridge		Pg. 56	10 reps each side
Straight-leg abduction		Pg. 61	10 reps each side
Seated hip flexor with overhead reach		Pg. 65	10 reps each side with 3-sec hold
Mobility			
Quadruped thoracic spine rotation		Pg. 29	10 each side
Wall ankle mobilization		Pg. 30	10 reps each (front, right, left)
Split squat		Pg. 30	5 reps each side
Lateral squat		Pg. 31	5 reps each side
Transverse plane squat		Pg. 32	5 reps each side
Movement preparation			
Linear movement prep		Pg. 34	20 yd each
Plyometric training			
One-leg hurdle hop with stabilization		Pg. 180	4 x 5
Complex training: speed and sled			
Lean, fall, and run + resisted march		Pg. 188, 195	25 yd + 25 yd x 6
Strength training			
Tri-set	Dumbbell snatch	Pg. 110	4 x 3 each side
	Hip flexor with band	Pg. 199	2 x 20 sec each side
	Quadruped straight-leg hip extension	Pg. 59	2 x 8 each side
Quad-set	Front squat + one-leg hurdle hop with stabilization superset	Pg. 120, 180	4 x 6 + 5 each side
	Mixed-grip pull-up	Pg. 139	3 x 6
	Stir the pot	Pg. 72	2 x 10 each side
	Chest stretch	Pg. 206	2 x 20 sec
Quad-set	Rear-foot elevated split squat	Pg. 125	3 x 8 each side
	Upper back dumbbell row	Pg. 143	3 x 8 each side
	Get up to hip extension	Pg. 83	2 x 5 each side
	Hamstring stretch	Pg. 200	2 x 20 sec each side
Conditioning			
Shuttle run		Pg. 210	7 x 150 yd in less than 30 sec with 90-sec rest

Table 10.20 Off-Season Training Program: Friday, Week 5

Foam rolling		Pg. 26	5 min
Static stretching		Pg. 198	5 min
Resets			
Seated cross crawl		Pg. 52	10 reps each side
Rolling (supine and prone)		Pg. 52	3 reps each side lower; 3 reps each side upper
Forearm rocking		Pg. 53	30 reps; on forearms
Core activation			
One-leg glute bridge		Pg. 56	10 reps each side
Straight-leg abduction		Pg. 61	10 reps each side
Seated hip flexor with overhead reach		Pg. 65	10 reps each side with 3-sec hold
Mobility			
Quadruped thoracic spine rotation		Pg. 29	10 reps each side
Wall ankle mobilization		Pg. 30	10 reps each (front, right, left)
Split squat		Pg. 30	5 reps each side
Lateral squat		Pg. 31	5 reps each side
Transverse plane squat		Pg. 32	5 reps each side
Exercise band work			
Monster walk		Pg. 33	15 yd each
Exercise band lateral shuffle		Pg. 34	15 yd each
Movement preparation			
Lateral movement prep		Pg. 44	20 yd each
Plyometric training			
Angle bound with stabilization		Pg. 176	4 x 5 each side
Complex training: speed and sled			
Lateral resisted crossover + lean, fall, crossover, and run		Pg. 195, 191	25 yd + 25 yd x 3 each side
Medicine ball work			
Half-kneeling side-twist throw		Pg. 96	3 x 10 each side
Half-kneeling overhead throw		Pg. 97	3 x 8 each side
Strength training			
Tri-set	Hang clean (light weight)	Pg. 106	4 x 5
	Squat stretch	Pg. 199	2 x 20 sec each side
	Plank with arm lift	Pg. 86	2 x 8 each side
Quad-set	Incline bench press + standing chest pass (medicine ball) superset	Pg. 148, 102	4 x 5 + 10
	One-leg skater squat	Pg. 126	3 x 6 each side
	Side bridge	Pg. 90	3 x 5 with side 10-sec hold
	Quad stretch	Pg. 200	2 x 20 sec each side
Tri-set	Half-kneeling dumbbell shoulder press	Pg. 157	3 x 6 each side
	Ball leg curl	Pg. 134	3 x 10
	Half-kneeling cable chop	Pg. 75	3 x 10 each side
Pairs	Dumbbell pullover	Pg. 163	3 x 8
	Farmer's walk	Pg. 165	3 x 40 yd
Conditioning			
Slide-board conditioning		Pg. 209	14 x 30 sec with 90-sec rest

Table 10.21 Off-Season Training Program: Monday, Week 6

	Exercise	Page	Reps/Sets
	Foam rolling	Pg. 26	5 min
	Static stretching	Pg. 198	5 min
Resets			
	Seated cross crawl	Pg. 51	10 reps each side
	Rolling (supine and prone)	Pg. 52	3 reps each side lower; 3 reps each side upper
	Forearm rocking	Pg. 53	30 reps; on forearms
Core activation			
	One-leg glute bridge	Pg. 56	10 reps each side
	Straight-leg abduction	Pg. 61	10 reps each side
	Seated hip flexor with overhead reach	Pg. 65	10 reps each side with 3-sec hold
Mobility			
	Quadruped thoracic spine rotation	Pg. 29	10 each side
	Wall ankle mobilization	Pg. 30	10 reps each (front, right, left)
	Split squat	Pg. 30	5 reps each side
	Lateral squat	Pg. 31	5 reps each side
	Transverse plane squat	Pg. 32	5 reps each side
Movement preparation			
	Linear movement prep	Pg. 34	20 yd each
Plyometric training			
	Hurdle jump with stabilization	Pg. 178	4 x 5
Complex training: speed and sled			
	Lean, fall, and run + resisted march	Pg. 188, 195	25 yd + 25 yd x 6
Strength training			
Tri-set	Double kettlebell swing	Pg. 118	3 x 12
	Hip flexor stretch	Pg. 199	2 x 20 sec each side
	Quadruped straight-leg hip extension	Pg. 59	2 x 10 each side
Quad-set	Front squat + hurdle jump with stabilization superset	Pg. 120, 178	4 x 5 + 5
	Pull-up (weighted)	Pg. 136	3 x 5
	Stir the pot	Pg. 72	2 x 12 each side
	Chest stretch	Pg. 206	2 x 20 sec
Quad-set	One-leg box squat	Pg. 63	3 x 6 each side
	Dumbbell row	Pg. 142	3 x 6 each side
	Get up to hip extension	Pg. 83	2 x 5 each side
	Hamstring stretch	Pg. 200	2 x 20 sec each side
Conditioning			
	Tempo run	Pg. 208	15 x 110 yd

Table 10.22　Off-Season Training Program: Tuesday, Week 6

Foam rolling	Pg. 26	5 min
Static stretching	Pg. 198	5 min
Resets		
Seated cross crawl	Pg. 51	10 reps each side
Rolling (supine and prone)	Pg. 52	3 reps each side lower; 3 reps each side upper
Forearm rocking	Pg. 53	30 reps; on forearms
Core activation		
One-leg glute bridge	Pg. 56	10 reps each side
Straight-leg abduction	Pg. 61	10 reps each side
Seated hip flexor with overhead reach	Pg. 65	10 reps each side with 3-sec hold
Mobility		
Quadruped thoracic spine rotation	Pg. 29	10 each side
Wall ankle mobilization	Pg. 30	10 reps each (front, right, left)
Split squat	Pg. 30	5 reps each side
Lateral squat	Pg. 31	5 reps each side
Transverse plane squat	Pg. 32	5 reps each side
Exercise band work		
Monster walk	Pg. 33	15 yd each
Exercise band lateral shuffle	Pg. 34	15 yd each
Movement preparation		
Lateral movement prep	Pg. 44	20 yd each
Plyometric training		
One-leg lateral–medial hurdle hop with stabilization	Pg. 179	4 x 5 each side
Complex training: speed and sled		
Lateral resisted crossover + lean, fall, crossover, and run	Pg. 195, 191	25 yd + 25 yd x 3 each side
Medicine ball work		
Half-kneeling side-twist throw	Pg. 96	3 x 10 each side
Half-kneeling overhead throw	Pg. 97	3 x 10 each side
Strength training			
Tri-set	Hang clean	Pg. 106	4 x 3 each side
	Squat stretch	Pg. 199	2 x 20 sec each side
	Plank with arm lift	Pg. 86	2 x 10 each side
Quad-set	Bench press + standing chest pass (medicine ball) superset	Pg. 147, 102	4 x 5 + 10
	One-leg straight-leg deadlift	Pg. 132	3 x6 each side
	Side bridge	Pg. 90	2 x 5 each side with 10-sec hold
	Quad stretch	Pg. 200	2 x 20 sec each side
Tri-set	Half-kneeling dumbbell shoulder press	Pg. 157	3 x 6 each side
	Ball leg curl	Pg. 134	3 x 12
	Half-kneeling cable chop	Pg. 75	3 x 10 each side
Pairs	Dumbbell pullover	Pg. 163	3 x 8
	Farmer's walk	Pg. 165	3 x 40 yd
Conditioning			
Slide-board conditioning		Pg. 209	8 x 30 sec with 60-sec rest

Table 10.23   Off-Season Training Program: Thursday, Week 6

Foam rolling		Pg. 26	5 min
Static stretching		Pg. 198	5 min
Resets			
Seated cross crawl		Pg. 51	10 reps each side
Rolling (supine and prone)		Pg. 52	3 reps each side lower; 3 reps each side upper
Forearm rocking		Pg. 53	30 reps; on forearms
Core activation			
One-leg glute bridge		Pg. 56	10 reps each side
Straight-leg abduction		Pg. 61	10 reps each side
Seated hip flexor with overhead reach		Pg. 65	10 reps each side with 3-sec hold
Mobility			
Quadruped thoracic spine rotation		Pg. 29	10 each side
Wall ankle mobilization		Pg. 30	10 reps each (front, right, left)
Split squat		Pg. 30	5 reps each side
Lateral squat		Pg. 31	5 reps each side
Transverse plane squat		Pg. 32	5 reps each side
Movement preparation			
Linear movement prep		Pg. 34	20 yd each
Plyometric training			
One-leg hurdle hop with stabilization		Pg. 180	4 x 5 each side
Complex training: speed and sled			
Lean, fall, and run + resisted march		Pg. 188, 195	25 yd + 25 yd x 6
Strength training			
Tri-set	Dumbbell snatch	Pg. 110	4 x 3 each side
	Hip flexor with band	Pg. 199	2 x 20 sec each side
	Quadruped straight-leg hip extension	Pg. 59	2 x 10 each side
Quad-set	Front split squat + one-leg hurdle hop with stabilization superset	Pg. 127, 180	4 x 6 + 5 each side
	Mixed-grip pull-up	Pg. 139	3 x 6
	Stir the pot	Pg. 72	2 x 12 each side
	Chest stretch	Pg. 206	2 x 20 sec
Quad-set	Rear-foot elevated split squat	Pg. 125	3 x 8 each side
	Upper back dumbbell row	Pg. 143	3 x 6 each side
	Get up to hip extension	Pg. 83	2 x 5 each side
	Hamstring stretch	Pg. 200	2 x 20 sec each side
Conditioning			
Shuttle run		Pg. 210	8 x 150 yd in less than 30 sec with 90-sec rest

Table 10.24 Off-Season Training Program: Friday, Week 6

Foam rolling		Pg. 26	5 min
Static stretching		Pg. 198	5 min
Resets			
Seated cross crawl		Pg. 51	10 reps each side
Rolling (supine and prone)		Pg. 52	3 reps each side lower; 3 reps each side upper
Rocking		Pg. 53	30 reps; on forearms
Core activation			
One-leg glute bridge		Pg. 56	10 reps each side
Straight-leg abduction		Pg. 61	10 reps each side
Seated hip flexor with overhead reach		Pg. 65	10 reps each side with 3-sec hold
Mobility			
Quadruped thoracic spine rotation		Pg. 29	10 reps each side
Wall ankle mobilization		Pg. 30	10 reps each (front, right, left)
Split squat		Pg. 30	5 reps each side
Lateral squat		Pg. 31	5 reps each side
Transverse plane squat		Pg. 32	5 reps each side
Exercise band work			
Monster walk		Pg. 33	15 yd each
Exercise band lateral shuffle		Pg. 34	15 yd each
Movement preparation			
Lateral movement prep		Pg. 44	20 yd each
Plyometric training			
Angle bound with stabilization		Pg. 176	4 x 5 each side
Complex training: speed and sled			
Lateral resisted crossover + lean, fall, crossover, and run		Pg. 195, 191	25 yd + 25 yd x 3 each side
Medicine ball work			
Half-kneeling side-twist throw		Pg. 96	3 x 10 each side
Half-kneeling overhead throw		Pg. 97	3 x 10 each side
Strength training			
Tri-set	Hang clean (light weight)	Pg. 106	4 x 5
	Squat stretch	Pg. 199	2 x 20 sec
	Plank with arm lift	Pg. 86	2 x 10 each side
Quad-set	Incline bench press + standing chest pass (medicine ball) superset	Pg. 148, 102	4 x 5 + 10
	One-leg skater squat	Pg. 126	3 x 6 each side
	Side bridge	Pg. 90	3 x 5 each side with 10-sec hold
	Quad stretch	Pg. 200	2 x 20 sec each side
Tri-set	Half-kneeling dumbbell shoulder press	Pg. 157	3 x 6 each side
	Ball leg curl	Pg. 134	3 x 12
	Half-kneeling cable chop	Pg. 75	3 x 10 each side
Pairs	Dumbbell pullover	Pg. 163	3 x 8
	Farmer's walk	Pg. 165	3 x 40 yd
Conditioning			
Slide-board conditioning		Pg. 209	8 x 30 sec with 60-sec rest

Table 10.25   Off-Season Training Program: Monday, Week 7

Foam rolling		Pg. 26	5 min
Static stretching		Pg. 198	5 min
Resets			
Standing cross crawl		Pg. 51	10 reps each side
Rolling (supine and prone)		Pg. 52	3 reps each side lower; 3 reps each side upper
Straight-arm rocking		Pg. 54	30 reps; on hands
Core activation			
Hands-free one-leg glute bridge		Pg. 56	10 reps each side
Straight-leg abduction		Pg. 61	10 reps each side
Standing hip flexor		Pg. 66	10 reps each side with 3-sec hold
Mobility			
Quadruped thoracic spine rotation		Pg. 29	10 each side
Wall ankle mobilization		Pg. 30	10 reps each (front, right, left)
Alternating leg lunge		Pg. 129	5 reps each side
Lateral lunge		Pg. 31	5 reps each side
Transverse plane squat		Pg. 32	5 reps each side
Movement preparation			
Linear movement prep		Pg. 34	20 yd each
Plyometric training			
Hurdle jump with bounce		Pg. 181	4 x 5
Speed training			
Ball drop		Pg. 189	6 x 5 yd
Sled training			
Sled push		Pg. 196	6 x 25 yd
Strength training			
Tri-set	One-arm kettlebell swing	Pg. 117	3 x 8 each side
	Hip flexor stretch	Pg. 199	2 x 20 sec each side
	Quadruped alternating arm–leg extension	Pg. 60	2 x 5 each side
Quad-set	Front squat	Pg. 120	3 x 8
	Chin-up	Pg. 137	3 x 5 with 4-sec hold
	Stir the pot	Pg. 72	2 x 8 each side
	Chest stretch	Pg. 206	2 x 20 sec
Quad-set	One-leg box squat	Pg. 63	3 x 8 each side
	Dumbbell row	Pg. 142	3 x 8 each side
	Get up to kneeling position	Pg. 84	2 x 5 each side
	Hamstring stretch	Pg. 200	2 x 20 sec each side
Conditioning			
Tempo run		Pg. 208	16 x 110 yd

Table 10.26   Off-Season Training Program: Tuesday, Week 7

Foam rolling		Pg. 26	5 min
Static stretching		Pg. 198	5 min
Resets			
Standing cross crawl		Pg. 51	10 reps each side
Rolling (supine and prone)		Pg. 52	3 reps each side lower; 3 reps each side upper
Straight-arm rocking		Pg. 54	30 reps; on hands
Core activation			
Hands-free one-leg glute bridge		Pg. 56	10 reps each side
Straight-leg abduction		Pg. 61	10 reps each side
Standing hip flexor		Pg. 66	10 reps each side with 3-sec hold
Mobility			
Quadruped thoracic spine rotation		Pg. 29	10 each side
Wall ankle mobilization		Pg. 30	10 reps each (front, right, left)
Alternating leg lunge		Pg. 129	5 reps each side
Lateral lunge		Pg. 31	5 reps each side
Transverse plane lunge		Pg. 32	5 reps each side
Exercise band work			
Monster walk		Pg. 33	15 yd each
Exercise band lateral shuffle		Pg. 34	15 yd each
Movement preparation			
Lateral movement prep		Pg. 44	20 yd each
Plyometric training			
One-leg lateral hurdle hop with bounce		Pg. 182	4 x 5 each side
Speed training			
Lateral crossover ball drop		Pg. 192	3 each side
Sled training			
Lateral resisted crossover		Pg. 195	3 x 25 yd each side
Medicine ball work			
Split side-twist throw		Pg. 98	3 x 10 each side
Split overhead throw		Pg. 99	3 x 6 each side
Strength training			
Tri-set	Hang clean	Pg. 106	3 x 5
	Squat stretch	Pg. 199	2 x 20 sec
	Plank with dumbbell row	Pg. 89	2 x 5 each side
Quad-set	Bench press	Pg. 147	3 x 8
	One-leg straight-leg deadlift	Pg. 132	3 x 8 each side
	Straddle side bridge	Pg. 92	2 x 5 each side with 10-sec hold
	Quad stretch	Pg. 200	2 x 20 sec each side
Tri-set	Dumbbell curl and press	Pg. 160	3 x 8
	Slide-board leg curl	Pg. 135	3 x 8 each side
	Lunge cable chop	Pg. 76	3 x 10 each side
Pairs	Y, T, W, L	Pg. 167	3 x 8
	Bottom's up kettlebell walk	Pg. 166	3 x 40 yd
Conditioning			
Slide-board conditioning		Pg. 209	9 x 30 sec with 60-sec rest

Table 10.27   Off-Season Training Program: Thursday, Week 7

Foam rolling		Pg. 26	5 min
Static stretching		Pg. 198	5 min
Resets			
Seated cross crawl		Pg. 51	10 reps each side
Rolling (supine and prone)		Pg. 52	3 reps each side lower; 3 reps each side upper
Forearm rocking		Pg. 53	30 reps; on forearms
Core activation			
Glute bridge		Pg. 55	10 reps each side
Straight-leg abduction		Pg. 61	10 reps each side
Seated hip flexor with overhead reach		Pg. 65	10 reps each side with 3-sec hold
Mobility			
Quadruped thoracic spine rotation		Pg. 29	10 reps each side
Wall ankle mobilization		Pg. 30	10 reps each (front, right, left)
Split squat		Pg. 30	5 reps each side
Lateral squat		Pg. 31	5 reps each side
Transverse plane squat		Pg. 32	5 reps each side
Movement preparation			
Linear movement prep		Pg. 34	20 yd each
Plyometric training			
One-leg hurdle hop with bounce		Pg. 183	4 x 5
Speed training			
Ball drop		Pg. 189	6 x 5 yd
Sled training			
Sled push		Pg. 196	6 x 25 yd
Strength training			
Tri-set	Dumbbell snatch	Pg. 110	3 x 5 each side
	Hip flexor stretch	Pg. 199	2 x 20 sec each side
	Quadruped alternating arm–leg extension	Pg. 60	2 x 5 each side
Quad-set	Rear-foot elevated split squat	Pg. 125	3 x 8 each side
	Basic pull-up	Pg. 136	3 x 8
	Stir the pot	Pg. 72	2 x 8 each side
	Chest stretch	Pg. 206	2 x 20 sec
Quad-set	Lateral squat	Pg. 124	3 x 8 each side
	One-arm, one-leg cable row	Pg. 145	3 x 8 each side
	Get up to kneeling position	Pg. 84	2 x 5 each side
	Hamstring stretch	Pg. 200	2 x 20 sec each side
Conditioning			
Shuttle run		Pg. 210	9 x 150 yd in less than 30 sec with 90-sec rest

Table 10.28 Off-Season Training Program: Friday, Week 7

Foam rolling		Pg. 26	5 min
Static stretching		Pg. 198	5 min
Resets			
Seated cross crawl		Pg. 51	10 reps each side
Rolling (supine and prone)		Pg. 52	3 reps each side lower; 3 reps each side upper
Forearm rocking		Pg. 53	30 reps; on forearms
Core activation			
Glute bridge		Pg. 55	10 reps each side
Straight-leg abduction		Pg. 61	10 reps each side
Seated hip flexor with overhead reach		Pg. 65	10 reps each side with 3-sec hold
Mobility			
Quadruped thoracic spine rotation		Pg. 29	10 reps each side
Wall ankle mobilization		Pg. 30	10 reps each (front, right, left)
Split squat		Pg. 30	5 reps each side
Lateral squat		Pg. 31	5 reps each side
Transverse plane squat		Pg. 32	5 reps each side
Exercise band work			
Monster walk		Pg. 33	15 yd each
Exercise band lateral shuffle		Pg. 34	15 yd each
Movement preparation			
Lateral movement prep		Pg. 44	20 yd each
Plyometric training			
Heiden hop		Pg. 177	4 x 5 each side
Speed training			
Ball drop		Pg. 189	3 each side
Medicine ball work			
Split side-twist throw		Pg. 98	3 x 10 each side
Split overhead throw		Pg. 99	3 x 6 each side
Strength training			
Tri-set	Hang clean (light weight)	Pg. 106	3 x 5
	Squat stretch	Pg. 199	2 x 20 sec
	Plank with dumbbell row	Pg. 89	2 x 5 each side
Quad-set	Dumbbell incline press	Pg. 151	3 x 8
	One-leg squat	Pg. 126	3 x 8 each side
	Straddle side bridge	Pg. 92	2 x 5 each side with 10-sec hold
	Quad stretch	Pg. 200	2 x 20 sec each side
Tri-set	Alternating-arm dumbbell shoulder press	Pg. 159	3 x 8 each side
	Slide-board leg curl	Pg. 135	3 x 8 each side
	Lunge cable chop	Pg. 76	3 x 10 each side
Pairs	Y, T, W, L	Pg. 167	3 x 8 each side
	Bottom's up kettlebell walk	Pg. 166	3 x 40 yd
Conditioning			
Slide-board conditioning		Pg. 209	10 x 30 sec with 60-sec rest

Table 10.29　Off-Season Training Program: Monday, Week 8

Foam rolling		Pg. 26	5 min
Static stretching		Pg. 198	5 min
Resets			
Standing cross crawl		Pg. 51	10 reps each side
Rolling (supine and prone)		Pg. 52	3 reps each side lower; 3 reps each side upper
Straight-arm rocking		Pg. 54	30 reps; on hands
Core activation			
Hands-free one-leg glute bridge		Pg. 56	10 reps each side
Straight-leg abduction		Pg. 61	10 reps each side
Standing hip flexor		Pg. 66	10 reps each side with 3-sec hold
Mobility			
Quadruped thoracic spine rotation		Pg. 29	10 each side
Wall ankle mobilization		Pg. 30	10 reps each (front, right, left)
Alternating leg lunge		Pg. 129	5 reps each side
Lateral lunge		Pg. 31	5 reps each side
Transverse plane squat		Pg. 32	5 reps each side
Movement preparation			
Linear movement prep		Pg. 34	20 yd each
Plyometric training			
Hurdle jump with bounce		Pg. 181	4 x 5
Speed training			
Ball drop		Pg. 189	6 x 5 yd
Sled training			
Sled push		Pg. 196	6 x 25 yd
Strength training			
Tri-set	One-arm kettlebell swing	Pg. 117	3 x 10 each side
	Hip flexor stretch	Pg. 199	2 x 20 sec each side
	Quadruped alternating arm–leg extension	Pg. 60	2 x 8 each side
Quad-set	Front squat	Pg. 120	3 x 8
	Chin-up	Pg. 137	3 x 6 with 4-sec hold
	Stir the pot (feet only)	Pg. 72	2 x 10 each side
	Chest stretch	Pg. 206	2 x 20 sec
Quad-set	One-leg box squat	Pg. 63	3 x 8 each side
	Dumbbell row	Pg. 142	3 x 10 each side
	Get up to kneeling position	Pg. 84	2 x 5 each side
	Hamstring stretch	Pg. 200	2 x 20 sec each side
Conditioning			
Tempo run		Pg. 208	16 x 110 yd

Table 10.30 Off-Season Training Program: Tuesday, Week 8

Foam rolling		Pg. 26	5 min
Static stretching		Pg. 198	5 min
Resets			
Standing cross crawl		Pg. 51	10 reps each side
Rolling (supine and prone)		Pg. 52	3 reps each side lower; 3 reps each side upper
Forearm rocking		Pg. 53	30 reps; on hands
Core activation			
Hands-free one-leg glute bridge		Pg. 56	10 reps each side
Straight-leg abduction		Pg. 61	10 reps each side
Standing hip flexor		Pg. 66	10 reps each side with 3-sec hold
Mobility			
Quadruped thoracic spine rotation		Pg. 29	10 each side
Wall ankle mobilization		Pg. 30	10 reps each (front, right, left)
Alternating leg lunge		Pg. 129	5 reps each side
Lateral lunge		Pg. 31	5 reps each side
Transverse plane lunge		Pg. 32	5 reps each side
Exercise band work			
Monster walk		Pg. 33	15 yd each
Exercise band lateral shuffle		Pg. 34	15 yd each
Movement preparation			
Lateral movement prep		Pg. 44	20 yd each
Plyometric training			
One-leg lateral–medial hop with bounce		Pg. 179	4 x 5 each leg
Speed training			
Ball drop		Pg. 189	3 each side
Sled training			
Lateral resisted crossover		Pg. 195	3 x 25 yd each side
Medicine ball work			
Split side-twist throw		Pg. 98	3 x 10 each side
Split overhead throw		Pg. 99	3 x 8 each side
Strength training			
Tri-set	Hang clean	Pg. 106	4 x 5
	Squat stretch	Pg. 199	2 x 20 sec
	Dumbbell row	Pg. 142	2 x 8 each side
Quad-set	Bench press	Pg. 147	3 x 8
	One-leg straight-leg deadlift	Pg. 132	3 x 8 each side
	Straddle side bridge	Pg. 92	2 x 5 each side with 10-sec hold
	Quad stretch	Pg. 200	2 x 20 sec each side
Tri-set	Dumbbell curl and press	Pg. 160	3 x 8
	Slide-board leg curl	Pg. 135	3 x 10 each side
	Lunge cable chop	Pg. 76	3 x 10 each side
Pairs	Y, T, W, L	Pg. 167	3 x 10 each side
	Bottom's up kettlebell walk	Pg. 166	3 x 40 yd
Conditioning			
Slide-board conditioning		Pg. 209	8 x 45 sec with 75-sec rest

Table 10.31 Off-Season Training Program: Thursday, Week 8

Foam rolling		Pg. 26	5 min
Static stretching		Pg. 198	5 min
Resets			
Seated cross crawl		Pg. 51	10 reps each side
Rolling (supine and prone)		Pg. 52	3 reps each side lower; 3 reps each side upper
Forearm rocking		Pg. 53	30 reps; on forearms
Core activation			
One-leg glute bridge		Pg. 56	10 reps each side
Straight-leg abduction		Pg. 61	10 reps each side
Seated hip flexor with overhead reach		Pg. 65	10 reps each side with 3-sec hold
Mobility			
Quadruped thoracic spine rotation		Pg. 29	10 each side
Wall ankle mobilization		Pg. 30	10 reps each (front, right, left)
Split squat		Pg. 30	5 reps each side
Lateral squat		Pg. 31	5 reps each side
Transverse plane squat		Pg. 32	5 reps each side
Movement preparation			
Linear movement prep		Pg. 34	20 yd each
Plyometric training			
One-leg hurdle hop with bounce		Pg. 183	4 x 5
Speed training			
Ball drop		Pg. 189	6 x 5 yd
Sled training			
Sled push		Pg. 196	6 x 25 yd
Strength training			
Tri-set	Dumbbell snatch	Pg. 110	4 x 3 each side
	Hip flexor stretch	Pg. 199	2 x 20 sec each side
	Quadruped alternating arm–leg extension	Pg. 60	2 x 8 each side
Quad-set	Rear-foot elevated split squat	Pg. 125	3 x 8 each side
	Basic pull-up	Pg. 136	3 x 8
	Stir the pot (feet only)	Pg. 72	2 x 10 each side
	Chest stretch	Pg. 206	2 x 20 sec
Quad-set	Lateral squat	Pg. 124	3 x 10 each side
	One-arm, one-leg cable row	Pg. 145	3 x 10 each side
	Get up to kneeling position	Pg. 84	2 x 5 each side
	Hamstring stretch	Pg. 200	2 x 20 sec each side
Conditioning			
Shuttle run		Pg. 210	10 x 150 yd in less than 30 sec with 90-sec rest

Table 10.32   Off-Season Training Program: Friday, Week 8

Foam rolling		Pg. 26	5 min
Static stretching		Pg. 198	5 min
Resets			
Seated cross crawl		Pg. 51	10 reps each side
Rolling (supine and prone)		Pg. 52	3 reps each side lower; 3 reps each side upper
Rocking		Pg. 53	30 reps; on forearms
Core activation			
Glute bridge		Pg. 55	10 reps each side
Straight-leg abduction		Pg. 61	10 reps each side
Seated hip flexor with overhead reach		Pg. 65	10 reps each side with 3-sec hold
Mobility			
Quadruped thoracic spine rotation		Pg. 29	10 each side
Wall ankle mobilization		Pg. 30	10 reps each (front, right, left)
Split squat		Pg. 30	5 reps each side
Lateral squat		Pg. 31	5 reps each side
Transverse plane squat		Pg. 32	5 reps each side
Exercise band work			
Monster walk		Pg. 33	15 yd each
Exercise band lateral shuffle		Pg. 34	15 yd each
Movement preparation			
Lateral movement prep		Pg. 44	20 yd each
Plyometric training			
Heiden hop		Pg. 177	4 x 5 each side
Speed training			
Ball drop		Pg. 189	3 each side
Medicine ball work			
Split side-twist throw		Pg. 98	3 x 10 each side
Split overhead throw		Pg. 99	3 x 8 each side
Strength training			
Tri-set	Hang clean (light weight)	Pg. 106	4 x 5
	Squat stretch	Pg. 199	2 x 20 sec
	Plank with dumbbell row	Pg. 89	2 x 8 each side
Quad-set	Dumbbell incline press	Pg. 151	3 x 10
	One-leg squat	Pg. 126	3 x 8 each side
	Straddle side bridge	Pg. 92	2 x 5 each side with 10-sec hold
	Quad stretch	Pg. 200	2 x 20 sec each side
Tri-set	Alternating-arm dumbbell shoulder press	Pg. 159	3 x 8 each side
	Slide-board leg curl	Pg. 135	3 x 10 each side
	Lunge cable chop	Pg. 76	3 x 10 each side
Pairs	Y, T, W, L	Pg. 167	3 x 10 each side
	Bottom's up kettlebell walk	Pg. 166	3 x 40 yd
Conditioning			
Slide-board conditioning		Pg. 209	8 x 45 sec with 75-sec rest

Table 10.33 Off-Season Training Program: Monday, Week 9

Foam rolling		Pg. 26	5 min
Static stretching		Pg. 198	5 min
Resets			
Standing cross crawl		Pg. 51	10 reps each side
Rolling (supine and prone)		Pg. 52	3 reps each side lower; 3 reps each side upper
Straight-arm rocking		Pg. 54	30 reps; on hands
Core activation			
Hands-free one-leg glute bridge		Pg. 56	10 reps each side
Straight-leg abduction		Pg. 61	10 reps each side
Standing hip flexor		Pg. 66	10 reps each side with 3-sec hold
Mobility			
Quadruped thoracic spine rotation		Pg. 29	10 each side
Wall ankle mobilization		Pg. 30	10 reps each (front, right, left)
Alternating leg lunge		Pg. 129	5 reps each side
Lateral lunge		Pg. 31	5 reps each side
Transverse plane squat		Pg. 32	5 reps each side
Movement preparation			
Linear movement prep		Pg. 34	20 yd each
Plyometric training			
Hurdle jump with bounce		Pg. 181	4 x 5
Speed training			
Ball drop		Pg. 189	6 x 5 yd
Sled training			
Sled push		Pg. 196	6 x 25 yd
Strength training			
Tri-set	One-arm kettlebell swing	Pg. 117	3 x 12 each side
	Hip flexor stretch	Pg. 199	2 x 20 sec each side
	Quadruped alternating arm–leg extension	Pg. 60	2 x 10 each side
Quad-set	Front squat	Pg. 120	3 x 8
	Chin-up	Pg. 137	3 x 7 with 4-sec hold
	Stir the pot (feet only)	Pg. 72	2 x 12 each side
	Chest stretch	Pg. 206	2 x 20 sec
Quad-set	One-leg box squat	Pg. 63	3 x 8 each side
	Dumbbell row	Pg. 142	3 x 12 each side
	Get up to kneeling position	Pg. 84	2 x 5 each side
	Hamstring stretch	Pg. 200	2 x 20 sec each side
Conditioning			
Tempo run		Pg. 208	17 x 110 yd

Table 10.34   Off-Season Training Program: Tuesday, Week 9

Foam rolling		Pg. 26	5 min
Static stretching		Pg. 198	5 min
Resets			
Standing cross crawl		Pg. 51	10 reps each side
Rolling (supine and prone)		Pg. 52	3 reps each side lower; 3 reps each side upper
Straight-arm rocking		Pg. 54	30 reps; on hands
Core activation			
Hands-free one-leg glute bridge		Pg. 56	10 reps each side
Straight-leg abduction		Pg. 61	10 reps each side
Standing hip flexor		Pg. 66	10 reps each side with 3-sec hold
Mobility			
Quadruped thoracic spine rotation		Pg. 29	10 each side
Wall ankle mobilization		Pg. 30	10 reps each (front, right, left)
Alternating leg lunge		Pg. 129	5 reps each side
Lateral squat		Pg. 31	5 reps each side
Transverse plane squat		Pg. 32	5 reps each side
Exercise band work			
Monster walk		Pg. 33	15 yd each
Exercise band lateral shuffle		Pg. 34	15 yd each
Movement preparation			
Lateral movement prep		Pg. 44	20 yd each
Plyometric training			
One-leg lateral hurdle hop with bounce		Pg. 183	4 x 5 each leg
Speed training			
Ball drop		Pg. 189	3 each side
Sled training			
Lateral resisted crossover		Pg. 195	3 x 25 yd each side
Medicine ball work			
Split side-twist throw		Pg. 98	3 x 10 each side
Split overhead throw		Pg. 99	3 x 10 each side
Strength training			
Tri-set	Hang clean	Pg. 106	4 x 5
	Squat stretch	Pg. 199	2 x 20 sec
	Plank with dumbbell row	Pg. 89	2 x 10 each side
Quad-set	Bench press	Pg. 147	3 x 8
	One-leg straight-leg deadlift	Pg. 132	3 x 8 each side
	Straddle side bridge	Pg. 92	2 x 5 each side with 10-sec hold
	Quad stretch	Pg. 200	2 x 20 sec each side
Tri-set	Dumbbell curl and press	Pg. 160	3 x 8
	Slide-board leg curl	Pg. 135	3 x 12 each side
	Lunge cable chop	Pg. 76	3 x 10 each side
Pairs	Y, T, W, L	Pg. 167	3 x 12 each side
	Bottom's up kettlebell walk	Pg. 166	3 x 40 yd
Conditioning			
Slide-board conditioning		Pg. 207	9 x 45 sec with 75-sec rest

Table 10.35   Off-Season Training Program: Thursday, Week 9

Foam rolling		Pg. 26	5 min
Static stretching		Pg. 198	5 min
Resets			
Seated cross crawl		Pg. 51	10 reps each side
Rolling (supine and prone)		Pg. 52	3 reps each side lower; 3 reps each side upper
Forearm rocking		Pg. 53	30 reps; on forearms
Core activation			
One-leg glute bridge		Pg. 56	10 reps each side
Straight-leg abduction		Pg. 61	10 reps each side
Seated hip flexor with overhead reach		Pg. 65	10 reps each side with 3-sec hold
Mobility			
Quadruped thoracic spine rotation		Pg. 29	10 each side
Wall ankle mobilization		Pg. 30	10 reps each (front, right, left)
Split squat		Pg. 30	5 reps each side
Lateral squat		Pg. 31	5 reps each side
Transverse plane squat		Pg. 32	5 reps each side
Movement preparation			
Linear movement prep		Pg. 34	20 yd each
Plyometric training			
One-leg hurdle hop with bounce		Pg. 183	4 x 5
Speed training			
Ball drop		Pg. 189	6 x 5 yd
Sled training			
Sled push		Pg. 196	6 x 25 yd
Strength training			
Tri-set	Dumbbell snatch	Pg. 110	4 x 5 each side
	Hip flexor stretch	Pg. 199	2 x 20 sec each side
	Quadruped alternating arm–leg extension	Pg. 60	2 x 10 each side
Quad-set	Rear-foot elevated split squat	Pg. 125	3 x 8 each side
	Basic pull-up	Pg. 136	3 x 8
	Stir the pot (feet only)	Pg. 72	2 x 12 each side
	Chest stretch	Pg. 206	2 x 20 sec
Quad-set	Lateral squat	Pg. 124	3 x 12 each side
	One-arm, one-leg cable row	Pg. 145	3 x 10 each side
	Get up to kneeling position	Pg. 84	2 x 5 each side
	Hamstring stretch	Pg. 200	2 x 20 sec each side
Conditioning			
Shuttle run		Pg. 210	11 x 150 yd in less than 30 sec with 90-sec rest

Table 10.36   Off-Season Training Program: Friday, Week 9

Foam rolling		Pg. 26	5 min
Static stretching		Pg. 198	5 min
Resets			
Seated cross crawl		Pg. 51	10 reps each side
Rolling (supine and prone)		Pg. 52	3 reps each side lower; 3 reps each side upper
Forearm rocking		Pg. 53	30 reps; on forearms
Core activation			
One-leg glute bridge		Pg. 56	10 reps each side
Straight-leg abduction		Pg. 61	10 reps each side
Seated hip flexor with overhead reach		Pg. 65	10 reps each side with 3-sec hold
Mobility			
Quadruped thoracic spine rotation		Pg. 29	10 reps each side
Wall ankle mobilization		Pg. 30	10 reps each (front, right, left)
Split squat		Pg. 30	5 reps each side
Lateral squat		Pg. 31	5 reps each side
Transverse plane squat		Pg. 32	5 reps each side
Exercise band work			
Monster walk		Pg. 33	15 yd each
Exercise band lateral shuffle		Pg. 34	15 yd each
Movement preparation			
Lateral movement prep		Pg. 44	20 yd each
Plyometric training			
Heiden hop		Pg. 177	4 x 5 each side
Speed training			
Ball drop		Pg. 189	3 each side
Medicine ball work			
Split side-twist toss		Pg. 98	3 x 10 each side
Split overhead throw		Pg. 99	3 x 10 each side
Strength training			
Tri-set	Hang clean (light weight)	Pg. 106	4 x 5
	Squat stretch	Pg. 199	2 x 20 sec
	Plank with dumbbell row	Pg. 89	2 x 10 each side
Quad-set	Dumbbell incline press	Pg. 151	3 x 12
	One-leg squat	Pg. 126	3 x 8 each side
	Straddle side bridge	Pg. 92	2 x 5 each side with 10-sec hold
	Quad stretch	Pg. 200	2 x 20 sec each side
Tri-set	Alternating-arm dumbbell shoulder press	Pg. 159	3 x 8 each side
	Slide-board leg curl	Pg. 135	3 x 12 each side
	Lunge cable chop	Pg. 76	3 x 10 each side
Pairs	Y, T, W, L	Pg. 167	3 x 12 each side
	Bottom's up kettlebell walk	Pg. 166	3 x 40 yd
Conditioning			
Slide-board conditioning		Pg. 209	9 x 45 sec with 75-sec rest

Table 10.37 Off-Season Training Program: Monday, Week 10

	Foam rolling	Pg. 26	5 min
	Static stretching	Pg. 198	5 min
Resets			
	Standing cross crawl (eyes closed)	Pg. 51	10 reps each side
	Rolling (supine and prone)	Pg. 52	3 reps each side lower; 3 reps each side upper
	Straight-arm rocking	Pg. 54	30 reps; on hands
Core activation			
	Medicine ball one-leg glute bridge	Pg. 57	10 reps each side
	One-leg box squat	Pg. 63	10 reps each side
	Mountain climber	Pg. 67	10 reps each side with 30-sec hold
Mobility			
	Quadruped thoracic spine rotation	Pg. 29	10 each side
	Wall ankle mobilization	Pg. 30	10 reps each (front, right, left)
	Alternating leg lunge	Pg. 129	5 reps each side
	Lateral lunge	Pg. 31	5 reps each side
	Transverse plane lunge	Pg. 32	5 reps each side
Movement preparation			
	Linear movement prep	Pg. 34	20 yd each
Plyometric training			
	Hurdle jump	Pg. 184	4 x 5
Speed training			
	Push-up start	Pg. 190	3 lead; 3 chase
Strength training			
Tri-set	Double kettlebell swing	Pg. 118	3 x 8
	Hip flexor stretch	Pg. 199	2 x 20 sec each side
	Quadruped alternating arm–leg extension (2.5 lb; 1 kg)	Pg. 60	2 x 5 each side
Quad-set	Front squat	Pg. 120	3 x 5
	Chin-up (weighted)	Pg. 137	3 x 3
	Wheel rollout	Pg. 71	2 x 10
	Chest stretch	Pg. 206	2 x 20 sec
Quad-set	One-leg box squat	Pg. 63	3 x 8 each side
	One-arm, one-leg cable row	Pg. 145	3 x 8 each side
	Full get-up	Pg. 85	2 x 5 each side
	Hamstring stretch	Pg. 200	2 x 20 sec each side
Conditioning			
	Tempo run	Pg. 208	18 x 110 yd

Table 10.38   Off-Season Training Program: Tuesday, Week 10

Foam rolling		Pg. 26	5 min
Static stretching		Pg. 198	5 min
Resets			
Standing cross crawl (eyes closed)		Pg. 51	10 reps each side
Rolling (supine and prone)		Pg. 52	3 reps each side lower; 3 reps each side upper
Rocking		Pg. 53	30 reps; on hands
Core activation			
Medicine ball one-leg glute bridge		Pg. 57	10 reps each side
One-leg box squat		Pg. 63	10 reps each side
Mountain climber		Pg. 67	10 reps each side with 3-sec hold
Mobility			
Quadruped thoracic spine rotation		Pg. 29	10 each side
Wall ankle mobilization		Pg. 30	10 reps each (front, right, left)
Alternating leg lunge		Pg. 129	5 reps each side
Lateral lunge		Pg. 31	5 reps each side
Transverse plane lunge		Pg. 32	5 reps each side
Exercise band work			
Monster walk		Pg. 33	15 yd each
Exercise band lateral shuffle		Pg. 34	15 yd each
Movement preparation			
Lateral movement prep		Pg. 44	20 yd each
Plyometric training			
One-leg lateral hurdle hop		Pg. 185	4 x 5 each leg
Speed training			
Partner agility mirror drill		Pg. 194	3 each direction
Medicine ball work			
Standing side-twist throw		Pg. 100	3 x 10 each side
Standing overhead throw		Pg. 101	3 x 10
Strength training			
Tri-set	Hang clean	Pg. 106	3 x 3
	Squat stretch	Pg. 199	2 x 20 sec
	Quadraped alternating arm–leg extension (2.5 lb; 1 kg)	Pg. 60	2 x 5 each side
Quad-set	Bench press	Pg. 147	3 x 3
	Two-arm, one-leg straight-leg deadlift	Pg. 132	3 x 6 each side
	Transitional straddle side bridge	Pg. 92	2 x 5 each side with 10-sec hold
	Quad stretch	Pg. 200	2 x 20 sec each side
Tri-set	Standing one-arm kettlebell press	Pg. 158	3 x 6 each side
	Ball leg curl	Pg. 134	3 x 6 each side
	Standing cable chop	Pg. 77	3 x 10 each side
Pairs	Dumbbell triceps extension	Pg. 162	3 x 8
	Cross walk	Pg. 166	3 x 40 yd each side
Conditioning			
Slide-board conditioning		Pg. 209	10 x 45 sec with 75-sec rest

Table 10.39 Off-Season Training Program: Thursday, Week 10

Foam rolling		Pg. 26	5 min
Static stretching		Pg. 198	5 min
Resets			
Standing cross crawl (eyes closed)		Pg. 51	10 reps each side
Rolling (supine and prone)		Pg. 52	3 reps each side lower; 3 reps each side upper
Straight-arm rocking		Pg. 54	30 reps; on hands
Core activation			
Medicine ball one-leg glute bridge		Pg. 57	10 reps each side
One-leg box squat		Pg. 63	10 reps each side
Mountain climber		Pg. 67	10 reps each side with 30-sec hold
Mobility			
Quadruped thoracic spine rotation		Pg. 29	10 each side
Wall ankle mobilization		Pg. 30	10 reps each (front, right, left)
Alternating leg lunge		Pg. 129	5 reps each side
Lateral lunge		Pg. 31	5 reps each side
Transverse plane lunge		Pg. 32	5 reps each side
Movement preparation			
Linear movement prep		Pg. 34	20 yd each
Plyometric training			
One-leg hurdle jump		Pg. 185	4 x 5
Speed training			
Push-up start		Pg. 190	3 lead; 3 chase
Strength training			
Tri-set	Dumbbell snatch	Pg. 110	3 x 3 each side
	Hip flexor stretch	Pg. 199	2 x 20 sec each side
	Quadruped alternating arm–leg extension	Pg. 60	2 x 5 each side
Quad-set	Front split squat	Pg. 127	3 x 6 each side
	Basic pull-up (weighted)	Pg. 136	3 x 5
	Wheel rollout	Pg. 71	2 x 10
	Chest stretch	Pg. 206	2 x 20 sec
Quad-set	One-leg box squat	Pg. 63	3 x 6 each side
	One-arm, one-leg cable row	Pg. 145	3 x 8 each side
	Full get-up	Pg. 85	2 x 5 each side
	Hamstring stretch	Pg. 200	2 x 20 sec each side
Conditioning			
Shuttle run		Pg. 210	2 x 300 yd in less than 60 sec with 3-min rest and 2 x 150 yd in less than 30 sec with 90-sec rest

Table 10.40 Off-Season Training Program: Tuesday, Week 10

Foam rolling		Pg. 26	5 min
Static stretching		Pg. 198	5 min
Resets			
Standing cross crawl (eyes closed)		Pg. 51	10 reps each side
Rolling (supine and prone)		Pg. 52	3 reps each side lower; 3 reps each side upper
Straight-arm rocking		Pg. 54	30 reps; on hands
Core activation			
Medicine ball one-leg glute bridge		Pg. 57	10 reps each side
One-leg box squat		Pg. 63	10 reps each side
Mountain climber		Pg. 67	10 reps each side with 3-sec hold
Mobility			
Quadruped thoracic spine rotation		Pg. 29	10 each side
Wall ankle mobilization		Pg. 30	10 reps each (front, right, left)
Alternating leg lunge		Pg. 129	5 reps each side
Lateral lunge		Pg. 31	5 reps each side
Transverse plane lunge		Pg. 32	5 reps each side
Exercise band work			
Monster walk		Pg. 33	15 yd each
Exercise band lateral shuffle		Pg. 34	15 yd each
Movement preparation			
Lateral movement prep		Pg. 44	20 yd each
Plyometric training			
Angle bound		Pg. 187	4 x 5 each side
Speed training			
Partner agility mirror drill		Pg. 194	3 each direction
Medicine ball work			
Standing side-twist throw		Pg. 100	3 x 10 each side
Standing overhead throw		Pg. 101	3 x 10
Strength training			
Tri-set	Hang clean (light weight)	Pg. 106	3 x 5
	Squat stretch	Pg. 199	2 x 20 sec
	Quadruped alternating arm–leg extension (2.5 lb; 1 kg)	Pg. 60	2 x 5 each side
Quad-set	Incline bench press	Pg. 148	3 x 3
	One-leg squat	Pg. 92	3 x 6 each side
	Transitional straddle side bridge	Pg. 92	2 x 5 each side with 10-sec hold
	Quad stretch	Pg. 200	2 x 20 sec each side
Tri-set	Alternating-arm dumbbell curl and press	Pg. 161	3 x 8 each side
	Slide-board leg curl	Pg. 135	3 x 8 each side
	Standing cable chop	Pg. 77	3 x 10 each side
Pairs	Dumbbell triceps extension	Pg. 162	3 x 8
	Cross walk	Pg. 166	3 x 40 yd each side
Conditioning			
Slide-board conditioning		Pg. 209	10 x 45 sec with 75-sec rest

Table 10.41 Off-Season Training Program: Thursday, Week 11

Foam rolling		Pg. 26	5 min
Static stretching		Pg. 198	5 min
Resets			
Standing cross crawl (eyes closed)		Pg. 51	10 reps each side
Rolling (supine and prone)		Pg. 52	3 reps each side lower; 3 reps each side upper
Straight-arm rocking		Pg. 54	30 reps; on hands
Core activation			
Medicine ball one-leg glute bridge		Pg. 57	10 reps each side
One-leg box squat		Pg. 63	10 reps each side
Mountain climber		Pg. 67	10 reps each side with 30-sec hold
Mobility			
Quadruped thoracic spine rotation		Pg. 29	10 each side
Wall ankle mobilization		Pg. 30	10 reps each (front, right, left)
Alternating leg lunge		Pg. 129	5 reps each side
Lateral lunge		Pg. 31	5 reps each side
Transverse plane lunge		Pg. 32	5 reps each side
Movement preparation			
Linear movement prep		Pg. 34	20 yd each
Plyometric training			
Hurdle jump		Pg. 184	4 x 5
Speed training			
Push-up start		Pg. 190	3 lead; 3 chase
Strength training			
Tri-set	Double kettlebell swing	Pg. 118	3 x 10
	Hip flexor stretch	Pg. 199	2 x 20 sec each side
	Quadruped alternating arm–leg extension (2.5 lb; 1 kg)	Pg. 60	2 x 8 each side
Quad-set	Front squat	Pg. 120	4 x 5
	Chin-up (weighted)	Pg. 137	4 x 3
	Wheel rollout	Pg. 71	2 x 12
	Chest stretch	Pg. 206	2 x 20 sec
Quad-set	One-leg box squat	Pg. 63	3 x 8 each side
	One-arm, one-leg cable row	Pg. 145	3 x 8 each side
	Full get-up	Pg. 85	2 x 5 each side
	Hamstring stretch	Pg. 200	2 x 20 sec each side
Conditioning			
Tempo run		Pg. 208	19 x 110 yd

Table 10.42　Off-Season Training Program: Tuesday, Week 11

Foam rolling		Pg. 26	5 min
Static stretching		Pg. 198	5 min
Resets			
Standing cross crawl (eyes closed)		Pg. 51	10 reps each side
Rolling (supine and prone)		Pg. 52	3 reps each side lower; 3 reps each side upper
Straight-arm rocking		Pg. 54	30 reps; on hands
Core activation			
Medicine ball one-leg glute bridge		Pg. 57	10 reps each side
One-leg box squat		Pg. 63	10 reps each side
Mountain climber		Pg. 67	10 reps each side with 30-sec hold
Mobility			
Quadruped thoracic spine rotation		Pg. 29	10 each side
Wall ankle mobilization		Pg. 30	10 reps each (front, right, left)
Alternating leg lunge		Pg. 129	5 reps each side
Lateral lunge		Pg. 31	5 reps each side
Transverse plane lunge		Pg. 32	5 reps each side
Exercise band work			
Monster walk		Pg. 33	15 yd each
Exercise band lateral shuffle		Pg. 34	15 yd each
Movement preparation			
Lateral movement prep		Pg. 44	20 yd each
Plyometric training			
One-leg lateral hurdle hop		Pg. 185	4 x 5 each side
Speed training			
Partner agility mirror drill		Pg. 194	3 each direction
Medicine ball work			
Standing side-twist throw		Pg. 100	3 x 10 each side
Standing overhead throw		Pg. 101	3 x 10
Strength training			
Tri-set	Hang clean	Pg. 106	4 x 3
	Squat stretch	Pg. 199	2 x 20 sec
	Quadruped alternating arm–leg extension (2.5 lb; 1 kg)	Pg. 60	2 x 8 each side
Quad-set	Bench press	Pg. 147	4 x 3
	Two-arm, one-leg straight-leg deadlift	Pg. 132	4 x 6 each side
	Transitional straddle side bridge	Pg. 92	2 x 5 each side with 10-sec hold
	Quad stretch	Pg. 200	2 x 20 sec each side
Tri-set	Standing one-arm kettlebell press	Pg. 158	3 x 6 each side
	Ball leg curl	Pg. 134	3 x 10 each side
	Standing cable chop	Pg. 77	3 x 10 each side
Pairs	Dumbbell triceps extension	Pg. 162	3 x 8
	Cross walk	Pg. 166	3 x 40 yd each side
Conditioning			
Slide-board conditioning		Pg. 209	11 x 45 sec with 75-sec rest

Table 10.43 Off-Season Training Program: Thursday, Week 11

Foam rolling		Pg. 26	5 min
Static stretching		Pg. 198	5 min
Resets			
Standing cross crawl (eyes closed)		Pg. 51	10 reps each side
Rolling (supine and prone)		Pg. 52	3 reps each side lower; 3 reps each side upper
Straight-arm rocking		Pg. 54	30 reps; on hands
Core activation			
Medicine ball one-leg glute bridge		Pg. 57	10 reps each side
One-leg box squat		Pg. 63	10 reps each side
Mountain climber		Pg. 67	10 reps each side with 30-sec hold
Mobility			
Quadruped thoracic spine rotation		Pg. 29	10 each side
Wall ankle mobilization		Pg. 30	10 reps each (front, right, left)
Alternating leg lunge		Pg. 129	5 reps each side
Lateral lunge		Pg. 31	5 reps each side
Transverse plane lunge		Pg. 32	5 reps each side
Movement preparation			
Linear movement prep		Pg. 34	20 yd each
Plyometric training			
One-leg hurdle hop		Pg. 186	4 x 5
Speed training			
Push-up start		Pg. 190	3 lead; 3 chase
Strength training			
Tri-set	Dumbbell snatch	Pg. 110	4 x 3 each side
	Hip flexor stretch	Pg. 199	2 x 20 sec each side
	Quadruped alternating arm–leg extension	Pg. 60	2 x 8 each side
Quad-set	Front split squat	Pg. 127	4 x 6 each side
	Basic pull-up (weighted)	Pg. 136	4 x 5 each side
	Wheel rollout	Pg. 71	2 x 12
	Chest stretch	Pg. 206	2 x 20 sec
Quad-set	One-leg box squat	Pg. 63	3 x 6 each side
	One-arm, one-leg cable row	Pg. 145	3 x 8 each side
	Full get-up	Pg. 85	2 x 5 each side
	Hamstring stretch	Pg. 200	2 x 20 sec each side
Conditioning			
300-yd shuttle run		Pg. 210	3 x 60 sec or less with 3-min rest
150-yd shuttle run		Pg. 210	2 x 30 sec or less with 90-sec rest

Table 10.44   Off-Season Training Program: Friday, Week 11

Foam rolling		Pg. 26	5 min
Static stretching		Pg. 198	5 min
Resets			
Standing cross crawl (eyes closed)		Pg. 51	10 reps each side
Rolling (supine and prone)		Pg. 52	3 reps each side lower; 3 reps each side upper
Rocking		Pg. 53	30 reps; on hands
Core activation			
Medicine ball one-leg glute bridge		Pg. 57	10 reps each side
One-leg box squat		Pg. 63	10 reps each side
Mountain climber		Pg. 67	10 reps each side with 30-sec hold
Mobility			
Quadruped thoracic spine rotation		Pg. 29	10 each side
Wall ankle mobilization		Pg. 30	10 reps each (front, right, left)
Alternating leg lunge		Pg. 129	5 reps each side
Lateral lunge		Pg. 31	5 reps each side
Transverse plane lunge		Pg. 32	5 reps each side
Exercise band work			
Monster walk		Pg. 33	15 yd each
Exercise band lateral shuffle		Pg. 34	15 yd each
Movement preparation			
Lateral movement prep		Pg. 44	20 yd each
Plyometric training			
Angle bound		Pg. 187	4 x 5 each leg
Speed training			
Partner agility mirror drill		Pg. 194	3 each direction
Medicine ball work			
Standing side-twist throw		Pg. 100	3 x 10 each side
Standing overhead throw		Pg. 101	3 x 10
Strength training			
Tri-set	Hang clean (light weight)	Pg. 106	4 x 5
	Squat stretch	Pg. 199	2 x 20 sec
	Quadruped alternating arm–leg extension (2.5 lb; 1 kg)	Pg. 60	2 x 8 each side
Quad-set	Incline bench press	Pg. 148	4 x 3
	One-leg squat	Pg. 126	4 x 6 each side
	Transitional straddle side bridge	Pg. 92	2 x 5 each side with 10-sec hold
	Quad stretch	Pg. 200	2 x 20 sec each side
Tri-set	Alternating-arm dumbbell curl and press	Pg. 161	3 x 8 each side
	Slide-board leg curl	Pg. 135	3 x 10 each side
	Standing cable chop	Pg. 77	3 x 10 each side
Pairs	Dumbbell triceps extension	Pg. 162	3 x 8
	Cross walk	Pg. 166	3 x 40 yd each side
Conditioning			
Slide-board conditioning		Pg. 209	11 x 45 sec with 75-sec rest

Table 10.45　Off-Season Training Program: Monday, Week 12

Foam rolling		Pg. 26	5 min
Static stretching		Pg. 198	5 min
Resets			
Standing cross crawl (eyes closed)		Pg. 51	10 reps each side
Rolling (supine and prone)		Pg. 52	3 reps each side lower; 3 reps each side upper
Straight-arm rocking		Pg. 54	30 reps; on hands
Core activation			
Medicine ball one-leg glute bridge		Pg. 57	10 reps each side
One-leg box squat		Pg. 63	10 reps each side
Mountain climber		Pg. 67	10 reps each side with 30-sec hold
Mobility			
Quadruped thoracic spine rotation		Pg. 29	10 each side
Wall ankle mobilization		Pg. 30	10 reps each (front, right, left)
Alternating leg lunge		Pg. 129	5 reps each side
Lateral lunge		Pg. 31	5 reps each side
Transverse plane lunge		Pg. 32	5 reps each side
Movement preparation			
Linear movement prep		Pg. 34	20 yd each
Plyometric training			
Hurdle jump		Pg. 184	4 x 5
Speed training			
Push-up start		Pg. 190	3 lead; 3 chase
Strength training			
Tri-set	Double kettlebell swing	Pg. 118	3 x 12
	Hip flexor stretch	Pg. 199	2 x 20 sec each side
	Quadruped alternating arm–leg extension (2.5 lb; 1 kg)	Pg. 60	2 x 10 each side
Quad-set	Front squat	Pg. 120	4 x 5
	Chin-up (weighted)	Pg. 137	4 x 3
	Wheel rollout	Pg. 71	2 x 15
	Chest stretch	Pg. 206	2 x 20 sec
Quad-set	One-leg box squat	Pg. 63	3 x 8 each side
	One-arm, one-leg cable row	Pg. 145	3 x 8 each side
	Full get-up	Pg. 85	2 x 5 each side
	Hamstring stretch	Pg. 200	2 x 20 sec each side
Conditioning			
Tempo run		Pg. 208	20 x 110 yd

Table 10.46   Off-Season Training Program: Tuesday, Week 12

Foam rolling		Pg. 26	5 min
Static stretching		Pg. 198	5 min
Resets			
Standing cross crawl (eyes closed)		Pg. 51	10 reps each side
Rolling (supine and prone)		Pg. 52	3 reps each side lower; 3 reps each side upper
Straight-arm rocking		Pg. 54	30 reps; on hands
Core activation			
Medicine ball one-leg glute bridge		Pg. 57	10 reps each side
One-leg box squat		Pg. 63	10 reps each side
Mountain climber		Pg. 67	10 reps each side with 30-sec hold
Mobility			
Quadruped thoracic spine rotation		Pg. 29	10 each side
Wall ankle mobilization		Pg. 30	10 reps each (front, right, left)
Alternating leg lunge		Pg. 129	5 reps each side
Lateral lunge		Pg. 31	5 reps each side
Transverse plane lunge		Pg. 32	5 reps each side
Exercise band work			
Monster walk		Pg. 33	15 yd each
Exercise band lateral shuffle		Pg. 34	15 yd each
Movement preparation			
Lateral movement prep		Pg. 44	20 yd each
Plyometric training			
One-leg lateral hurdle hop		Pg. 185	4 x 5 each side
Speed training			
Partner agility mirror drill		Pg. 194	3 each direction
Medicine ball work			
Standing side-twist throw		Pg. 100	3 x 10 each side
Standing overhead throw		Pg. 101	3 x 10
Strength training			
Tri-set	Hang clean	Pg. 106	4 x 3
	Squat stretch	Pg. 199	2 x 20 sec
	Quadruped alternating arm–leg extension (2.5 lb; 1 kg)	Pg. 60	2 x 10 each side
Quad-set	Bench press	Pg. 147	4 x 3
	Two-arm, one-leg straight-leg deadlift	Pg. 132	4 x 6 each side
	Transitional straddle side bridge	Pg. 92	2 x 5 each side with 10-sec hold
	Quad stretch	Pg. 200	2 x 20 sec each side
Tri-set	Standing one-arm kettlebell press	Pg. 158	3 x 6 each side
	Ball leg curl	Pg. 134	3 x 12 each side
	Standing cable chop	Pg. 77	3 x 10 each side
Pairs	Dumbbell triceps extension	Pg. 162	3 x 8
	Cross walk	Pg. 166	3 x 40 yd each side
Conditioning			
Slide-board conditioning		Pg. 209	12 x 45 sec with 75-sec rest

Table 10.47 Off-Season Training Program: Thursday, Week 12

Foam rolling		Pg. 26	5 min
Static stretching		Pg. 198	5 min
Resets			
Standing cross crawl (eyes closed)		Pg. 51	10 reps each side
Rolling (supine and prone)		Pg. 52	3 reps each side lower; 3 reps each side upper
Straight-arm rocking		Pg. 54	30 reps; on hands
Core activation			
Medicine ball one-leg glute bridge		Pg. 57	10 reps each side
One-leg box squat		Pg. 63	10 reps each side
Mountain climber		Pg. 67	10 reps each side with 30-sec hold
Mobility			
Quadruped thoracic spine rotation		Pg. 29	10 each side
Wall ankle mobilization		Pg. 30	10 reps each (front, right, left)
Alternating leg lunge		Pg. 129	5 reps each side
Lateral lunge		Pg. 31	5 reps each side
Transverse plane lunge		Pg. 32	5 reps each side
Movement preparation			
Linear movement prep		Pg. 34	20 yd each
Plyometric training			
One-leg hurdle hop		Pg. 186	4 x 5
Speed training			
Push-up start		Pg. 190	3 lead; 3 chase
Strength training			
Tri-set	Dumbbell snatch	Pg. 110	4 x 3 each side
	Hip flexor stretch	Pg. 199	2 x 20 sec each side
	Quadruped alternating arm–leg extension	Pg. 60	2 x 10 each side
Quad-set	Front split squat	Pg. 127	4 x 6 each side
	Basic pull-up (weighted)	Pg. 136	4 x 5
	Wheel rollout	Pg. 71	2 x 15
	Chest stretch	Pg. 206	2 x 20 sec
Quad-set	One-leg squat	Pg. 126	3 x 6 each side
	One-arm, one-leg cable row	Pg. 145	3 x 8 each side
	Full get-up	Pg. 85	2 x 5 each side
	Hamstring stretch	Pg. 200	2 x 20 sec each side
Conditioning			
Shuttle run		Pg. 210	4 x 300 yd in less than 60 sec with 3-min rest

Table 10.48   Off-Season Training Program: Friday, Week 12

Foam rolling		Pg. 26	5 min
Static stretching		Pg. 198	5 min
Resets			
Standing cross crawl (eyes closed)		Pg. 51	10 reps each side
Rolling (supine and prone)		Pg. 52	3 reps each side lower; 3 reps each side upper
Straight-arm rocking		Pg. 54	30 reps; on hands
Core activation			
Medicine ball one-leg glute bridge		Pg. 57	10 reps each side
One-leg box squat		Pg. 63	10 reps each side
Mountain climber		Pg. 67	10 reps each side with 30-sec hold
Mobility			
Quadruped thoracic spine rotation		Pg. 29	10 each side
Wall ankle mobilization		Pg. 30	10 reps each (front, right, left)
Alternating leg lunge		Pg. 129	5 reps each side
Lateral lunge		Pg. 31	5 reps each side
Transverse plane lunge		Pg. 32	5 reps each side
Exercise band work			
Monster walk		Pg. 33	15 yd each
Exercise band lateral shuffle		Pg. 34	15 yd each
Movement preparation			
Lateral movement prep		Pg. 44	20 yd each
Plyometric training			
Angle bound		Pg. 187	4 x 5 each leg
Speed training			
Partner agility mirror drill		Pg. 194	3 each direction
Medicine ball work			
Standing side-twist throw		Pg. 100	3 x 10 each side
Standing overhead throw		Pg. 101	3 x 10
Strength training			
Tri-set	Hang clean (light weight)	Pg. 106	4 x 5
	Squat stretch	Pg. 199	2 x 20 sec
	Quadruped alternating arm–leg extension (2.5 lb; 1 kg)	Pg. 60	2 x 10 each side
Quad-set	Incline bench press	Pg. 148	4 x 3
	One-leg squat	Pg. 126	4 x 6 each side
	Transitional straddle side bridge	Pg. 92	2 x 5 each side with 10-sec hold
	Quad stretch	Pg. 200	2 x 20 sec each side
Tri-set	Alternating-arm dumbbell curl and press	Pg. 161	3 x 8 each side
	Slide-board leg curl	Pg. 135	3 x 12 each side
	Standing cable chop	Pg. 77	3 x 10 each side
Pairs	Dumbbell triceps extension	Pg. 162	3 x 8
	Cross walk	Pg. 166	3 x 40 yd each side
Conditioning			
Slide-board conditioning		Pg. 209	12 x 45 sec with 75-sec rest

Chapter 11

Preseason Training Programs

The goals of preseason strength and conditioning for hockey are to prepare the players for the demands of the regular season and to bridge the gap between the off-season and in-season strength and conditioning phases. The intensity level is upgraded, and the strength and conditioning program is ramped up in terms of volume. The preseason is the time for players to start doing more work to prepare their bodies for both physical and mental stressors.

This phase has two parts. The first is pretraining camp, when there is no interaction with on-ice coaches. Rules at the collegiate and professional level prohibit on-ice coaches from working with the team before a specific date on the calendar. The strength and conditioning coach organizes and operates the strength and conditioning sessions and sometimes the on-ice sessions, but the on-ice component can also be organized and operated by the players themselves. The term *captains' practice* is the best way to describe the on-ice sessions because the captain and leaders of the team are involved in planning the practices. The second part of the preseason phase starts when the coaches can officially get involved in the practices. Preseason games begin, and strength and conditioning sessions continue.

Since most players at the NCAA and major junior levels and above are in different locations throughout the off-season, the preseason is the strength and conditioning coach's first chance to implement the program with the entire team. This is an important time to build camaraderie and get every player on the same page before the season begins. (Ideally, a high school team's or midget team's members have been training with each other throughout the entire off-season, unless they are affiliated with a boarding school or prep school, with players from different parts of the world.)

A typical preseason at the professional and major junior levels is usually three or four weeks from late August through late September. During the first part of the preseason, players spend three days a week in the weight room in addition to being on the ice for four to six days. *Total Hockey Training* recommends scheduling strength training before on-ice practice on Monday, Wednesday, and Friday, with conditioning on the bike before skating on Tuesday and Thursday. When practices officially begin, the frequency of strength training is scaled back because the number of practices and exhibition games increases.

Training volume is much higher, as both lifting and skating are added accordingly. This is much different from the off-season phase when training is primarily off the ice each day. Some of the activities that were done during the off-season are stopped to allow for a smooth transition to on-ice training. This includes speed work, working with sleds, and running and slide-boarding for conditioning. At this point, speed, agility, and conditioning most likely take place on the ice. Some players may have already begun on-ice training—it is not unusual for players to skate near their off-season homes before reporting to their team's training camp.

Players at all levels are expected to report for training camps in excellent physical condition. This is not the time for getting into shape. The priority of camp is to get the team sorted out and ready to go. It is the time for evaluating players and working on line combinations, special teams, and defensive systems.

DESIGNING A PRESEASON STRENGTH AND CONDITIONING PROGRAM

The strength and conditioning during the pre-season will transition from a late off-season of higher intensity strength training and a great amount of running for conditioning to an approach of lesser intensity strength training (but more volume) and no running for conditioning. The conditioning is primarily on-ice and also consists of more sessions of exercise bike work.

Strength Training

Total Hockey Training advocates circuit training for building strength in the preseason. Twelve exercises are completed straight through, unlike other times in the calendar year where five or six exercises are paired with each other, while core exercises are performed during the rest periods. Each player is assigned to an exercise station from 1 to 12, and the players move through the circuit, resting for 90 seconds after they have done all 12 exercises. They complete three circuits. When prescribing loads for the exercises, the emphasis is still on getting strong. However, the athlete and coach need to let the number of repetitions prescribed determine the load. For example, if an exercise calls for 10 repetitions, then a load the athlete can lift 15 times wouldn't be acceptable. In this situation, a load that allows for 10 to 12 repetitions with excellent technique should be used.

During circuit training, exercises are put in an order that allows for adequate rest periods between movements while also elevating the heart rate so that work demand is increased. The prescribed exercise format is double-leg push, upper pull (vertical), upper push (horizontal), core/anterior chain, lower explosive lower, single-leg push, upper pull (horizontal), upper press (vertical), single-leg lower (glute/hamstring emphasis), single-arm pull, core stabilization, and upper explosive. These circuits are done twice per week, on Mondays and Fridays. The format stays the same, but the selection of exercises is different. For example, on Monday, pull-ups (hands facing away) are completed, while chin-ups (palms facing) are done on Friday. On Wednesdays, each player completes a circuit while using a 25-pound (11.3 kg) weight plate as resistance. The format of these exercises is slightly different from on Mondays and Fridays.

During the Monday and Friday circuits, each player performs the prescribed number of reps for each exercise. Regressions are allowed for athletes who are not ready for a given exercise (e.g., players who are injured or unable to perform a specific exercise). For example, the goblet squat can be substituted for the front squat, or a split squat for a one-leg squat. This is common practice for new players as well, such as a walk-on player at the NCAA level, a tryout player at the professional level, or a new player added via trade or free agency. The strength and conditioning coach decides what level of exercises the players are ready for in all situations.

During the Wednesday circuit, each player is given a 25-pound (11.3 kg) plate and completes the entire circuit without resting. All the athletes perform the last exercise together. Like the other circuits, the plate circuit consists of alternating upper, lower, and core exercises to create a conditioning effect during the training session.

Conditioning

The off-ice conditioning sessions take place on stationary bikes on Tuesdays, Thursdays, and Saturdays. Monday's session consists of 1-minute sprints at a high level of resistance. The goal is to enhance the players' resistance to fatigue, especially after the 30- to 40-second mark. At the end of the sprint, they recover to 130 bpm while at level 1 on the bike. As soon as their heart rate drops below 130 bpm, they start their next sprint at the highest resistance. The players start with 6 reps in week 1 and add one more rep each week. Thursday's session is a steady-state cardiac output ride where the emphasis is on keeping the heart rate in the 130- to 140-bpm range. This 30- to 60-minute-ride enhances the players' ability to recover from bouts of high-intensity work. Saturday bike rides should be optional and also prescribed based on how each player feels and what her needs may be. For example, a player who reported to camp with inadequate conditioning or a high body fat percentage may be included in Saturday bike rides.

Before training camp officially begins, the players operate their own on-ice practices. This is common at the professional, collegiate, and major junior levels. Usually, the teams' captains plan the practice, using drills that mimic a regular practice session. A 45-minute team practice followed by a 45-minute scrimmage is typical. It is also not uncommon for strength and conditioning coaches to run conditioning drills after some of these practices. They may also help the players prepare for any on-ice conditioning tests when training camp officially begins. The strength and conditioning coach can coach and interact with the players while making a smooth transition into the in-season phase.

Full participation from everyone on the team is important. Players should believe in the preseason program and its importance during the team-building process. Getting the athletes to buy into the prescribed plan is much more important than providing a state-of-the-art program that not everyone will want to do. When the players are given a basic program in an environment where they are training hard together, the on-ice results can be positive.

SAMPLE PRESEASON TRAINING PROGRAMS

Following are three weeks of sample preseason training programs that bring together everything that has been discussed in *Total Hockey Training*. These sample programs are for any player at any level.

During the preseason, the concepts that were introduced in chapter 4 should be utilized. At this point, all pretraining methods with the exception of plyometric training, speed training, and sled training should still be utilized. It is up to the strength and conditioning coach to determine how much time and what exercises should be used. Time is valuable during the preseason.

Table 11.1   Preseason Training Program: Monday, Week 1

Strength training			
Dumbbell snatch + hip flexor stretch		Pg. 110, 199	3 × 5 + 2 each side
Strength circuit (3 sets with 90-sec rest between sets)	Front squat	Pg. 120	8
	Basic pull-up	Pg. 136	6
	Dumbbell bench press	Pg. 149	8
	Wheel rollout	Pg. 71	10
	Squat jump	Pg. 176	10
	Inverted row	Pg. 140	8
	Alternating-arm dumbbell shoulder press	Pg. 159	8 each side
	One-leg straight-leg deadlift	Pg. 132	8 each side
	One-arm cable row	Pg. 144	8 each side
Conditioning			
On-ice practice			Variable

Table 11.2   Preseason Training Program: Tuesday, Week 1

Conditioning	
On-ice practice	Variable
Postpractice conditioning	
Stationary bike	After a 5-min warm-up, sprint as hard as possible at the highest level for 1 min. Then set the bike to the easiest level and recover to a heart rate of 130 bpm or less. Repeat for 8 reps.

Table 11.3   Preseason Training Program: Wednesday, Week 1

Strength training			
Body-weight leg circuit (3 sets with 90-sec rest between sets)	Squat jump	Pg. 176	10
	Alternating leg lunge	Pg. 129	10 each side
	Step-up	Pg. 130	10 each side
	Front squat	Pg. 120	20
Plate circuit (3 sets with 90-sec rest between sets)	Plate overhead squat	Pg. 121	10
	Plate row	Pg. 142	10 each side
	Push-up (with plate on back)	Pg. 152	10
	Straight-leg sit-up (with plate across chest)	Pg. 73	10
	One-leg straight-leg deadlift (with plate)	Pg. 132	10 each side
	Plate upright row	Pg. 141	10
	Staggered push-up (with plate on back)	Pg. 153	10 each side
	Overhead plate squat plus triceps extension	Pg. 122	10
	Plate steering wheel	Pg. 164	30 sec
Conditioning			
On-ice practice			Variable

Table 11.4   Preseason Training Program: Thursday, Week 1

Conditioning	
On-ice practice	Variable
Postpractice conditioning	
Stationary bike	45-60 min of steady-state work with a heart rate in the 120-140 bpm range

Table 11.5   Preseason Training Program: Friday, Week 1

Strength training			
Barbell complex (3 sets with 90-sec rest between sets)	Upright row	Pg. 111	6
	Muscle snatch	Pg. 112	6
	Good morning	Pg. 113	6
	Squat plus press	Pg. 114	6
	Bent-over row	Pg. 115	6
Strength circuit (3 sets with 90-sec rest between sets)	One-leg squat	Pg. 126	6 each
	Inverted row	Pg. 140	8
	Push-up (with feet elevated)	Pg. 152	10
	Wheel rollout	Pg. 71	10
	Front split squat	Pg. 127	8 each
	One-arm, one-leg cable row	Pg. 145	8 each
	Dumbbell curl and press	Pg. 160	8
	Slide-board leg curl	Pg. 135	8
	Half-kneeling cable chop	Pg. 75	10 each
Conditioning			
On-ice practice			Variable

Table 11.6   Preseason Training Program: Monday, Week 2

Strength training			
Dumbbell snatch + standing hip flexor stretch		Pg. 110, 199	4 × 5 + 2 each side
Strength circuit (3 sets with 90-sec rest between sets)	Front squat	Pg. 120	10
	Basic pull-up	Pg. 136	7
	Dumbbell bench press	Pg. 149	10
	Wheel rollout	Pg. 71	12
	Squat jump	Pg. 176	12
	Inverted row	Pg. 140	10
	Alternating-arm dumbbell shoulder press	Pg. 159	10 each
	One-leg straight-leg deadlift	Pg. 132	8 each
	One-arm cable row	Pg. 144	10 each
Conditioning			
On-ice practice			Variable

Table 11.7   Preseason Training Program: Tuesday, Week 2

Conditioning	
On-ice practice	Variable
Postpractice conditioning	
Stationary bike	After a 5-min warm-up, sprint as hard as possible at the highest level for 1 min. Then set the bike to the easiest level and recover to a heart rate of 130 bpm or less. Repeat for 10 reps.

Table 11.8   Preseason Training Program: Wednesday, Week 2

Strength training			
Leg circuit with empty barbell (3 sets with 90 sec rest between sets)	Squat jump	Pg. 176	10
	Alternating leg lunge	Pg. 129	10 each
	Step-up	Pg. 130	10 each
	Front squat	Pg. 120	20
Plate circuit (3 sets with 90-sec rest between sets)	Plate overhead squat	Pg. 121	12
	Plate row	Pg. 142	12 each
	Push-up (with plate on back)	Pg. 152	12
	Straight-leg sit-up (with plate across chest)	Pg. 73	12
	One-leg straight-leg deadlift (with plate)	Pg. 132	10 each
	Plate upright row	Pg. 141	12
	Staggered push-up (with plate on back)	Pg. 153	12 each
	Plate overhead squat plus triceps extension	Pg. 122	12
	Plate steering wheel	Pg. 164	45 sec
Conditioning			
On-ice practice			Variable

Table 11.9   Preseason Training Program: Thursday, Week 2

Conditioning	
On-ice practice	Variable
Postpractice conditioning	
Stationary bike	45-60 min of steady-state work with a heart rate in the 120-140 bpm range

Table 11.10 Preseason Training Program: Friday, Week 2

Strength training			
Barbell complex with 10 lb (4.5 kg) total added to the barbell (3 sets with 90-sec rest between sets)	Upright row	Pg. 111	6
	Muscle snatch	Pg. 112	6
	Good morning	Pg. 113	6
	Squat and press	Pg. 114	6
	Bent-over row	Pg. 115	6
Strength circuit (3 sets with 90-sec rest between sets)	One-leg squat	Pg. 126	8 each
	Inverted row	Pg. 140	8
	Push-up (with feet elevated)	Pg. 152	12
	Wheel rollout	Pg. 71	12
	Front split squat	Pg. 127	10 each
	One-arm, one-leg cable row	Pg. 145	10 each
	Dumbbell curl and press	Pg. 160	10
	Slide-board leg curl	Pg. 135	10
	Half-kneeling cable chop	Pg. 75	10 each
Conditioning			
On-ice practice			Variable

Table 11.11 Preseason Training Program: Monday, Week 3

Strength training			
Dumbbell snatch + standing hip flexor stretch		Pg. 110, 199	4 × 5 + 2 each side
Strength circuit (3 sets with 90-sec rest between sets)	Front squat	Pg. 120	12
	Basic pull-up	Pg. 136	8
	Dumbbell bench press	Pg. 199	12
	Wheel rollout	Pg. 71	14
	Squat jump	Pg. 176	14
	Inverted row	Pg. 140	12
	Alternating-arm dumbbell shoulder press	Pg. 159	10 each
	One-leg straight-leg deadlift	Pg. 132	8 each
	One-arm cable row	Pg. 144	10 each
Conditioning			
On-ice practice			Variable

Table 11.12   Preseason Training Program: Tuesday, Week 3

Conditioning	
On-ice practice	Variable
Postpractice conditioning	
Stationary bike	After a 5-min warm-up, sprint as hard as possible at the highest level for 1 min. Then set the bike to the easiest level and recover to a heart rate of 130 bpm or less. Repeat for 12 reps.

Table 11.13   Preseason Training Program: Wednesday, Week 3

Strength training			
Leg circuit with 10 lb (4.5 kg) total added to the barbell (3 sets with 90-sec rest between sets)	Squat jump	Pg. 176	10
	Alternating leg lunge	Pg. 129	10 each
	Step-up	Pg. 130	10 each
	Front squat	Pg. 120	20
Plate circuit (3 sets with 90-sec rest between sets)	Plate overhead squat	Pg. 121	14
	Plate row	Pg. 142	14 each
	Push-up (with plate on back)	Pg. 152	14
	Straight-leg sit-up (with plate across chest)	Pg. 73	14
	One-leg straight-leg deadlift (with plate)	Pg. 132	10 each
	Plate upright row	Pg. 141	14
	Staggered push-up (with plate on back)	Pg. 153	14 each
	Plate overhead squat plus triceps extension	Pg. 122	14
	Plate steering wheel	Pg. 164	1 min
Conditioning			
On-ice practice			Variable

Table 11.14   Preseason Training Program: Thursday, Week 3

Conditioning	
On-ice practice	Variable
Postpractice conditioning	
Stationary bike	45-60 min of steady-state work with a heart rate in the 120-140 bpm range

Table 11.15   Preseason Training Program: Friday, Week 3

Strength training				
Barbell complex with 20 lb (9 kg) total added to the barbell (3 sets with 90-sec rest between sets)	Upright row	Pg. 111	6	
	Muscle snatch	Pg. 112	6	
	Good morning	Pg. 113	6	
	Squat + press	Pg. 114	6	
	Bent-over row	Pg. 115	6	
Strength circuit (3 sets with 90-sec rest between sets)	One-leg squat	Pg. 126	10 each	
	Inverted row	Pg. 140	8	
	Push-up (with feet elevated)	Pg. 152	14	
	Wheel rollout	Pg. 71	14	
	Split squat with kettlebell	Pg. 127	12 each	
	One-arm, one-leg cable row	Pg. 145	12 each	
	Dumbbell curl and press	Pg. 160	12	
	Slide-board leg curl	Pg. 135	12	
	Half-kneeling cable chop	Pg. 75	10 each	
Conditioning				
On-ice practice			Variable	

Chapter 12

In-Season Training Programs

In-season strength and conditioning is important at all levels of ice hockey. The hockey season can span from early fall of one year to late spring of the next. Ideally, the strength and conditioning work put in throughout the off-season will help individual players and the team during the season. However, a program needs to be in place to improve or at least maintain strength and conditioning levels throughout the season. It is certainly a challenge, but it is possible if the strength and conditioning coach comes up with appropriate strategies based on the team's schedule. A stronger and better conditioned player is going to be durable and more resistant to injury throughout the season.

DESIGNING AN IN-SEASON STRENGTH AND CONDITIONING PROGRAM

At this point in the yearly plan, the volume of on-ice practices and games is more important than the volume in the weight room. The work in the weight room needs to complement what is happening on the ice in practices and games; it must be scaled back so that on-ice results are the priority.

In college hockey, for the most part, games are played on the weekends (there will always be an occasional midweek game). This gives college hockey players enough time to get in quality strength and conditioning sessions during the week. For example, if the team plays on both Friday and Saturday nights, they could perform a strength and conditioning session and an on-ice practice on Sunday, then take Monday off (NCAA rules mandate that one day of the week be free of hockey activities), and then strength train again on Tuesday or Wednesday before or after practice. This allows the team to work hard on Sunday so the players can recover on Monday. Some college programs take their mandatory day off on Sunday and do their strength training on Monday and Wednesday. Either way, the team can get more work in at the beginning of the week since the players will have a few days to recover.

At the professional level, for players who are healthy and playing regularly in games, postgame strength and conditioning sessions allow the strength and conditioning coach to individualize aspects of each player's program.

Strength Training

At the professional and major junior levels, one of the most difficult challenges for the strength and conditioning coach is scheduling strength training sessions. At the professional level, the regular season schedule starts in October and ends in April. There are 76 to 82 games on the schedule (depending on the league), with half played at home and the other half on the road. At the major junior level, there are usually 72 games from September through March. Teams often face less than ideal situations throughout the season. Back-to-back games, three games in three nights, and three games in four nights are all common at the professional and major junior levels. This makes scheduling training sessions difficult.

At the professional level, one option is to strength train immediately after games when there isn't a scheduled game the next day. This alternative is available only when the team is at home and has access to an adequate facility. Having a strength training session on the road immediately after a game is nearly impossible. Inadequate facilities and the reality that visiting teams usually depart quickly after road games prohibit quality training sessions on the road.

Although postgame training sessions may not be the best option, in many cases they are the only way to get work in. Some strength training done after a game is better than no strength and conditioning work. The emphasis is on getting the players in and out of the weight room as quickly and as efficiently as possible because the recovery process for the next game will start immediately after training. Since the team has just played a 60-minute game, there is no need for other parts of a complete training program such as a dynamic warm-up, plyometrics, sprints, core training, or sled work. For postgame strength training, four or five exercises are sufficient.

Strength training sessions completed on practice days (especially prepractice) can include the dynamic warm-up, plyometrics, and core training. Training volume can be increased in the strength training portion because the athletes won't be playing a hockey game before the session. The team will be able to get a better strength training session in because each player will have more energy than he would postgame.

When planning and organizing the in-season program, it is important to consider the demands of the different parts of the regular season. At the beginning of the season, players may be able to spend more time in the weight room since they will be transitioning from an off-season training program and will simply have more energy. The volume (i.e., number of exercises, sets, and reps) can be higher. At this point, the objective is to delay the breakdown of the gains the players made in the off-season. Exercises such as the dumbbell snatch, front squat, bench press, weighted pull-up, and straight-leg deadlift can be implemented successfully at the beginning of the season.

At the midpoint of the season, the number of exercises, sets, and repetitions prescribed can be reduced. Trying to increase or maintain strength is the priority. Compound, multijoint exercises such as one-leg squats, bench presses, weighted chin-ups, and one-leg straight-leg deadlifts can continue to be done.

Near the later months of the season, strength training sessions can use body weight only, dumbbells, or weight vests. The volume may be lower in sets but higher in reps. Exercises such as kettlebell swings, jump squats, dumbbell snatches, pull-ups, push-ups, one-leg squats, and slide-board split squats are all included. Usually 1 or 2 sets of 5 to 8 repetitions for power movements, 1 or 2 sets of 10 reps for traditional strength training, and max number of reps for push-ups and pull-ups are sufficient. Again, it is important that the players get some training work in and then recover.

WORKING WITH INJURED PLAYERS

When injuries do occur, after the initial healing process and evaluation, the rehab process begins. The player will spend time with the team's athletic trainer or physical therapist, and the strength and conditioning coach should design a program that trains the rest of the athlete's body. If a player has an injury to an upper limb, then a one-arm, two-leg program can begin. If the injury is to a lower limb, then a one-leg, two-arm program can begin. The most important thing to remember is ensuring the safety of the athlete. Exercises that cause any pain or discomfort are not to be done.

The strength and conditioning coach can and should be a significant part of the process during a major injury. In addition, the strength and conditioning coach can use this time to demonstrate a level of care for the athlete that he is potentially unable to show in group settings. Some of the best relationships between strength and conditioning coaches and athletes often come out of serious injury.

As the season goes on, the training sessions should become shorter. However, all hockey players should continue to strength train all the way to the season's end. The more a team trains throughout the season, the stronger it will be during playoff time—when it counts the most.

Conditioning

Like strength training, in-season conditioning is very important. However, in most cases, in-season conditioning should be the by-product of on-ice practices (which should include on-ice conditioning drills) and games. The emphasis should be on rest and recovery rather than on conditioning work. Where conditioning work can and should be implemented is with those who don't play as much, such as third- and fourth-line players, fifth and sixth defensemen, healthy scratched players, and injured players. As you learned in chapter 3, each position has unique conditioning needs based on ice time during the game.

SAMPLE IN-SEASON TRAINING PROGRAMS

Following are sample in-season training programs that bring together everything that has been discussed in *Total Hockey Training*. Again, in-season training sessions need to be shorter than off-season and preseason training sessions. The strength and conditioning work off the ice needs to support the work on the ice.

Sample In-Season Workouts for High-School Hockey

Following are four weeks of sample preseason training programs for high school players (see tables 12.1 to 12.4). Training occurs two days per week.

During the in-season period, the concepts that were introduced in chapter 4 should be utilized when a training session is done prior to practice. At this point, all pretraining methods with the exception of plyometric training, speed training, and sled training should still be utilized. It is up to the strength and conditioning coach to determine how much time and what exercises should be used. Like the preseason, time is valuable during the in-season period.

Table 12.1　In-Season Program: High School Phase 1

	Strength training: day 1						
			Rest	Week 1	Week 2	Week 3	Week 4
Tri-set	Dumbbell snatch	Pg. 110	2:00	3 × 5 each side	3 × 5 each side	3 × 5 each side	3 × 5 each side
	Hip flexor stretch	Pg. 199	1:00	2 × 5 each side	2 × 5 each side	2 × 8 each side	2 × 10 each side
	Quadruped bent-knee hip extension	Pg. 58	1:00	2 × 5 each side	2 × 5 each side	2 × 8 each side	2 × 10 each side
Quad-set	Front squat	Pg. 120	1:00	3 × 8	3 × 8	3 × 8	3 × 8
	Dumbbell incline press	Pg. 151	1:00	3 × 8	3 × 8	3 × 8	3 × 8
	Stability ball rollout	Pg. 70	1:00	2 × 12	2 × 12	2 × 12	2 × 12
	Hamstring stretch	Pg. 200	1:00	2 × 30 sec	2 × 30 sec	2 × 30 sec	2 × 30 sec
Quad-set	Chin-up	Pg. 137	1:00	3 × 8 with 10-sec hold	3 × 8 with 10-sec hold	3 × 8 with 10-sec hold	3 × 8 with 10-sec hold
	Ball leg curl	Pg. 134	1:00	3 × 8	3 × 10	3 × 12	3 × 14
	Get up to hand	Pg. 82	1:00	2 × 5 each side	2 × 5 each side	2 × 5 each side	2 × 5 each side
	Quad stretch	Pg. 200	1:00	2 × 30 sec	2 × 30 sec	2 × 30 sec	2 × 30 sec
	Strength training: day 2						
			Rest	Week 1	Week 2	Week 3	Week 4
Tri-set	Hang clean	Pg. 106	2:00	3 × 5	3 × 5	3 × 5	3 × 5
	Squat stretch	Pg. 199	1:00	2 × 30 sec	2 × 30 sec	2 × 30 sec	2 × 30 sec
	Plank	Pg. 86	1:00	2 × 30 sec	2 × 30 sec	2 × 30 sec	2 × 30 sec
Quad-set	Split squat	Pg. 124	1:00	3 × 8 each side	3 × 8 each side	3 × 8 each side	3 × 8 each side
	Bench press	Pg. 147	1:00	3 × 8	3 × 8	3 × 8	3 × 8
	Bent-knee side bridge	Pg. 90	1:00	2 × 5 with 10-sec hold	2 × 5 with 10-sec hold	2 × 5 with 10-sec hold	2 × 5 with 10-sec hold
	Lat stretch	Pg. 205	1:00	2 × 30 sec each side	2 × 30 sec each side	2 × 30 sec each side	2 × 30 sec each side
Tri-set	Back extension	Pg. 131	1:00	3 × 8	3 × 10	3 × 12	3 × 14
	Dumbbell row	Pg. 142	1:00	3 × 10 each side	3 × 10 each side	3 × 10 each side	3 × 10 each side
	Chest stretch	Pg. 206	1:00	2 × 30 sec	2 × 30 sec	2 × 30 sec	2 × 30 sec
Y,T,W,L		Pg. 167	1:00	2 × 8 each	2 × 10 each	2 × 12 each	2 × 14 each

Table 12.2 In-Season Program: High School Phase 2

	Strength training: day 1						
			Rest	Week 1	Week 2	Week 3	Week 4
Tri-set	Dumbbell snatch	Pg. 110	2:00	3 × 3 each side	3 × 3 each side	3 × 3 each side	3 × 3 each side
	Hip flexor stretch	Pg. 199	1:00	2 × 30 sec each side	2 × 30 sec each side	2 × 30 sec each side	2 × 30 sec each side
	Quadruped straight-leg hip extension	Pg. 58	1:00	2 × 5 each side	2 × 5 each side	2 × 8 each side	2 × 10 each side
Quad-set	Front squat	Pg. 120	1:00	3 × 5	3 × 5	3 × 5	3 × 5
	Dumbbell incline press	Pg. 151	1:00	3 × 6	3 × 6	3 × 6	3 × 6
	Stability ball rollout	Pg. 70	1:00	2 × 12	2 × 12	2 × 12	2 × 12
	Hamstring stretch	Pg. 200	1:00	2 × 30 sec each side	2 × 30 sec each side	2 × 30 sec each side	2 × 30 sec each side
Quad-set	Chin-up (weighted)	Pg. 137	1:00	3 × 5 with 10-sec hold	3 × 5 with 10-sec hold	3 × 5 with 10-sec hold	3 × 5 with 10-sec hold
	Ball leg curl	Pg. 134	1:00	3 × 8	3 × 8	3 × 8	3 × 8
	Get up to hip extension	Pg. 83	1:00	2 × 5 each side	2 × 5 each side	2 × 5 each side	2 × 5 each side
	Quad stretch	Pg. 200	1:00	2 × 30 sec each side	2 × 30 sec each side	2 × 30 sec each side	2 × 30 sec each side
	Strength training: day 2						
			Rest	Week 1	Week 2	Week 3	Week 4
Tri-set	Hang clean	Pg. 106	2:00	3 × 3	3 × 3	3 × 3	3 × 3
	Squat stretch	Pg. 199	1:00	2 × 30 sec	2 × 30 sec	2 × 30 sec	2 × 30 sec
	Plank with leg lift	Pg. 87	1:00	2 × 5 each side	2 × 5 each side	2 × 5 each side	2 × 5 each side
Quad-set	Rear-foot elevated split squat	Pg. 125	1:00	3 × 6 each side	3 × 6 each side	3 × 6 each side	3 × 6 each side
	Bench press	Pg. 147	1:00	3 × 5	3 × 5	3 × 5	3 × 5
	Bent-knee side bridge	Pg. 90	1:00	2 × 5 each side with 10-sec hold	2 × 5 each side with 10-sec hold	2 × 5 each side with 10-sec hold	2 × 5 each side with 10-sec hold
	Lat stretch	Pg. 205	1:00	2 × 30 sec each side	2 × 30 sec each side	2 × 30 sec each side	2 × 30 sec each side
Tri-set	Two-arm, two-leg straight-leg deadlift	Pg. 133	1:00	3 × 8	3 × 8	3 × 8	3 × 8
	Dumbbell row	Pg. 142	1:00	3 × 8 each side	3 × 8 each side	3 × 8 each side	3 × 8 each side
	Chest stretch	Pg. 206	1:00	2 × 30 sec	2 × 30 sec	2 × 30 sec	2 × 30 sec
	Y,T,W,L (weighted)	Pg. 167	1:00	2 × 8 each	2 × 10 each	2 × 12 each	2 × 14 each

Table 12.3　In-Season Program: High School Phase 3

	Strength training: day 1						
		Rest		**Week 1**	**Week 2**	**Week 3**	**Week 4**
Tri-set	Kettlebell swing	Pg. 116	2:00	3 × 8	3 × 10	3 × 12	3 × 14
	Hip flexor stretch	Pg. 199	1:00	2 × 30 sec each side	2 × 30 sec each side	2 × 30 sec each side	2 × 30 sec each side
	Quadruped alternating arm–leg extension	Pg. 60	1:00	2 × 5 each side	2 × 5 each side	2 × 8 each side	2 × 10 each side
Quad-set	Front Squat	Pg. 120	1:00	3 × 6	3 × 6	3 × 6	3 × 6
	Dumbbell incline press	Pg. 151	1:00	3 × 6	3 × 6	3 × 6	3 × 6
	Stir the pot (on knees)	Pg. 72	1:00	2 × 5 each direction	2 × 5 each direction	2 × 5 each direction	2 × 5 each direction
	Hamstring stretch	Pg. 200	1:00	2 × 30 sec each side	2 × 30 sec each side	2 × 30 sec each side	2 × 30 sec each side
Quad-set	Parallel-grip pull-up (weighted)	Pg. 138	1:00	3 × 6 with 10-sec hold	3 × 6 with 10-sec hold	3 × 6 with 10-sec hold	3 × 6 with 10-sec hold
	Slide-board leg curl	Pg. 135	1:00	3 × 8	3 × 8	3 × 8	3 × 8
	Get up to kneeling position	Pg. 84	1:00	2 × 5 each side	2 × 5 each side	2 × 5 each side	2 × 5 each side
	Quad stretch	Pg. 200	1:00	2 × 30 sec each side	2 × 30 sec each side	2 × 30 sec each side	2 × 30 sec each side
	Strength training: day 2						
		Rest		**Week 1**	**Week 2**	**Week 3**	**Week 4**
Tri-set	Hang clean	Pg. 106	2:00	3 × 5	3 × 5	3 × 5	3 × 5
	Squat stretch	Pg. 199	1:00	2 × 30 sec	2 × 30 sec	2 × 30 sec	2 × 30 sec
	Plank with arm lift	Pg. 86	1:00	2 × 5 each side	2 × 5 each side	2 × 5 each side	2 × 5 each side
Quad-set	One-leg box squat	Pg. 63	1:00	3 × 6 each side	3 × 6 each side	3 × 6 each side	3 × 6 each side
	Bench press	Pg. 147	1:00	3 × 6	3 × 6	3 × 6	3 × 6
	Bent-knee side bridge	Pg. 90	1:00	2 × 5 each side with 10-sec hold	2 × 5 each side with 10-sec hold	2 × 5 each side with 10-sec hold	2 × 5 each side with 10-sec hold
	Lat stretch	Pg. 205	1:00	2 × 30 sec each side	2 × 30 sec each side	2 × 30 sec each side	2 × 30 sec each side
Tri-set	One-leg straight-leg deadlift	Pg. 132	1:00	3 × 6 each side	3 × 6 each side	3 × 6 each side	3 × 6 each side
	Inverted row	Pg. 140	1:00	3 × 8	3 × 8	3 × 8	3 × 8
	Chest stretch	Pg. 206	1:00	2 × 30 sec	2 × 30 sec	2 × 30 sec	2 × 30 sec

Table 12.4   In-Season Program: High School Phase 4

			Rest	Week 1	Week 2	Week 3	Week 4
Strength training: day 1							
Tri-set	Double kettlebell swing	Pg. 118	2:00	3 × 8	3 × 10	3 × 12	3 × 14
	Hip flexor stretch	Pg. 199	1:00	2 × 30 sec each side	2 × 30 sec each side	2 × 30 sec each side	2 × 30 sec each side
	Quadruped alternating arm–leg extension (weighted)	Pg. 60	1:00	2 × 5 each side	2 × 5 each side	2 × 8 each side	2 × 10 each side
Quad-set	Front squat	Pg. 120	1:00	3 × 5	3 × 5	3 × 5	3 × 5
	Dumbbell incline press	Pg. 151	1:00	3 × 5	3 × 5	3 × 5	3 × 5
	Stir the pot (on knees)	Pg. 72	1:00	2 × 5 each direction	2 × 5 each direction	2 × 5 each direction	2 × 5 each direction
	Hamstring stretch	Pg. 200	1:00	2 × 30 sec each side	2 × 30 sec each side	2 × 30 sec each side	2 × 30 sec each side
Quad-set	Basic pull-up (weighted)	Pg. 136	1:00	3 × 5 with 10 sec hold	3 × 5 with 10 sec hold	3 × 5 with 10 sec hold	3 × 5 with 10 sec hold
	Slide-board leg curl	Pg. 135	1:00	3 × 8	3 × 8	3 × 8	3 × 8
	Full get-up	Pg. 85	1:00	2 × 5 each side	2 × 5 each side	2 × 5 each side	2 × 5 each side
	Quad stretch	Pg. 200	1:00	2 × 30 sec each side	2 × 30 sec each side	2 × 30 sec each side	2 × 30 sec each side
Strength training: day 2							
			Rest	Week 1	Week 2	Week 3	Week 4
Tri-set	Hang clean	Pg. 106	2:00	3 × 3	3 × 3	3 × 3	3 × 3
	Squat stretch	Pg. 199	1:00	2 × 30 sec	2 × 30 sec	2 × 30 sec	2 × 30 sec
	Plank with alternating arm and leg lift	Pg. 88	1:00	2 × 5 each side	2 × 5 each side	2 × 5 each side	2 × 5 each side
Quad-set	Front split squat	Pg. 127	1:00	3 × 6 each side	3 × 6 each side	3 × 6 each side	3 × 6 each side
	Bench press	Pg. 147	1:00	3 × 5	3 × 5	3 × 5	3 × 5
	Bent-knee side bridge	Pg. 90	1:00	2 × 5 each side with 10 sec hold	2 × 5 each side with 10 sec hold	2 × 5 each side with 10 sec hold	2 × 5 each side with 10 sec hold
	Lat stretch	Pg. 205	1:00	2 × 30 sec each side	2 × 30 sec each side	2 × 30 sec each side	2 × 30 sec each side
Tri-set	One-leg straight leg deadlift	Pg. 132	1:00	3 × 6 each side	3 × 6 each side	3 × 6 each side	3 × 6 each side
	Inverted row (weighted)	Pg. 140	1:00	3 × 6	3 × 6	3 × 6	3 × 6
	Chest stretch	Pg. 206	1:00	2 × 30 sec	2 × 30 sec	2 × 30 sec	2 × 30 sec

Sample In-Season Workouts for Juniors and College Hockey

Following are six weeks of sample in-season training programs for junior/college-level players (see tables 12.5 to 12.10). Training occurs two days per week.

Table 12.5 In-Season Program: Juniors and College Phase 1

Strength training: day 1			Rest	Week 1	Week 2	Week 3	Week 4
Tri-set	Dumbbell snatch	p. 110	2:00	3 × 5 each side	3 × 5 each side	3 × 5 each side	3 × 5 each side
	Hip flexor stretch	Pg. 199	1:00	2 × 30 sec each side	2 × 30 sec each side	2 × 30 sec each side	2 × 30 sec each side
	Quadruped bent-knee hip extension	Pg. 58	1:00	2 × 5 each side	2 × 5 each side	2 × 8 each side	2 × 10 each side
Quad-set	Front squat	Pg. 120	1:00	3 × 8	3 × 8	3 × 8	3 × 8
	Dumbbell incline press	Pg. 151	1:00	3 × 8	3 × 8	3 × 8	3 × 8
	Stability ball rollout	Pg. 70	1:00	2 × 12	2 × 12	2 × 12	2 × 12
	Hamstring stretch	Pg. 200	1:00	2 × 30 sec each side	2 × 30 sec each side	2 × 30 sec each side	2 × 30 sec each side
Quad-set	Chin-up	Pg. 137	1:00	3 × 8 with 10-sec hold	3 × 8 with 10-sec hold	3 × 8 with 10-sec hold	3 × 8 with 10-sec hold
	Ball leg curl	Pg. 134	1:00	3 × 8	3 × 8	3 × 8	3 × 8
	Get up to hand	Pg. 82	1:00	2 × 5 each side	2 × 5 each side	2 × 5 each side	2 × 5 each side
	Quad stretch	Pg. 200	1:00	2 × 30 sec each side	2 × 30 sec each side	2 × 30 sec each side	2 × 30 sec each side
Strength training: day 2			Rest	Week 1	Week 2	Week 3	Week 4
Tri-set	Hang clean	Pg. 106	2:00	3 × 5	3 × 5	3 × 5	3 × 5
	Squat stretch	Pg. 199	1:00	2 × 30 sec	2 × 30 sec	2 × 30 sec	2 × 30 sec
	Plank	Pg. 86	1:00	2 × 30 sec	2 × 30 sec	2 × 30 sec	2 × 30 sec
Quad-set	One-leg box squat	Pg. 63	1:00	3 × 6 each side	3 × 6 each side	3 × 6 each side	3 × 6 each side
	Bench press	Pg. 147	1:00	3 × 8	3 × 8	3 × 8	3 × 8
	Bent-knee side bridge	Pg. 90	1:00	2 × 5 with 10-sec hold	2 × 5 with 10-sec hold	2 × 5 with 10-sec hold	2 × 5 with 10-sec hold
	Lat stretch	Pg. 205	1:00	2 × 30 sec each side	2 × 30 sec each side	2 × 30 sec each side	2 × 30 sec each side
Tri-set	Two-arm, two-leg straight-leg deadlift	Pg. 133	1:00	3 × 8	3 × 8	3 × 8	3 × 8
	Dumbbell row	Pg. 142	1:00	3 × 8 each side	3 × 8 each side	3 × 8 each side	3 × 8 each side
	Chest stretch	Pg. 206	1:00	2 × 30 sec	2 × 30 sec	2 × 30 sec	2 × 30 sec
Y,T,W,L		Pg. 167	1:00	2 × 8 each	2 × 10 each	2 × 12 each	2 × 14 each

Table 12.6 In-Season Program: Juniors and College Phase 2

			Rest	Week 1	Week 2	Week 3	Week 4
Strength training: day 1							
Tri-set	Dumbbell snatch	Pg. 110	2:00	3 × 3 each side	3 × 3 each side	3 × 3 each side	3 × 3 each side
	Hip flexor stretch	Pg. 199	1:00	2 × 30 sec each side	2 × 30 sec each side	2 × 30 sec each side	2 × 30 sec each side
	Quadruped bent-knee hip extension.	Pg. 58	1:00	2 × 5 each side	2 × 5 each side	2 × 8 each side	2 × 10 each side
Quad-set	Front squat	Pg. 120	1:00	3 × 5	3 × 5	3 × 5	3 × 5
	Dumbbell incline press	Pg. 151	1:00	3 × 6	3 × 6	3 × 6	3 × 6
	Stability ball rollout	Pg. 70	1:00	2 × 12	2 × 12	2 × 12	2 × 12
	Hamstring stretch	Pg. 200	1:00	2 × 30 sec each side	2 × 30 sec each side	2 × 30 sec each side	2 × 30 sec each side
Quad-set	Chin-up (weighted)	Pg. 137	1:00	3 × 5 with 10-sec hold	3 × 5 with 10-sec hold	3 × 5 with 10-sec hold	3 × 5 with 10-sec hold
	Ball leg curl	Pg. 134	1:00	3 × 8	3 × 8	3 × 8	3 × 8
	Get up to hand	Pg. 82	1:00	2 × 5 each side	2 × 5 each side	2 × 5 each side	2 × 5 each side
	Quad stretch	Pg. 200	1:00	2 × 30 sec each side	2 × 30 sec each side	2 × 30 sec each side	2 × 30 sec each side
Strength training: day 2							
			Rest	Week 1	Week 2	Week 3	Week 4
Tri-set	Hang clean	Pg. 106	2:00	3 × 3	3 × 3	3 × 3	3 × 3
	Squat stretch	Pg. 199	1:00	2 × 30 sec	2 × 30 sec	2 × 30 sec	2 × 30 sec
	Plank	Pg. 86	1:00	2 × 30 sec	2 × 30 sec	2 × 30 sec	2 × 30 sec
Quad-set	One-leg box squat	Pg. 63	1:00	3 × 6 each side	3 × 6 each side	3 × 6 each side	3 × 6 each side
	Bench press	Pg. 147	1:00	3 × 5	3 × 5	3 × 5	3 × 5
	Bent-knee side bridge	Pg. 90	1:00	2 × 5 each side with 10-sec hold	2 × 5 each side with 10-sec hold	2 × 5 each side with 10-sec hold	2 × 5 each side with 10-sec hold
	Lat stretch	Pg. 205	1:00	2 × 30 sec each side	2 × 30 sec each side	2 × 30 sec each side	2 × 30 sec each side
Tri-set	Two-arm, two-leg straight-leg deadlift	Pg. 133	1:00	3 × 8	3 × 8	3 × 8	3 × 8
	Dumbbell row	Pg. 142	1:00	3 × 8 each side	3 × 8 each side	3 × 8 each side	3 × 8 each side
	Chest stretch	Pg. 206	1:00	2 × 30 sec	2 × 30 sec	2 × 30 sec	2 × 30 sec
Y,T,W,L (weighted)		Pg. 167	1:00	2 × 8 each	2 × 10 each	2 × 12 each	2 × 14 each

Table 12.7 In-Season Program: Juniors and College Phase 3

			Rest	Week 1	Week 2	Week 3	Week 4
Strength training: day 1							
Tri-set	Kettlebell swing	Pg. 116	2:00	3 × 8	3 × 10	3 × 12	3 × 14
	Hip flexor stretch	Pg. 199	1:00	2 × 30 sec each side	2 × 30 sec each side	2 × 30 sec each side	2 × 30 sec each side
	Quadruped straight-leg hip extension	Pg. 59	1:00	2 × 5 each side	2 × 5 each side	2 × 5 each side	2 × 5 each side
Quad-set	Front split squat	Pg. 127	1:00	3 × 8 each side	3 × 8 each side	3 × 8 each side	3 × 8 each side
	Incline bench press	Pg. 148	1:00	3 × 8	3 × 8	3 × 8	3 × 8
	Stir the pot (on knees)	Pg. 72	1:00	2 × 5 each direction	2 × 5 each direction	2 × 5 each direction	2 × 5 each direction
	Hamstring stretch	Pg. 200	1:00	2 × 30 sec each side	2 × 30 sec each side	2 × 30 sec each side	2 × 30 sec each side
Quad-set	Parallel-grip pull-up	Pg. 138	1:00	3 × 8 with 10-sec hold	3 × 8 with 10-sec hold	3 × 8 with 10-sec hold	3 × 8 with 10-sec hold
	Slide-board leg curl	Pg. 135	1:00	3 × 8	3 × 8	3 × 8	3 × 8
	Get up to hip extension	Pg. 83	1:00	2 × 5 each side	2 × 5 each side	2 × 5 each side	2 × 5 each side
	Quad stretch	Pg. 200	1:00	2 × 30 sec each side	2 × 30 sec each side	2 × 30 sec each side	2 × 30 sec each side
Strength training: day 2							
Tri-set	Hang clean	Pg. 106	200	3 × 5	3 × 5	3 × 5	3 × 5
	Squat stretch	Pg. 199	1:00	2 × 30 sec	2 × 30 sec	2 × 30 sec	2 × 30 sec
	Plank with arm lift	Pg. 87	1:00	2 × 5 each side	2 × 5 each side	2 × 5 each side	2 × 5 each side
Quad-set	Front split squat	Pg. 127	1:00	3 × 6 each side	3 × 6 each side	3 × 6 each side	3 × 6 each side
	Bench press	Pg. 147	1:00	3 × 8	3 × 8	3 × 8	3 × 8
	Bent-knee side bridge	Pg. 90	1:00	2 × 5 each side with 10-sec hold	2 × 5 each side with 10-sec hold	2 × 5 each side with 10-sec hold	2 × 5 each side with 10-sec hold
	Lat stretch	Pg. 205	1:00	2 × 30 sec each side	2 × 30 sec each side	2 × 30 sec each side	2 × 30 sec each side
Tri-set	One-leg straight-leg deadlift	Pg. 132	1:00	3 × 6 each side	3 × 6 each side	3 × 6 each side	3 × 6 each side
	Inverted row	Pg. 140	1:00	3 × 8	3 × 8	3 × 8	3 × 8
	Chest stretch	Pg. 206	1:00	2 × 30 sec	2 × 30 sec	2 × 30 sec	2 × 30 sec

Table 12.8 In-Season Program: Juniors and College Phase 4

	Strength training: day 1						
			Rest	Week 1	Week 2	Week 3	Week 4
Tri-set	Double kettlebell swing	Pg. 118	2:00	3 × 8	3 × 10	3 × 12	3 × 14
	Hip flexor stretch	Pg. 199	1:00	2 × 30 sec each side	2 × 30 sec each side	2 × 30 sec each side	2 × 30 sec each side
	Quadruped straight-leg hip extension	Pg. 59	1:00	2 × 10 each side	2 × 10 each side	2 × 10 each side	2 × 10 each side
Quad-set	Front split squat	Pg. 127	1:00	3 × 6 each side	3 × 6 each side	3 × 6 each side	3 × 6 each side
	Incline bench press	Pg. 148	1:00	3 × 5	3 × 5	3 × 5	3 × 5
	Stir the pot (on knees)	Pg. 72	1:00	2 × 5 each direction	2 × 5 each direction	2 × 5 each direction	2 × 5 each direction
	Hamstring stretch	Pg. 200	1:00	2 × 30 sec each side	2 × 30 sec each side	2 × 30 sec each side	2 × 30 sec each side
Quad-set	Parallel-grip pull-up (weighted)	Pg. 138	1:00	3 × 5 with 10-sec hold	3 × 5 with 10-sec hold	3 × 5 with 10-sec hold	3 × 5 with 10-sec hold
	Slide-board leg curl	Pg. 135	1:00	3 × 8	3 × 8	3 × 8	3 × 8
	Get up to hip extension	Pg. 83	1:00	2 × 5 each side	2 × 5 each side	2 × 5 each side	2 × 5 each side
	Quad stretch	Pg. 200	1:00	2 × 30 sec each side	2 × 30 sec each side	2 × 30 sec each side	2 × 30 sec each side
	Strength training: day 2						
			Rest	Week 1	Week 2	Week 3	Week 4
Tri-set	Hang clean	Pg. 106	2:00	3 × 3	3 × 3	3 × 3	3 × 3
	Squat stretch	Pg. 199	1:00	2 × 30 sec	2 × 30 sec	2 × 30 sec	2 × 30 sec
	Plank with arm lift	Pg. 87	1:00	2 × 5 each side	2 × 5 each side	2 × 5 each side	2 × 5 each side
Quad-set	Front split squat	Pg. 127	1:00	3 × 6 each side	3 × 6 each side	3 × 6 each side	3 × 6 each side
	Bench press	Pg. 147	1:00	3 × 5	3 × 5	3 × 5	3 × 5
	Bent-knee side bridge	Pg. 90	1:00	2 × 5 each side with 10-sec hold	2 × 5 each side with 10-sec hold	2 × 5 each side with 10-sec hold	2 × 5 each side with 10-sec hold
	Lat stretch	Pg. 205	1:00	2 × 30 sec each side	2 × 30 sec each side	2 × 30 sec each side	2 × 30 sec each side
Tri-set	One-leg straight-leg deadlift	Pg. 132	1:00	3 × 6 each side	3 × 6 each side	3 × 6 each side	3 × 6 each side
	Inverted row (weighted)	Pg. 140	1:00	3 × 6	3 × 6	3 × 6	3 × 6
	Chest stretch	Pg. 206	1:00	2 × 30 sec	2 × 30 sec	2 × 30 sec	2 × 30 sec

Table 12.9   In-Season Program: Juniors and College Phase 5

			Rest	Week 1	Week 2	Week 3	Week 4
Strength training: day 1							
Tri-set	Dumbbell snatch	Pg. 110	2:00	3 × 5 each side	3 × 5 each side	3 × 5 each side	3 × 5 each side
	Hip flexor stretch	Pg. 199	1:00	2 × 30 each side	2 × 30 each side	2 × 30 each side	2 × 30 each side
	Quadruped alternating arm–leg extension	Pg. 60		2 × 10 each side	2 × 10 each side	2 × 10 each side	2 × 10 each side
Quad-set	Trap bar deadlift	Pg. 123	1:00	3 × 6	3 × 6	3 × 6	3 × 6
	Dumbbell incline press	Pg. 151	1:00	3 × 8	3 × 8	3 × 8	3 × 8
	Stir the pot (on feet)	Pg. 72	1:00	2 × 5 each direction	2 × 5 each direction	2 × 5 each direction	2 × 5 each direction
	Hamstring stretch	Pg. 200	1:00	2 × 30 sec each side	2 × 30 sec each side	2 × 30 sec each side	2 × 30 sec each side
Quad-set	Basic pull-up	Pg. 136	1:00	3 × 8 with 10-sec hold	3 × 8 with 10-sec hold	3 × 8 with 10-sec hold	3 × 8 with 10-sec hold
	Slide-board leg curl	Pg. 135	1:00	3 × 8	3 × 8	3 × 8	3 × 8
	Get up to kneeling position	Pg. 84	1:00	2 × 5 each side	2 × 5 each side	2 × 5 each side	2 × 5 each side
	Quad stretch	Pg. 200	1:00	2 × 30 sec each side	2 × 30 sec each side	2 × 30 sec each side	2 × 30 sec each side
Strength training: day 2							
Tri-set	Hang clean + front squat	Pg. 106, 120	2:00	3 × 5 + 5	3 × 5 + 5	3 × 5 + 5	3 × 5 + 5
	Squat stretch	Pg. 199	1:00	2 × 30 sec	2 × 30 sec	2 × 30 sec	2 × 30 sec
	Plank	Pg. 86	1:00	2 × 30 sec	2 × 30 sec	2 × 30 sec	2 × 30 sec
Quad-set	One-leg skater squat	Pg. 126	1:00	3 × 6 each side	3 × 6 each side	3 × 6 each side	3 × 6 each side
	Dumbbell bench press	Pg. 149	1:00	3 × 8	3 × 8	3 × 8	3 × 8
	Straddle side bridge	Pg. 92	1:00	2 × 5 each side with 10-sec hold	2 × 5 each side with 10-sec hold	2 × 5 each side with 10-sec hold	2 × 5 each side with 10-sec hold
	Lat stretch	Pg. 205	1:00	2 × 30 sec each side	2 × 30 sec each side	2 × 30 sec each side	2 × 30 sec each side
Tri-set	One-leg straight-leg deadlift	Pg. 132	1:00	3 × 6 each side	3 × 6 each side	3 × 6 each side	3 × 6 each side
	Dumbbell row	Pg. 142	1:00	3 × 8 each side	3 × 8 each side	3 × 8 each side	3 × 8 each side
	Chest stretch	Pg. 206	1:00	2 × 30 sec	2 × 30 sec	2 × 30 sec	2 × 30 sec
Y,T,W,L		Pg. 167	1:00	2 × 8 each	2 × 10 each	2 × 12 each	2 × 14 each

Table 12.10   In-Season Program: Juniors and College Phase 6

			Rest	Week 1	Week 2	Week 3	Week 4
Strength training: day 1							
Tri-set	Dumbbell snatch	Pg. 110	2:00	3 × 3 each side	3 × 3 each side	3 × 3 each side	3 × 3 each side
	Hip flexor stretch	Pg. 199	1:00	2 × 30 sec each side	2 × 30 sec each side	2 × 30 sec each side	2 × 30 sec each side
	Quadruped alternating arm–leg extension	Pg. 60	1:00	2 × 10 each side	2 × 10 each side	2 × 10 each side	2 × 10 each side
Quad-set	Trap bar deadlift	Pg. 123	1:00	3 × 5	3 × 5	3 × 5	3 × 5
	Dumbbell incline press	Pg. 151	1:00	3 × 6	3 × 6	3 × 6	3 × 6
	Stir the pot (on feet)	Pg. 72	1:00	2 × 5 each direction	2 × 5 each direction	2 × 5 each direction	2 × 5 each direction
	Hamstring stretch	Pg. 200	1:00	2 × 30 sec each side	2 × 30 sec each side	2 × 30 sec each side	2 × 30 sec each side
Quad-set	Basic pull-up (weighted)	Pg. 136	1:00	3 × 5 with 10-sec hold	3 × 5 with 10-sec hold	3 × 5 with 10-sec hold	3 × 5 with 10-sec hold
	Slide-board leg curl	Pg. 135	1:00	3 × 8	3 × 8	3 × 8	3 × 8
	Get up to kneeling position	Pg. 84	1:00	2 × 5 each side	2 × 5 each side	2 × 5 each side	2 × 5 each side
	Quad stretch	Pg. 200	1:00	2 × 30 sec each side	2 × 30 sec each side	2 × 30 sec each side	2 × 30 sec each side
Strength training: day 2							
			Rest	Week 1	Week 2	Week 3	Week 4
Tri-set	Hang clean + front squat	Pg. 106, 120	2:00	3 × 5 + 5	3 × 5 + 5	3 × 5 + 5	3 × 5 + 5
	Squat stretch	Pg. 199	1:00	2 × 30 sec	2 × 30 sec	2 × 30 sec	2 × 30 sec
	Plank	Pg. 86	1:00	2 × 30 sec	2 × 30 sec	2 × 30 sec	2 × 30 sec
Quad-set	One-leg squat	Pg. 126	1:00	3 × 6 each side	3 × 6 each side	3 × 6 each side	3 × 6 each side
	Dumbbell bench press	Pg. 149	1:00	3 × 6	3 × 6	3 × 6	3 × 6
	Straddle side bridge	Pg. 92	1:00	2 × 5 each side with 10-sec hold	2 × 5 each side with 10-sec hold	2 × 5 each side with 10-sec hold	2 × 5 each side with 10-sec hold
	Lat stretch	Pg. 205	1:00	2 × 30 sec each side	2 × 30 sec each side	2 × 30 sec each side	2 × 30 sec each side
Tri-set	One-leg straight-leg deadlift	Pg. 132	1:00	3 × 6 each side	3 × 6 each side	3 × 6 each side	3 × 6 each side
	Dumbbell row	Pg. 142	1:00	3 × 6 each side	3 × 6 each side	3 × 6 each side	3 × 6 each side
	Chest stretch	Pg. 206	1:00	2 × 30 sec	2 × 30 sec	2 × 30 sec	2 × 30 sec
Y,T,W,L (weighted)		Pg. 167	1:00	2 × 8 each	2 × 10 each	2 × 12 each	2 × 14 each

Bibliography

Anderson, T., and M. McNiff. 2011. Becoming bulletproof: An uncommon approach to building a resilient body. Amazon Digital Services.

Boyle, M. November 7, 2001. Sliding through. Training and Conditioning. www.momentummedia.com/articles/tc/tc1107/sliding.htm.

Christie, H.J., S. Kumar, and S.A. Warren. 1995. Postural aberrations in low back pain. *Archives of Physical Medicine and Rehabilitation* 76(3):218–24.

Hodges, P.W., and C.A. Richardson. 1996. Inefficient muscular stabilization of the lumbar spine associated with low back pain: A motor control evaluation of transversus abdominis. *Spine* 15;21(22):2640-50.

Hough, P.A., E.Z. Ross, and G.J. Howatson. 2009. Effects of dynamic and static stretching on vertical jump performance and electromyographic activity. *Journal of Strength and Conditioning* 23(2):507–12.

Jamieson, J. 2009. *Ultimate MMA conditioning*. www.8weeksout.com.

Kyndall, L., P.T. Boyle, J. Olinick, and C. Lewis. 2010. The value of blowing up a balloon. *North American Journal of Sports Physical Therapy* 5(3):179–88.

Luoto, S., M. Heliovaara, H.L. Hurri, et al. 1995. Static back endurance and the risk of low back pain. *Clinical Biomechanics* 10:323–4.

Mascaro, T., B.L. Seaver, and L. Swanson. 1992. Prediction of skating speed with off-ice testing in professional hockey players. *Journal of Orthopaedic and Sports Physical Therapy* 15(2):92–8.

McGill, S. 2010. Core training: Evidence translating to better performance and injury prevention. *Strength and Conditioning Journal* 32(3):35.

Montgomery, D.L. 1982. The effect of added weight on ice hockey performance. *Physician and Sportsmedicine* 10(11):91–99.

Page, P., C.C. Frank, and R. Lardner. 2010. *Assessment and treatment of muscle imbalance: The Janda approach*. Champaign, IL: Human Kinetics.

Sahrmann, S. 2002. *Diagnosis and treatment of movement impairment syndromes*. St. Louis: Mosby.

Tabata, I., K. Nishimura, M. Kouzaki, Y. Hirai, F. Ogita, M. Miyachi, and K. Yamamoto. 1996. Effects of moderate-intensity endurance and high-intensity intermittent training on anaerobic capacity and VO2max. *Medicine & Science in Sports & Exercise* 28(10):1327-30.

Tomlin, D.L., and H.A. Wenger. 2001. The relationship between aerobic fitness and recovery from high intensity intermittent exercise. *Sports Medicine* 31(1):1–11.

About the Author

Sean Skahan was named the strength and conditioning coach for men's hockey at Boston University in 2015. Prior to taking the position, Skahan was the strength and conditioning coach for the National Hockey League's (NHL) Anaheim Ducks for 13 seasons, where he was responsible for the overall strength and conditioning program for all players in the Ducks' system.

Before working with the Ducks, Skahan was the assistant strength and conditioning coach at Boston College and at the University of North Dakota. While earning his master's degree in kinesiology, Skahan worked as a graduate assistant strength and conditioning coach at the University of Minnesota. He earned his bachelor's degree in exercise physiology from the University of Massachusetts at Boston.

Skahan holds certifications from the National Strength and Conditioning Association (NSCA), Functional Movement Screen (FMS), and USA Weightlifting. He is also certified as a kettlebell movement specialist (CK-FMS) and a StrongFirst level 1 instructor. Skahan presents at strength and conditioning conferences worldwide when his schedule permits. He lives in Boston.

You'll find other outstanding hockey resources at

www.HumanKinetics.com/icehockey

In the U.S. call 1-800-747-4457

Australia 08 8372 0999 • Canada 1-800-465-7301
Europe +44 (0) 113 255 5665 • New Zealand 0800 222 062

HUMAN KINETICS
The Premier Publisher for Sports & Fitness
P.O. Box 5076 • Champaign, IL 61825-5076 USA

eBook
available at
HumanKinetics.com